"Simultaneously touching and comic."

—The New York Times

"Regularly throws out rich, dazzling images which delight and surprise with their simplicity. But Miss Angelou's book is more than a tour de force of language or the story of childhood suffering: it quietly and gracefully portrays and pays tribute to the courage, dignity and endurance of the small, rural community in which she spent most of her early years in the 1930's . . . Some of the incidents she depicts are wonderfully funny. But a summary of the incidents cannot do this book justice; one has to read it to appreciate its sensitivity and life."

—Robert A. Gross, Newsweek

"A work of art which eludes description because the black aesthetic—another way of saying 'the black experience'—has too long been neglected to be formalized by weary cliches . . . Anyone who doesn't read Maya Angelou doesn't want to know where it was, much less where it's at."

—Julian Mayfield

"It is a heroic and beautiful book."

—Cleveland Plain Dealer

"Maya Angelou is a natural writer with an inordinate sense of life and she has written an exceptional autobiographical narrative . . . a beautiful book—an unconditionally involving memoir for our time or any time."

—The Kirkus Reviews

I KNOW WHY THE CAGED BIRD SINGS

MAYA ANGELOU

BANTAM BOOKS

TORONTO · NEW YORK · LONDON · SYDNEY

I KNOW WHY THE CAGED BIRD SINGS

*A Bantam Book / published by arrangement with
Random House, Inc.*

PRINTING HISTORY

Random House edition published February 1970

2nd printing .... April 1970	4th printing .... July 1970
3rd printing .... May 1970	5th printing .... August 1970
6th printing .... September 1970	

Book-of-the-Month Club edition published March 1970

Ebony Book Club edition published April 1970

A portion of this book appeared in EBONY *magazine April 1970*

*Bantam edition / March 1971
21 printings through February 1980*

ACKNOWLEDGMENTS

*The title, I Know Why the Caged Bird Sings, is from the
poem "Sympathy," by Paul Laurence Dunbar.
"Lift Ev'ry Voice and Sing," words by James Weldon Johnson, music by J. Rosamond Johnson. Copyright Edward B.
Marks Music Corporation.*

ISBN 0-553-13904-5

Published simultaneously in the United States and Canada

PRINTED IN THE UNITED STATES OF AMERICA

30 29 28 27 26

This book is dedicated to
MY SON, GUY JOHNSON,
and all the strong
black birds of promise
who defy the odds and gods
and sing their songs

ACKNOWLEDGMENTS

I thank my mother, **Vivian Baxter**, and my brother, **Bailey Johnson**, who encouraged me to remember. Thanks to the **Harlem Writers' Guild** for concern and to **John O. Killens** who told me I could write. To **Nana Kobina Nketsia IV** who insisted that I must. Lasting gratitude to **Gerard Purcell** who believed concretely and to **Tony D'Amato** who understood. Thanks to **Abbey Lincoln Roach** for naming my book. A final thanks to my editor at Random House, **Robert Loomis,** who gently prodded me back into the lost years.

"What you looking at me for?
  I didn't come to stay . . ."

I HADN'T so much forgot as I couldn't bring myself to remember. Other things were more important.

"What you looking at me for?
  I didn't come to stay . . ."

Whether I could remember the rest of the poem or not was immaterial. The truth of the statement was like a wadded-up handkerchief, sopping wet in my fists, and the sooner they accepted it the quicker I could let my hands open and the air would cool my palms.

"What you looking at me for . . . ?"

The children's section of the Colored Methodist Episcopal Church was wiggling and giggling over my well-known forgetfulness.

The dress I wore was lavender taffeta, and each time I breathed it rustled, and now that I was sucking in air to breathe out shame it sounded like crepe paper on the back of hearses.

As I'd watched Momma put ruffles on the hem and cute little tucks around the waist, I knew that once I put it on I'd look like a movie star. (It was silk and that made up for the awful color.) I was going to look like one of the sweet little white girls who were everybody's dream of what was right with the world. Hanging softly over the black Singer sew-

1

ing machine, it looked like magic, and when people saw me wearing it they were going to run up to me and say, "Marguerite [sometimes it was 'dear Marguerite'], forgive us, please, we didn't know who you were," and I would answer generously, "No, you couldn't have known. Of course I forgive you."

Just thinking about it made me go around with angel's dust sprinkled over my face for days. But Easter's early morning sun had shown the dress to be a plain ugly cut-down from a white woman's once-was-purple throwaway. It was old-lady-long too, but it didn't hide my skinny legs, which had been greased with Blue Seal Vaseline and powdered with the Arkansas red clay. The age-faded color made my skin look dirty like mud, and everyone in church was looking at my skinny legs.

Wouldn't they be surprised when one day I woke out of my black ugly dream, and my real hair, which was long and blond, would take the place of the kinky mass that Momma wouldn't let me straighten? My light-blue eyes were going to hypnotize them, after all the things they said about "my daddy must of been a Chinaman" (I thought they meant made out of china, like a cup) because my eyes were so small and squinty. Then they would understand why I had never picked up a Southern accent, or spoke the common slang, and why I had to be forced to eat pigs' tails and snouts. Because I was really white and because a cruel fairy stepmother, who was understandably jealous of my beauty, had turned me into a too-big Negro girl, with nappy black hair, broad feet and a space between her teeth that would hold a number-two pencil.

"What you looking ..." The minister's wife leaned toward me, her long yellow face full of sorry. She whispered, "I just come to tell you, it's Easter Day." I repeated, jamming the words together, "Ijustcometo tellyouit'sEasterDay," as low as possible. The giggles hung in the air like melting clouds that were waiting to rain on me. I held up two fingers, close to my chest, which meant that I had to go to the toilet, and tiptoed toward the rear of the church. Dimly, somewhere over my head, I heard ladies saying, "Lord bless the child," and "Praise God." My head was up and my eyes were open, but I didn't see anything. Halfway down the aisle, the church exploded with "Were you there when they crucified my Lord?" and I tripped over a foot stuck out from the children's pew. I stumbled and started to say something, or maybe to scream, but a green persimmon, or it could have been a lemon, caught me between the legs and squeezed. I tasted the sour on my tongue and felt it in the back of my mouth. Then before I reached the door, the sting was burning down my legs and into my Sunday socks. I tried to hold, to squeeze it back, to keep it from speeding, but when I reached the church porch I knew I'd have to let it go, or it would probably run right back up to my head and my poor head would burst like a dropped watermelon, and all the brains and spit and tongue and eyes would roll all over the place. So I ran down into the yard and let it go. I ran, peeing and crying, not toward the toilet out back but to our house. I'd get a whipping for it, to be sure, and the nasty children would have something new to tease me about. I laughed anyway, partially for the sweet release; still, the greater joy came not only from being liberated from the silly church but from the knowledge that I wouldn't die from a busted head.

If growing up is painful for the Southern Black girl, being aware of her displacement is the rust on the razor that threatens the throat.

It is an unnecessary insult.

1

WHEN I WAS three and Bailey four, we had arrived in the musty little town, wearing tags on our wrists

which instructed—"To Whom It May Concern"—
that we were Marguerite and Bailey Johnson Jr., from
Long Beach, California, en route to Stamps, Arkansas, c/o Mrs. Annie Henderson.

Our parents had decided to put an end to their
calamitous marriage, and Father shipped us home to
his mother. A porter had been charged with our
welfare—he got off the train the next day in Arizona—and our tickets were pinned to my brother's
inside coat pocket.

I don't remember much of the trip, but after we
reached the segregated southern part of the journey,
things must have looked up. Negro passengers, who
always traveled with loaded lunch boxes, felt sorry
for "the poor little motherless darlings" and plied us
with cold fried chicken and potato salad.

Years later I discovered that the United States
had been crossed thousands of times by frightened
Black children traveling alone to their newly
affluent parents in Northern cities, or back to grandmothers in Southern towns when the urban North
reneged on its economic promises.

The town reacted to us as its inhabitants had
reacted to all things new before our coming. It re-
garded us a while without curiosity but with caution, and after we were seen to be harmless (and
children) it closed in around us, as a real mother
embraces a stranger's child. Warmly, but not too
familiarly.

We lived with our grandmother and uncle in the
rear of the Store (it was always spoken of with a
capital s), which she had owned some twenty-five
years.

Early in the century, Momma (we soon stopped
calling her Grandmother) sold lunches to the saw-
men in the lumberyard (east Stamps) and the
seedmen at the cotton gin (west Stamps). Her crisp
meat pies and cool lemonade, when joined to her
miraculous ability to be in two places at the same
time, assured her business success. From being a

mobile lunch counter, she set up a stand between the two points of fiscal interest and supplied the workers' needs for a few years. Then she had the Store built in the heart of the Negro area. Over the years it became the lay center of activities in town. On Saturdays, barbers sat their customers in the shade on the porch of the Store, and troubadours on their ceaseless crawlings through the South leaned across its benches and sang their sad songs of The Brazos while they played juice harps and cigar-box guitars.

The formal name of the Store was the Wm. Johnson General Merchandise Store. Customers could find food staples, a good variety of colored thread, mash for hogs, corn for chickens, coal oil for lamps, light bulbs for the wealthy, shoestrings, hair dressing, balloons, and flower seeds. Anything not visible had only to be ordered.

Until we became familiar enough to belong to the Store and it to us, we were locked up in a Fun House of Things where the attendant had gone home for life.

Each year I watched the field across from the Store turn caterpillar green, then gradually frosty white. I knew exactly how long it would be before the big wagons would pull into the front yard and load on the cotton pickers at daybreak to carry them to the remains of slavery's plantations.

During the picking season my grandmother would get out of bed at four o'clock (she never used an alarm clock) and creak down to her knees and chant in a sleep-filled voice, "Our Father, thank you for letting me see this New Day. Thank you that you didn't allow the bed I lay on last night to be my cooling board, nor my blanket my winding sheet. Guide my feet this day along the straight and narrow, and help me to put a bridle on my tongue. Bless this house, and everybody in it. Thank you, in the name of your Son, Jesus Christ, Amen."

Before she had quite arisen, she called our names and issued orders, and pushed her large feet into homemade slippers and across the bare lye-washed wooden floor to light the coal-oil lamp.

The lamplight in the Store gave a soft make-believe feeling to our world which made me want to whisper and walk about on tiptoe. The odors of onions and oranges and kerosene had been mixing all night and wouldn't be disturbed until the wooded slat was removed from the door and the early morning air forced its way in with the bodies of people who had walked miles to reach the pickup place.

"Sister, I'll have two cans of sardines."

"I'm gonna work so fast today I'm gonna make you look like you standing still."

"Lemme have a hunk uh cheese and some sody crackers."

"Just gimme a coupla them fat peanut paddies." That would be from a picker who was taking his lunch. The greasy brown paper sack was stuck behind the bib of his overalls. He'd use the candy as a snack before the noon sun called the workers to rest.

In those tender mornings the Store was full of laughing, joking, boasting and bragging. One man was going to pick two hundred pounds of cotton, and another three hundred. Even the children were promising to bring home fo' bits and six bits.

The champion picker of the day before was the hero of the dawn. If he prophesied that the cotton in today's field was going to be sparse and stick to the bolls like glue, every listener would grunt a hearty agreement.

The sound of the empty cotton sacks dragging over the floor and the murmurs of waking people were sliced by the cash register as we rang up the five-cent sales.

If the morning sounds and smells were touched with the supernatural, the late afternoon had all the features of the normal Arkansas life. In the dying sunlight the people dragged, rather than their empty cotton sacks.

Brought back to the Store, the pickers would step out of the backs of trucks and fold down, dirt-disappointed, to the ground. No matter how much they had picked, it wasn't enough. Their wages wouldn't even get them out of debt to my grandmother, not to mention the staggering bill that waited on them at the white commissary downtown.

The sounds of the new morning had been replaced with grumbles about cheating houses, weighted scales, snakes, skimpy cotton and dusty rows. In later years I was to confront the stereotyped picture of gay song-singing cotton pickers with such inordinate rage that I was told even by fellow Blacks that my paranoia was embarrassing. But I had seen the fingers cut by the mean little cotton bolls, and I had witnessed the backs and shoulders and arms and legs resisting any further demands.

Some of the workers would leave their sacks at the Store to be picked up the following morning, but a few had to take them home for repairs. I winced to picture them sewing the coarse material under a coal-oil lamp with fingers stiffening from the day's work. In too few hours they would have to walk back to Sister Henderson's Store, get vittles and load, again, onto the trucks. Then they would face another day of trying to earn enough for the whole year with the heavy knowledge that they were going to end the season as they started it. Without the money or credit necessary to sustain a family for three months. In cotton-picking time the late afternoons revealed the harshness of Black Southern life, which in the early morning had been softened by nature's blessing of grogginess, forgetfulness and the soft lamplight.

2

WHEN BAILEY WAS six and I a year younger, we used to rattle off the times tables with the speed I was later to see Chinese children in San Francisco employ on their abacuses. Our summer-gray pot-bellied stove bloomed rosy red during winter, and became a severe disciplinarian threat if we were so foolish as to indulge in making mistakes.

Uncle Willie used to sit, like a giant black Z (he had been crippled as a child), and hear us testify to the Lafayette County Training Schools' abilities. His face pulled down on the left side, as if a pulley had been attached to his lower teeth, and his left hand was only a mite bigger than Bailey's, but on the second mistake or on the third hesitation his big overgrown right hand would catch one of us behind the collar, and in the same moment would thrust the culprit toward the dull red heater, which throbbed like a devil's toothache. We were never burned, although once I might have been when I was so terrified I tried to jump onto the stove to remove the possibility of its remaining a threat. Like most children, I thought if I could face the worst danger voluntarily, and *triumph*, I would forever have power over it. But in my case of sacrificial effort I was thwarted. Uncle Willie held tight to my dress and I only got close enough to smell the clean dry scent of hot iron. We learned the times tables without understanding their grand principle, simply because we had the capacity and no alternative.

The tragedy of lameness seems so unfair to children that they are embarrassed in its presence. And they, most recently off nature's mold, sense that they have only narrowly missed being another of her jokes. In relief at the narrow escape, they vent their emotions in impatience and criticism of the unlucky cripple.

Momma related times without end, and without any show of emotion, how Uncle Willie had been dropped when he was three years old by a woman who was minding him. She seemed to hold no rancor against the baby-sitter, nor for her just God who allowed the accident. She felt it necessary to explain over and over again to those who knew the story by heart that he wasn't "born that way."

In our society, where two-legged, two-armed strong Black men were able at best to eke out only the necessities of life, Uncle Willie, with his starched shirts, shined shoes and shelves full of food, was the whipping boy and butt of jokes of the underemployed and underpaid. Fate not only disabled him but laid a double-tiered barrier in his path. He was also proud and sensitive. Therefore he couldn't pretend that he wasn't crippled, nor could he deceive himself that people were not repelled by his defect.

Only once in all the years of trying not to watch him, I saw him pretend to himself and others that he wasn't lame.

Coming home from school one day, I saw a dark car in our front yard. I rushed in to find a strange man and woman (Uncle Willie said later they were schoolteachers from Little Rock) drinking Dr. Pepper in the cool of the Store. I sensed a wrongness around me, like an alarm clock that had gone off without being set.

I knew it couldn't be the strangers. Not frequently, but often enough, travelers pulled off the main road to buy tobacco or soft drinks in the only Negro store in Stamps. When I looked at Uncle Willie, I knew what was pulling my mind's coattails. He was standing erect behind the counter, not leaning forward or resting on the small shelf that had been built for him. Erect. His eyes seemed to hold me with a mixture of threats and appeal.

I dutifully greeted the strangers and roamed my

eyes around for his walking stick. It was nowhere to be seen. He said, "Uh ... this this ... this ... uh, my niece. She's ... uh ... just come from school." Then to the couple—"You know ... how, uh, children are ... th-th-these days ... they play all d-d-day at school and c-c-can't wait to get home and pl-play some more."

The people smiled, very friendly.

He added, "Go on out and pl-play, Sister."

The lady laughed in a soft Arkansas voice and said, "Well, you know, Mr. Johnson, they say, you're only a child once. Have you children of your own?"

Uncle Willie looked at me with an impatience I hadn't seen in his face even when he took thirty minutes to loop the laces over his high-topped shoes. "I ... I thought I told you to go ... go outside and play."

Before I left I saw him lean back on the shelves of Garret Snuff, Prince Albert and Spark Plug chewing tobacco.

"No, ma'am ... no ch-children and no wife." He tried a laugh. "I have an old m-m-mother and my brother's t-two children to l-look after."

I didn't mind his using us to make himself look good. In fact, I would have pretended to be his daughter if he wanted me to. Not only did I not feel any loyalty to my own father, I figured that if I had been Uncle Willie's child I would have received much better treatment.

The couple left after a few minutes, and from the back of the house I watched the red car scare chickens, raise dust and disappear toward Magnolia.

Uncle Willie was making his way down the long shadowed aisle between the shelves and the counter—hand over hand, like a man climbing out of a dream. I stayed quiet and watched him lurch from one side, bumping to the other, until he reached the coal-oil tank. He put his hand behind that dark recess and took his cane in the strong fist and shifted his weight on the wooden support. He thought he had pulled it off.

I'll never know why it was important to him that the couple (he said later that he'd never seen them before) would take a picture of a whole Mr. Johnson back to Little Rock.

He must have tired of being crippled, as prisoners tire of penitentiary bars and the guilty tire of blame. The high-topped shoes and the cane, his uncontrollable muscles and thick tongue, and the looks he suffered of either contempt or pity had simply worn him out, and for one afternoon, one part of an afternoon, he wanted no part of them.

I understood and felt closer to him at that moment than ever before or since.

During these years in Stamps, I met and fell in love with William Shakespeare. He was my first white love. Although I enjoyed and respected Kipling, Poe, Butler, Thackeray and Henley, I saved my young and loyal passion for Paul Lawrence Dunbar, Langston Hughes, James Weldon Johnson and W.E.B. Du Bois' "Litany at Atlanta." But it was Shakespeare who said, "When in disgrace with fortune and men's eyes." It was a state with which I felt myself most familiar. I pacified myself about his whiteness by saying that after all he had been dead so long it couldn't matter to anyone any more.

Bailey and I decided to memorize a scene from *The Merchant of Venice*, but we realized that Momma would question us about the author and that we'd have to tell her that Shakespeare was white, and it wouldn't matter to her whether he was dead or not. So we chose "The Creation" by James Weldon Johnson instead.

3

WEIGHING THE half-pounds of flour, excluding the scoop, and depositing them dust-free into the thin paper sacks held a simple kind of adventure for me. I developed an eye for measuring how full a silver-looking ladle of flour, mash, meal, sugar or corn had to be to push the scale indicator over to eight ounces or one pound. When I was absolutely accurate our appreciative customers used to admire: "Sister Henderson sure got some smart grandchildrens." If I was off in the Store's favor, the eagle-eyed women would say, "Put some more in that sack, child. Don't you try to make your profit offa me."

Then I would quietly but persistently punish myself. For every bad judgment, the fine was no silver-wrapped Kisses, the sweet chocolate drops that I loved more than anything in the world, except Bailey. And maybe canned pineapples. My obsession with pineapples nearly drove me mad. I dreamt of the days when I would be grown and able to buy a whole carton for myself alone.

Although the syrupy golden rings sat in their exotic cans on our shelves year round, we only tasted them during Christmas. Momma used the juice to make almost-black fruit cakes. Then she lined heavy soot-encrusted iron skillets with the pineapple rings for rich upside-down cakes. Bailey and I received one slice each, and I carried mine around for hours, shredding off the fruit until nothing was left except the perfume on my fingers. I'd like to think that my desire for pineapples was so sacred that I wouldn't allow myself to steal a can (which was possible) and eat it alone out in the garden, but I'm certain that I must have weighed the possibility of the scent exposing me and didn't have the nerve to attempt it.

Until I was thirteen and left Arkansas for good, the Store was my favorite place to be. Alone and empty in the mornings, it looked like an unopened present from a stranger. Opening the front doors was pulling the ribbon off the unexpected gift. The light would come in softly (we faced north), easing itself over the shelves of mackerel, salmon, tobacco, thread. It fell flat on the big vat of lard and by noontime during the summer the grease had softened to a thick soup. Whenever I walked into the Store in the afternoon, I sensed that it was tired. I alone could hear the slow pulse of its job half done. But just before bedtime, after numerous people had walked in and out, had argued over their bills, or joked about their neighbors, or just dropped in "to give Sister Henderson a 'Hi y'all,'" the promise of magic mornings returned to the Store and spread itself over the family in washed life waves.

Momma opened boxes of crispy crackers and we sat around the meat block at the rear of the Store. I sliced onions, and Bailey opened two or even three cans of sardines and allowed their juice of oil and fishing boats to ooze down and around the sides. That was supper. In the evening, when we were alone like that, Uncle Willie didn't stutter or shake or give any indication that he had an "affliction." It seemed that the peace of a day's ending was an assurance that the covenant God made with children, Negroes and the crippled was still in effect.

Throwing scoops of corn to the chickens and mixing sour dry mash with leftover food and oily dish water for the hogs were among our evening chores. Bailey and I sloshed down twilight trails to the pig pens, and standing on the first fence rungs we poured down the unappealing concoctions to our grateful hogs. They mashed their tender pink snouts down into the slop, and rooted and grunted their satisfaction. We always grunted a reply only half in jest. We were also grateful that we had concluded the dirtiest of chores and had only gotten the evil-smelling swill on our shoes, stockings, feet and hands.

Late one day, as we were attending to the pigs, I heard a horse in the front yard (it really should have been called a driveway, except that there was nothing to drive into it), and ran to find out who had come riding up on a Thursday evening when even Mr. Steward, the quiet, bitter man who owned a riding horse, would be resting by his warm fire until the morning called him out to turn over his field.

The used-to-be sheriff sat rakishly astraddle his horse. His nonchalance was meant to convey his authority and power over even dumb animals. How much more capable he would be with Negroes. It went without saying.

His twang jogged in the brittle air. From the side of the Store, Bailey and I heard him say to Momma, "Annie, tell Willie he better lay low tonight. A crazy nigger messed with a white lady today. Some of the boys'll be coming over here later." Even after the slow drag of years, I remember the sense of fear which filled my mouth with hot, dry air, and made my body light.

The "boys"? Those cement faces and eyes of hate that burned the clothes off you if they happened to see you lounging on the main street downtown on Saturday. Boys? It seemed that youth had never happened to them. Boys? No, rather men who were covered with graves' dust and age without beauty or learning. The ugliness and rottenness of old abominations.

If on Judgment Day I were summoned by St. Peter to give testimony to the used-to-be sheriff's act of kindness, I would be unable to say anything in his behalf. His confidence that my uncle and every other Black man who heard of the Klan's coming ride would scurry under their houses to hide in chicken droppings was too humiliating to hear. Without waiting for Momma's thanks, he rode out of the yard, sure that things were as they should be and that he was a gentle squire, saving those deserving serfs from the laws of the land, which he condoned.

Immediately, while his horse's hoofs were still loudly thudding the ground, Momma blew out the coal-oil lamps. She had a quiet, hard talk with Uncle Willie and called Bailey and me into the Store.

We were told to take the potatoes and onions out of their bins and knock out the dividing walls that kept them apart. Then with a tedious and fearful slowness Uncle Willie gave me his rubber-tipped cane and bent down to get into the now-enlarged empty bin. It took forever before he lay down flat, and then we covered him with potatoes and onions, layer upon layer, like a casserole. Grandmother knelt praying in the darkened Store.

It was fortunate that the "boys" didn't ride into our yard that evening and insist that Momma open the Store. They would have surely found Uncle Willie and just as surely lynched him. He moaned the whole night through as if he had, in fact, been guilty of some heinous crime. The heavy sounds pushed their way up out of the blanket of vegetables and I pictured his mouth pulling down on the right side and his saliva flowing into the eyes of new potatoes and waiting there like dew drops for the warmth of morning.

4

WHAT SETS ONE Southern town apart from another, or from a Northern town or hamlet, or city high-rise? The answer must be the experience shared between the unknowing majority (it) and the knowing minority (you). All of childhood's unanswered questions must finally be passed back to the town and answered there. Heroes and bogey men, values and dislikes, are first encountered and labeled in that early environment.

In later years they change faces, places and maybe races, tactics, intensities and goals, but beneath those penetrable masks they wear forever the stocking-capped faces of childhood.

Mr. McElroy, who lived in the big rambling house next to the Store, was very tall and broad, and although the years had eaten away the flesh from his shoulders, they had not, at the time of my knowing him, gotten to his high stomach, or his hands or feet.

He was the only Negro I knew, except for the school principal and the visiting teachers, who wore matching pants and jackets. When I learned that men's clothes were sold like that and called suits, I remember thinking that somebody had been very bright, for it made men look less manly, less threatening and a little more like women.

Mr. McElroy never laughed, and seldom smiled, and to his credit was the fact that he liked to talk to Uncle Willie. He never went to church, which Bailey and I thought also proved he was a very courageous person. How great it would be to grow up like that, to be able to stare religion down, especially living next door to a woman like Momma.

I watched him with the excitement of expecting him to do anything at any time. I never tired of this, or became disappointed or disenchanted with him, although from the perch of age, I see him now as a very simple and uninteresting man who sold patent medicine and tonics to the less sophisticated people in towns (villages) surrounding the metropolis of Stamps.

There seemed to be an understanding between Mr. McElroy and Grandmother. This was obvious to us because he never chased us off his land. In summer's late sunshine I often sat under the chinaberry tree in his yard, surrounded by the bitter aroma of its fruit and lulled by the drone of flies that fed on the berries. He sat in a slotted swing on his porch, rocking in his brown three-piece, his wide Panama nodding in time with the whir of insects.

One greeting a day was all that could be expected from Mr. McElroy. After his "Good morning, child," or "Good afternoon, child," he never said a word, even if I met him again on the road in front of his house or down by the well, or ran into him behind the house escaping in a game of hide-and-seek.

He remained a mystery in my childhood. A man who owned his land and the big many-windowed house with a porch that clung to its sides all around the house. An independent Black man. A near anachronism in Stamps.

Bailey was the greatest person in my world. And the fact that he was my brother, my only brother, and I had no sisters to share him with, was such good fortune that it made me want to live a Christian life just to show God that I was grateful. Where I was big, elbowy and grating, he was small, graceful and smooth. When I was described by our playmates as being shit color, he was lauded for his velvet-black skin. His hair fell down in black curls, and my head was covered with black steel wool. And yet he loved me.

When our elders said unkind things about my features (my family was handsome to a point of pain for me), Bailey would wink at me from across the room, and I knew that it was a matter of time before he would take revenge. He would allow the old ladies to finish wondering how on earth I came about, then he would ask, in a voice like cooling bacon grease, "Oh Mizeriz Coleman, how is your son? I saw him the other day, and he looked sick enough to die."

Aghast, the ladies would ask, "Die? From what? He ain't sick."

And in a voice oilier than the one before, he'd answer with a straight face, "From the Uglies."

I would hold my laugh, bite my tongue, grit my teeth and very seriously erase even the touch of a smile from my face. Later, behind the house by the black-walnut tree, we'd laugh and laugh and howl.

Bailey could count on very few punishments for his consistently outrageous behavior, for he was the pride of the Henderson/Johnson family.

His movements, as he was later to describe those of an acquaintance, were activated with oiled precision. He was also able to find more hours in the day than I thought existed. He finished chores, homework, read more books than I and played the group games on the side of the hill with the best of them. He could even pray out loud in church, and was apt at stealing pickles from the barrel that sat under the fruit counter and Uncle Willie's nose.

Once when the Store was full of lunchtime customers, he dipped the strainer, which we also used to sift weevils from meal and flour, into the barrel and fished for two fat pickles. He caught them and hooked the strainer onto the side of the barrel where they dripped until he was ready for them. When the last school bell rang, he picked the nearly dry pickles out of the strainer, jammed them into his pockets and threw the strainer behind the oranges. We ran out of the Store. It was summer and his pants were short, so the pickle juice made clean streams down his ashy legs, and he jumped with his pockets full of loot and his eyes laughing a "How about that?" He smelled like a vinegar barrel or a sour angel.

After our early chores were done, while Uncle Willie or Momma minded the Store, we were free to play the children's games as long as we stayed within yelling distance. Playing hide-and-seek, his voice was easily identified, singing, "Last night, night before, twenty-four robbers at my door. Who all is hid? Ask me to let them in, hit 'em in the head with a rolling pin. Who all is hid?" In follow the leader, naturally he was the one who created the most daring and interesting things to do. And when he was on the tail of the pop the whip, he would twirl off the end like a top, spinning, falling, laughing, finally stopping just before my heart beat its last, and then he was back in the game, still laughing.

Of all the needs (there are none imaginary) a lonely child has, the one that must be satisfied, if there is going to be hope and a hope of wholeness, is the unshaking need for an unshakable God. My pretty Black brother was my Kingdom Come.

In Stamps the custom was to can everything that could possibly be preserved. During the killing season, after the first frost, all neighbors helped each other to slaughter hogs and even the quiet, big-eyed cows if they had stopped giving milk.

The missionary ladies of the Christian Methodist Episcopal Church helped Momma prepare the pork for sausage. They squeezed their fat arms elbow deep in the ground meat, mixed it with gray nose-opening sage, pepper and salt, and made tasty little samples for all obedient children who brought wood for the slick black stove. The men chopped off the larger pieces of meat and laid them in the smoke-house to begin the curing process. They opened the knuckle of the hams with their deadly-looking knives, took out a certain round harmless bone ("it could make the meat go bad") and rubbed salt, coarse brown salt that looked like fine gravel, into the flesh, and the blood popped to the surface.

Throughout the year, until the next frost, we took our meals from the smokehouse, the little garden that lay cousin-close to the Store and from the shelves of canned foods. There were choices on the shelves that could set a hungry child's mouth to watering. Green beans, snapped always the right length, collards, cabbage, juicy red tomato preserves that came into their own on steaming buttered biscuits, and sausage, beets, berries and every fruit grown in Arkansas.

But at least twice yearly Momma would feel that as children we should have fresh meat included in our diets. We were then given money—pennies, nickels, and dimes entrusted to Bailey—and sent to town to buy liver. Since the whites had refrigerators, their butchers bought the meat from commercial slaughterhouses in Texarkana and sold it to the wealthy even in the peak of summer.

Crossing the Black area of Stamps which in childhood's narrow measure seemed a whole world, we were obliged by custom to stop and speak to every person we met, and Bailey felt constrained to spend a few minutes playing with each friend. There was a joy in going to town with money in our pockets (Bailey's pockets were as good as my own) and time on our hands. But the pleasure fled when we reached the white part of town. After we left Mr. Willie Williams' Do Drop Inn, the last stop before whitefolksville, we had to cross the pond and adventure the railroad tracks. We were explorers walking without weapons into man-eating animals' territory.

In Stamps the segregation was so complete that most Black children didn't really, absolutely know what whites looked like. Other than that they were different, to be dreaded, and in that dread was included the hostility of the powerless against the powerful, the poor against the rich, the worker against the worked for and the ragged against the well dressed.

I remember never believing that whites were really real.

Many women who worked in their kitchens traded at our Store, and when they carried their finished laundry back to town they often set the big baskets down on our front porch to pull a singular piece from the starched collection and show either how graceful was their ironing hand or how rich and opulent was the property of their employers.

I looked at the items that weren't on display. I knew, for instance, that white men wore shorts, as Uncle Willie did, and that they had an opening for taking out their "things" and peeing, and that white women's breasts weren't built into their dresses, as some people said, because I saw their brassieres in the baskets. But I couldn't force myself to think of them as people. People were Mrs. LaGrone, Mrs. Hendricks, Momma, Reverend Sneed, Lillie B, and Louise and Rex. Whitefolks couldn't be people because their feet were too small, their skin too white and see-throughy, and they didn't walk on the balls of their feet the way people did—they walked on their heels like horses.

People were those who lived on my side of town. I didn't like them all, or, in fact, any of them very much, but they were people. These others, the strange pale creatures that lived in their alien unlife, weren't considered folks. They were whitefolks.

5

"Thou shall not be dirty" and "Thou shall not be impudent" were the two commandments of Grandmother Henderson upon which hung our total salvation.

Each night in the bitterest winter we were forced to wash faces, arms, necks, legs and feet before going to bed. She used to add, with a smirk that unprofane people can't control when venturing into profanity, "and wash as far as possible, then wash possible."

We would go to the well and wash in the ice-cold, clear water, grease our legs with the equally cold stiff Vaseline, then tiptoe into the house. We wiped the dust from our toes and settled down for schoolwork, cornbread, clabbered milk, prayers and bed, always in that order. Momma was famous for pulling the quilts off after we had fallen asleep to examine our feet. If they weren't clean enough for her, she took the switch (she kept one behind the bedroom door for emergencies) and woke up the offender with a few aptly placed burning reminders.

The area around the well at night was dark and

slick, and boys told about how snakes love water, so
that anyone who had to draw water at night and
then stand there alone and wash knew that mocca-
sins and rattlers, puff adders and boa constrictors
were winding their way to the well and would arrive just as the person washing got soap in her eyes.
But Momma convinced us that not only was clean-
liness next to Godliness, dirtiness was the inventor of
misery.

The impudent child was detested by God and a
shame to its parents and could bring destruction to
its house and line. All adults had to be addressed as
Mister, Missus, Miss, Auntie, Cousin, Unk, Uncle,
Buhbah, Sister, Brother and a thousand other appel-
lations indicating familial relationship and the low-
liness of the addressor.

Everyone I knew respected these customary laws,
except for the powhitetrash children.

Some families of powhitetrash lived on Momma's
farm land behind the school. Sometimes a gaggle of
them came to the Store, filling the whole room, chas-
ing out the air and even changing the well-known
scents. The children crawled over the shelves and
into the potato and onion bins, twanging all the time
in their sharp voices like cigar-box guitars. They
took liberties in my Store that I would never dare.
Since Momma told us that the less you say to whitefolks (or even powhitetrash) the better, Bailey and
I would stand, solemn, quiet, in the displaced air.
But if one of the playful apparitions got close to us,
I pinched it. Partly out of angry frustration and
partly because I didn't believe in its flesh reality.

They called my uncle by his first name and ordered him around the Store. He, to my crying
shame, obeyed them in his limping dip-straight-dip
fashion.

My grandmother, too, followed their orders, except that she didn't seem to be servile because she
anticipated their needs.

"Here's sugar, Miz Potter, and here's baking powder. You didn't buy soda last month, you'll probably be needing some."

Momma always directed her statements to the adults, but sometimes, Oh painful sometimes, the grimy, snotty-nosed girls would answer her.

"Naw, Annie . . ."—to Momma? Who owned the land they lived on? Who forgot more than they would ever learn? If there was any justice in the world, God should strike them dumb at once!—"Just give us some extry sody crackers, and some more mackerel."

At least they never looked in her face, or I never caught them doing so. Nobody with a smidgen of training, not even the worst roustabout, would look right in a grown person's face. It meant the person was trying to take the words out before they were formed. The dirty little children didn't do that, but they threw their orders around the Store like lashes from a cat-o'-nine-tails.

When I was around ten years old, those scruffy children caused me the most painful and confusing experience I had ever had with my grandmother.

One summer morning, after I had swept the dirt yard of leaves, spearmint-gum wrappers and Vienna-sausage labels, I raked the yellow-red dirt, and made half-moons carefully, so that the design stood out clearly and mask-like. I put the rake behind the Store and came through the back of the house to find Grandmother on the front porch in her big, wide white apron. The apron was so stiff by virtue of the starch that it could have stood alone. Momma was admiring the yard, so I joined her. It truly looked like a flat redhead that had been raked with a big-toothed comb. Momma didn't say anything but I knew she liked it. She looked over toward the school principal's house and to the right at Mr. McElroy's. She was hoping one of those community pillars would see the design before the day's business wiped it out. Then she looked upward to the school. My head had swung with hers, so at just

about the same time we saw a troop of the powhitetrash kids marching over the hill and down by the
side of the school.

I looked to Momma for direction. She did an
excellent job of sagging from her waist down, but
from the waist up she seemed to be pulling for the
top of the oak tree across the road. Then she began
to moan a hymn. Maybe not to moan, but the tune
was so slow and the meter so strange that she could
have been moaning. She didn't look at me again.
When the children reached halfway down the hill,
halfway to the Store, she said without turning, "Sister, go on inside."

I wanted to beg her, "Momma, don't wait for
them. Come on inside with me. If they come in the
Store, you go to the bedroom and let me wait on
them. They only frighten me if you're around. Alone
I know how to handle them." But of course I
couldn't say anything, so I went in and stood behind
the screen door.

Before the girls got to the porch I heard their
laughter crackling and popping like pine logs in a
cooking stove. I suppose my lifelong paranoia was
born in those cold, molasses-slow minutes. They
came finally to stand on the ground in front of
Momma. At first they pretended seriousness. Then
one of them wrapped her right arm in the crook of
her left, pushed out her mouth and started to hum. I
realized that she was aping my grandmother. Another said, "Naw, Helen, you ain't standing like her.
This here's it." Then she lifted her chest, folded her
arms and mocked that strange carriage that was
Annie Henderson. Another laughed, "Naw, you can't
do it. Your mouth ain't pooched out enough. It's like
this."

I thought about the rifle behind the door, but I
knew I'd never be able to hold it straight, and the
.410, our sawed-off shotgun, which stayed loaded
and was fired every New Year's night, was locked in
the trunk and Uncle Willie had the key on his

chain. Through the fly-specked screen-door, I could
see that the arms of Momma's apron jiggled from
the vibrations of her humming. But her knees seemed
to have locked as if they would never bend again.

She sang on. No louder than before, but no softer
either. No slower or faster.

The dirt of the girls' cotton dresses continued on
their legs, feet, arms and faces to make them all of a
piece. Their greasy uncolored hair hung down,
uncombed, with a grim finality. I knelt to see them
better, to remember them for all time. The tears that
had slipped down my dress left unsurprising dark
spots, and made the front yard blurry and even more
unreal. The world had taken a deep breath and was
having doubts about continuing to revolve.

The girls had tired of mocking Momma and
turned to other means of agitation. One crossed her
eyes, stuck her thumbs in both sides of her mouth
and said, "Look here, Annie." Grandmother hummed
on and the apron strings trembled. I wanted to
throw a handful of black pepper in their faces, to
throw lye on them, to scream that they were dirty,
scummy peckerwoods, but I knew I was as clearly
imprisoned behind the scene as the actors outside
were confined to their roles.

One of the smaller girls did a kind of puppet
dance while her fellow clowns laughed at her. But
the tall one, who was almost a woman, said something very quietly, which I couldn't hear. They all
moved backward from the porch, still watching
Momma. For an awful second I thought they were
going to throw a rock at Momma, who seemed (except for the apron strings) to have turned into stone
herself. But the big girl turned her back, bent down
and put her hands flat on the ground—she didn't
pick up anything. She simply shifted her weight and
did a hand stand.

Her dirty bare feet and long legs went straight for
the sky. Her dress fell down around her shoulders,
and she had on no drawers. The slick pubic hair

made a brown triangle where her legs came together. She hung in the vacuum of that lifeless morning for only a few seconds, then wavered and tumbled. The other girls clapped her on the back and slapped their hands.

Momma changed her song to "Bread of Heaven, bread of Heaven, feed me till I want no more."

I found that I was praying too. How long could Momma hold out? What new indignity would they think of to subject her to? Would I be able to stay out of it? What would Momma really like me to do?

Then they were moving out of the yard, on their way to town. They bobbed their heads and shook their slack behinds and turned, one at a time:

" 'Bye, Annie."

" 'Bye, Annie."

" 'Bye, Annie."

Momma never turned her head or unfolded her arms, but she stopped singing and said, " 'Bye, Miz Helen, 'bye, Miz Ruth, 'bye, Miz Eloise."

I burst. A firecracker July-the-Fourth burst. How could Momma call them Miz? The mean nasty things. Why couldn't she have come inside the sweet, cool store when we saw them breasting the hill? What did she prove? And then if they were dirty, mean and impudent, why did Momma have to call them Miz?

She stood another whole song through and then opened the screen door to look down on me crying in rage. She looked until I looked up. Her face was a brown moon that shone on me. She was beautiful. Something had happened out there, which I couldn't completely understand, but I could see that she was happy. Then she bent down and touched me as mothers of the church "lay hands on the sick and afflicted" and I quieted.

"Go wash your face, Sister." And she went behind the candy counter and hummed, "Glory, glory, hallelujah, when I lay my burden down."

I threw the well water on my face and used the

weekday handkerchief to blow my nose. Whatever the contest had been out front, I knew Momma had won.

I took the rake back to the front yard. The smudged footprints were easy to erase. I worked for a long time on my new design and laid the rake behind the wash pot. When I came back in the Store, I took Momma's hand and we both walked outside to look at the pattern.

It was a large heart with lots of hearts growing smaller inside, and piercing from the outside rim to the smallest heart was an arrow. Momma said, "Sister, that's right pretty." Then she turned back to the Store and resumed, "Glory, glory, hallelujah, when I lay my burden down."

6

REVEREND HOWARD THOMAS was the presiding elder over a district in Arkansas that included Stamps. Every three months he visited our church, stayed at Momma's over the Saturday night and preached a loud passionate sermon on Sunday. He collected the money that had been taken in over the preceding months, heard reports from all the church groups and shook hands with the adults and kissed all small children. Then he went away. (I used to think that he went west to heaven, but Momma straightened me out. He just went to Texarkana.)

Bailey and I hated him unreservedly. He was ugly, fat, and he laughed like a hog with the colic. We were able to make each other burst with giggling when we did imitations of the thick-skinned preacher. Bailey was especially good at it. He could imitate Reverend Thomas right in front of Uncle Willie and never get caught because he did it soundlessly. He puffed out his cheeks until they looked like wet brown stones, and wobbled his head from side to side. Only he and I knew it, but that was old Reverend Thomas to a tree.

His obesity, while disgusting, was not enough to incur the intense hate that we felt for him. The fact that he never bothered to remember our names was insulting, but neither was that slight, alone, enough to make us despise him. But the crime that tipped the scale and made our hate not only just but imperative was his actions at the dinner table. He ate the biggest, brownest and best parts of the chicken at every Sunday meal.

The only good thing about his visits was the fact that he always arrived late on Saturday nights, after we had had dinner. I often wondered if he tried to catch us at the table. I believe so, for when he reached the front porch his little eyes would glitter toward the empty dining room and his face would fall with disappointment. Then immediately, a thin curtain would fall over his features and he'd laugh a few barks, "Uh, huh, uh, huh, Sister Henderson, just like a penny with a hole in it, I always turns up."

Right on cue every time, Momma would answer, "That's right, Elder Thomas, thank the blessed Jesus, come right in."

He'd step in the front door and put down his Gladstone (that's what he called it) and look around for Bailey and me. Then he opened his awful arms and groaned, "Suffer little children to come unto me, for such is the Kingdom of Heaven."

Bailey went to him each time with his hand stretched out, ready for a manly handshake, but Reverend Thomas would push away the hand and encircle my brother for a few seconds. "You still a boy, buddy. Remember that. They tell me the Good Book say, 'When I was a child I spake as a child, I thought as a child, but when I became a man, I put away childish things.' " Only then would he open his arms and release Bailey.

I never had the nerve to go up to him. I was quite afraid that if I tried to say, "Hello, Reverend Thomas," I would choke on the sin of mocking him. After all, the Bible did say, "God is not mocked," and the man was God's representative. He used to say to me, "Come on, little sister. Come and get this blessing." But I was so afraid and I also hated him so much that my emotions mixed themselves up and it was enough to start me crying. Momma told him time after time, "Don't pay her no mind, Elder Thomas, you know how tender-hearted she is."

He ate the leftovers from our dinner and he and Uncle Willie discussed the developments of the church programs. They talked about how the present minister was attending to his flock, who got married, who died and how many children had been born since his last visit.

Bailey and I stood like shadows in the rear of the Store near the coal-oil tank, waiting for the juicy parts. But when they were ready to talk about the latest scandal, Momma sent us to her bedroom with warnings to have our Sunday School lesson perfectly memorized or we knew what we could expect.

We had a system that never failed. I would sit in the big rocking chair by the stove and rock occasionally and stamp my feet. I changed voices, now soft and girlish, then a little deeper like Bailey's. Meanwhile, he would creep back into the Store. Many times he came flying back to sit on the bed and to hold the open lesson book just before Momma suddenly filled the doorway.

"You children get your lesson good, now. You know all the other children looks up to you all." Then, as she turned back into the Store Bailey followed right on her footsteps to crouch in the shadows and listen for the forbidden gossip.

Once, he heard how Mr. Coley Washington had a girl from Lewisville staying in his house. I didn't think that was so bad, but Bailey explained that Mr. Washington was probably "doing it" to her. He said that although "it" was bad just about everybody in the world did it to somebody, but no one else was supposed to know that. And once, we found out about a man who had been killed by whitefolks and thrown into the pond. Bailey said the man's things had been cut off and put in his pocket and he had been shot in the head, all because the whitefolks said he did "it" to a white woman.

Because of the kinds of news we filched from those hushed conversations, I was convinced that whenever Reverend Thomas came and Momma sent us to the back room they were going to discuss white-folks and "doing it." Two subjects about which I was very dim.

On Sunday mornings Momma served a breakfast that was geared to hold us quiet from 9:30 A.M. to 3 P.M. She fried thick pink slabs of home-cured ham and poured the grease over sliced red tomatoes. Eggs over easy, fried potatoes and onions, yellow hominy and crisp perch fried so hard we would pop them in our mouths and chew bones, fins and all. Her cathead biscuits were at least three inches in diame-ter and two inches thick. The trick to eating catheads was to get the butter on them before they got cold—then they were delicious. When, unlucki-ly, they were allowed to get cold, they tended to a gooeyness, not unlike a wad of tired gum.

We were able to reaffirm our findings on the catheads each Sunday that Reverend Thomas spent with us. Naturally enough, he was asked to bless the table. We would all stand; my uncle, leaning his walking stick against the wall, would lean his weight on the table. Then Reverend Thomas would begin. "Blessed Father, we thank you this morning . . ." and on and on and on. I'd stop listening after a while until Bailey kicked me and then I cracked my lids to see what had promised to be a meal that would make any Sunday proud. But as the Reverend droned on and on and on to a God who I thought must be bored to hear the same things over and over again, I saw that the ham grease had turned white on the tomatoes. The eggs had withdrawn from the edge of the platter to bunch in the center like children left out in the cold. And the catheads had sat down on themselves with the conclusiveness of a fat woman sitting in an easy chair. And still he talked on. When he finally stopped, our appetites were gone, but he feasted on the cold food with a non-talking but still noisy relish.

In the Christian Methodist Episcopal Church the children's section was on the right, cater-cornered from the pew that held those ominous women called the Mothers of the Church. In the young people's section the benches were placed close together, and when a child's legs no longer comfortably fitted in the narrow space, it was an indication to the elders that that person could now move into the intermediate area (center church). Bailey and I were allowed to sit with the other children only when there were informal meetings, church socials or the like. But on the Sundays when Reverend Thomas preached, it was ordained that we occupy the first row, called the mourners' bench. I thought we were placed in front because Momma was proud of us, but Bailey assured me that she just wanted to keep her grandchildren under her thumb and eye.

Reverend Thomas took his text from Deuteronomy. And I was stretched between loathing his voice and wanting to listen to the sermon. Deuteronomy was my favorite book in the Bible. The laws were so absolute, so clearly set down, that I knew if a person truly wanted to avoid hell and brimstone, and being roasted forever in the devil's fire, all she had to do was memorize Deuteronomy and follow its teaching, word for word. I also liked the way the word rolled off the tongue.

Bailey and I sat alone on the front bench, the wooden slats pressing hard on our behinds and the backs of our thighs. I would have wriggled just a bit, but each time I looked over at Momma, she seemed to threaten, "Move and I'll tear you up," so, obedient to the unvoiced command, I sat still. The church ladies were warming up behind me with a few hallelujahs and Praise the Lords and Amens, and the preacher hadn't really moved into the meat of the sermon.

It was going to be a hot service.

On my way into church, I saw Sister Monroe, her open-faced gold crown glinting when she opened her mouth to return a neighborly greeting. She lived in the country and couldn't get to church every Sunday, so she made up for her absences by shouting so hard when she did make it that she shook the whole church. As soon as she took her seat, all the ushers would move to her side of the church because it took three women and sometimes a man or two to hold her.

Once when she hadn't been to church for a few months (she had taken off to have a child), she got the spirit and started shouting, throwing her arms around and jerking her body, so that the ushers went over to hold her down, but she tore herself away from them and ran up to the pulpit. She stood in front of the altar, shaking like a freshly caught trout. She screamed at Reverend Taylor. "Preach it. I say, preach it." Naturally he kept on preaching as if she wasn't standing there telling him what to do. Then she screamed an extremely fierce "I said, preach it" and stepped up on the altar. The Reverend kept on throwing out phrases like home-run balls and Sister Monroe made a quick break and grasped for him. For just a second, everything and everyone in the church except Reverend Taylor and Sister Monroe hung loose like stockings on a washline. Then she caught the minister by the sleeve of his jacket and his coattail, then she rocked him from side to side.

I have to say this for our minister, he never stopped giving us the lesson. The usher board made its way to the pulpit, going up both aisles with a little more haste than is customarily seen in church. Truth to tell, they fairly ran to the minister's aid. Then two of the deacons, in their shiny Sunday suits, joined the ladies in white on the pulpit, and each time they pried Sister Monroe loose from the preacher he took another deep breath and kept on preaching, and Sister Monroe grabbed him in another place, and more firmly. Reverend Taylor was helping his rescuers as much as possible by jumping around when he got a chance. His voice at one point got so low it sounded like a roll of thunder, then Sister Monroe's "Preach it" cut through the roar, and we all wondered (I did, in any case) if it would ever end. Would they go on forever, or get tired out at last like a game of blindman's bluff that lasted too long, with nobody caring who was "it"?

I'll never know what might have happened, because magically the pandemonium spread. The spirit infused Deacon Jackson and Sister Willson, the chairman of the usher board, at the same time. Deacon Jackson, a tall, thin, quiet man, who was also a part-time Sunday school teacher, gave a scream like a falling tree, leaned back on thin air and punched Reverend Taylor on the arm. It must have hurt as much as it caught the Reverend unawares. There was a moment's break in the rolling sounds and Reverend Taylor jerked around surprised, and hauled off and punched Deacon Jackson. In the same second Sister Willson caught his tie, looped it over her fist a few times, and pressed down on him. There wasn't time to laugh or cry before all three of them were down on the floor behind the altar. Their legs spiked out like kindling wood.

Sister Monroe, who had been the cause of all the excitement, walked off the dais, cool and spent, and raised her flinty voice in the hymn, "I came to Jesus, as I was, worried, wound, and sad, I found in Him a resting place and He has made me glad."

The minister took advantage of already being on the floor and asked in a choky little voice if the church would kneel with him to offer a prayer of thanksgiving. He said we had been visited with a mighty spirit, and let the whole church say Amen.

On the next Sunday, he took his text from the eighteenth chapter of the Gospel according to St. Luke, and talked quietly but seriously about the Pharisees, who prayed in the streets so that the public would be impressed with their religious devotion. I doubt that anyone got the message—certainly not those to whom it was directed. The deacon board, however, did appropriate funds for him to buy a new suit. The other was a total loss.

Our presiding elder had heard the story of Reverend Taylor and Sister Monroe, but I was sure he didn't know her by sight. So my interest in the service's potential and my aversion to Reverend Thomas caused me to turn him off. Turning off or tuning out people was my highly developed art. The custom of letting obedient children be seen but not heard was so agreeable to me that I went one step further: Obedient children should not see or hear if they chose not to do so. I laid a handful of attention on my face and tuned up the sounds in the church.

Sister Monroe's fuse was already lit, and she sizzled somewhere to the right behind me. Elder Thomas jumped into the sermon, determined, I suppose, to give the members what they came for. I saw the ushers from the left side of the church near the big windows begin to move discreetly, like pallbearers, toward Sister Monroe's bench. Bailey jogged my knee. When the incident with Sister Monroe, which we always called simply "the incident," had taken place, we had been too astounded to laugh. But for weeks after, all we needed to send us into violent outbursts of laughter was a whispered "Preach it." Anyway, he pushed my knee, covered his mouth and whispered, "I say, preach it."

I looked toward Momma, across that square of stained boards, over the collection table, hoping that a look from her would root me safely to my sanity. But for the first time in memory Momma was staring behind me at Sister Monroe. I supposed that she was counting on bringing that emotional lady up short with a severe look or two. But Sister Monroe's voice had already reached the danger point. "Preach it!"

There were a few smothered giggles from the children's section, and Bailey nudged me again. "I say, preach it"—in a whisper. Sister Monroe echoed him loudly, "I say, preach it!"

Two deacons wedged themselves around Brother Jackson as a preventive measure and two large determined-looking men walked down the aisle toward Sister Monroe.

While the sounds in the church were increasing, Elder Thomas made the regrettable mistake of increasing his volume too. Then suddenly, like a summer rain, Sister Monroe broke through the cloud of people trying to hem her in, and flooded up to the pulpit. She didn't stop this time but continued immediately to the altar, bound for Elder Thomas, crying "I say, preach it."

Bailey said out loud, "Hot dog" and "Damn" and "She's going to beat his butt."

But Reverend Thomas didn't intend to wait for that eventuality, so as Sister Monroe approached the pulpit from the right he started descending from the left. He was not intimidated by his change of venue. He continued preaching and moving. He finally stopped right in front of the collection table, which put him almost in our laps, and Sister Monroe rounded the altar on his heels, followed by the deacons, ushers, some unofficial members and a few of the bigger children.

Just as the elder opened his mouth, pink tongue waving, and said, "Great God of Mount Nebo," Sister Monroe hit him on the back of his head with her purse. Twice. Before he could bring his lips together, his teeth fell, no, actually his teeth jumped, out of his mouth.

The grinning uppers and lowers lay by my right

shoe, looking empty and at the same time appearing to contain all the emptiness in the world. I could have stretched out a foot and kicked them under the bench or behind the collection table.

Sister Monroe was struggling with his coat, and the men had all but picked her up to remove her from the building. Bailey pinched me and said without moving his lips, "I'd like to see him eat dinner now."

I looked at Reverend Thomas desperately. If he appeared just a little sad or embarrassed, I could feel sorry for him and wouldn't be able to laugh. My sympathy for him would keep me from laughing. I dreaded laughing in church. If I lost control, two things were certain to happen. I would surely pee, and just as surely get a whipping. And this time I would probably die because everything was funny— Sister Monroe, and Momma trying to keep her quiet with those threatening looks, and Bailey whispering "Preach it" and Elder Thomas with his lips flapping loose like tired elastic.

But Reverend Thomas shrugged off Sister Monroe's weakening clutch, pulled out an extra-large white handkerchief and spread it over his nasty little teeth. Putting them in his pocket, he gummed, "Naked I came into the world, and naked I shall go out."

Bailey's laugh had worked its way up through his body and was escaping through his nose in short hoarse snorts. I didn't try any longer to hold back the laugh, I just opened my mouth and released sound. I heard the first titter jump up in the air over my head, over the pulpit and out the window. Momma said out loud, "Sister!" but the bench was greasy and I slid off onto the floor. There was more laughter in me trying to get out. I didn't know there was that much in the whole world. It pressed at all my body openings, forcing everything in its path. I cried and hollered, passed gas and urine. I didn't see Bailey descend to the floor, but I rolled over once and he was kicking and screaming too. Each time we looked at each other we howled louder than before, and though he tried to say something, the laughter attacked him and he was only able to get out "I say, preach." And then I rolled over onto Uncle Willie's rubber-tipped cane. My eyes followed the cane up to his good brown hand on the curve and up the long, long white sleeve to his face. The one side pulled down as it usually did when he cried (it also pulled down when he laughed). He stuttered, "I'm gonna whip you this time myself."

I have no memory of how we got out of church and into the parsonage next door, but in that over-stuffed parlor, Bailey and I received the whipping of our lives. Uncle Willie ordered us between licks to stop crying. I tried to, but Bailey refused to cooperate. Later he explained that when a person is beating you you should scream as loud as possible; maybe the whipper will become embarrassed or else some sympathetic soul might come to your rescue. Our savior came for neither of these reasons, but because Bailey yelled so loud and disturbed what was left of the service, the minister's wife came out and asked Uncle Willie to quiet us down.

Laughter so easily turns to hysteria for imaginative children. I felt for weeks after that I had been very, very sick, and until I completely recovered my strength I stood on laughter's cliff and any funny thing could hurl me off to my death far below.

Each time Bailey said "Preach it" to me, I hit him as hard as I could and cried.

7

MOMMA HAD MARRIED three times: Mr. Johnson, my grandfather, who left her around the turn of the century with two small sons to raise; Mr. Henderson, of whom I know nothing at all (Momma never

answered questions directly put to her on any subject except religion); then finally Mr. Murphy. I saw
him a fleeting once. He came through Stamps on a
Saturday night, and Grandmother gave me the
chore of making his pallet on the floor. He was a
stocky dark man who wore a snap-brim hat like
George Raft. The next morning he hung around the
Store until we returned from church. That marked
the first Sunday I knew Uncle Willie to miss services. Bailey said he stayed home to keep Mr. Murphy from stealing us blind. He left in the middle of
the afternoon after one of Momma's extensive Sunday dinners. His hat pushed back off his forehead, he
walked down the road whistling. I watched his thick
back until he turned the bend by the big white
church.

People spoke of Momma as a good-looking woman
and some, who remembered her youth, said she
used to be right pretty. I saw only her power and
strength. She was taller than any woman in my
personal world, and her hands were so large they
could span my head from ear to ear. Her voice was
soft only because she chose to keep it so. In church,
when she was called upon to sing, she seemed to pull
out plugs from behind her jaws and the huge, almost
rough sound would pour over the listeners and throb
in the air.

Each Sunday, after she had taken her seat, the
minister would announce, "We will now be led in a
hymn by Sister Henderson." And each Sunday she
looked up with amazement at the preacher and
asked silently, "Me?" After a second of assuring herself that she indeed was being called upon, she laid
down her handbag and slowly folded her handkerchief. This was placed neatly on top of the purse,
then she leaned on the bench in front and pushed
herself to a standing position, and then she opened
her mouth and the song jumped out as if it had only
been waiting for the right time to make an appearance. Week after week and year after year the

performance never changed, yet I don't remember anyone's ever remarking on her sincerity or readiness to sing.

Momma intended to teach Bailey and me to use the paths of life that she and her generation and all the Negroes gone before had found, and found to be safe ones. She didn't cotton to the idea that whitefolks could be talked to at all without risking one's life. And certainly they couldn't be spoken to insolently. In fact, even in their absence they could not be spoken of too harshly unless we used the sobriquet "They." If she had been asked and had chosen to answer the question of whether she was cowardly or not, she would have said that she was a realist. Didn't she stand up to "them" year after year? Wasn't she the only Negro woman in Stamps referred to once as Mrs.?

That incident became one of Stamps' little legends. Some years before Bailey and I arrived in town, a man was hunted down for assaulting white womanhood. In trying to escape he ran to the Store. Momma and Uncle Willie hid him behind the chifforobe until night, gave him supplies for an overland journey and sent him on his way. He was, however, apprehended, and in court when he was questioned as to his movements on the day of the crime, he replied that after he heard that he was being sought he took refuge in Mrs. Henderson's Store.

The judge asked that Mrs. Henderson be subpoenaed, and when Momma arrived and said she was Mrs. Henderson, the judge, the bailiff and other whites in the audience laughed. The judge had really made a gaffe calling a Negro woman Mrs., but then he was from Pine Bluff and couldn't have been expected to know that a woman who owned a store in that village would also turn out to be colored. The whites tickled their funny bones with the incident for a long time, and the Negroes thought it proved the worth and majesty of my grandmother.

8

Stamps, Arkansas, was Chitlin' Switch, Georgia; Hang 'Em High, Alabama; Don't Let the Sun Set on You Here, Nigger, Mississippi; or any other name just as descriptive. People in Stamps used to say that the whites in our town were so prejudiced that a Negro couldn't buy vanilla ice cream. Except on July Fourth. Other days he had to be satisfied with chocolate.

A light shade had been pulled down between the Black community and all things white, but one could see through it enough to develop a fear-admiration-contempt for the white "things"—white folks' cars and white glistening houses and their children and their women. But above all, their wealth that allowed them to waste was the most enviable. They had so many clothes they were able to give perfectly good dresses, worn just under the arms, to the sewing class at our school for the larger girls to practice on.

Although there was always generosity in the Negro neighborhood, it was indulged on pain of sacrifice. Whatever was given by Black people to other Blacks was most probably needed as desperately by the donor as by the receiver. A fact which made the giving or receiving a rich exchange.

I couldn't understand whites and where they got the right to spend money so lavishly. Of course, I knew God was white too, but no one could have made me believe he was prejudiced. My grandmother had more money than all the powhitetrash. We owned land and houses, but each day Bailey and I were cautioned, "Waste not, want not."

Momma bought two bolts of cloth each year for winter and summer clothes. She made my school dresses, underslips, bloomers, handkerchiefs, Bailey's shirts, shorts, her aprons, house dresses and waists from the rolls shipped to Stamps by Sears and Roebuck. Uncle Willie was the only person in the family who wore ready-to-wear clothes all the time. Each day, he wore fresh white shirts and flowered suspenders, and his special shoes cost twenty dollars. I thought Uncle Willie sinfully vain, especially when I had to iron seven stiff starched shirts and not leave a cat's face anywhere.

During the summer we went barefoot, except on Sunday, and we learned to resole our shoes when they "gave out," as Momma used to say. The Depression must have hit the white section of Stamps with cyclonic impact, but it seeped into the Black area slowly, like a thief with misgivings. The country had been in the throes of the Depression for two years before the Negroes in Stamps knew it. I think that everyone thought that the Depression, like everything else, was for the whitefolks, so it had nothing to do with them. Our people had lived off the land and counted on cotton-picking and hoeing and chopping seasons to bring in the cash needed to buy shoes, clothes, books and light farm equipment. It was when the owners of cotton fields dropped the payment of ten cents for a pound of cotton to eight, seven and finally five that the Negro community realized that the Depression, at least, did not discriminate.

Welfare agencies gave food to the poor families, Black and white. Gallons of lard, flour, salt, powdered eggs and powdered milk. People stopped trying to raise hogs because it was too difficult to get slop rich enough to feed them, and no one had the money to buy mash or fish meal.

Momma spent many nights figuring on our tablets, slowly. She was trying to find a way to keep her business going, although her customers had no money. When she came to her conclusions, she said, "Bailey, I want you to make me a nice clear sign.

Nice and neat. And Sister, you can color it with your Crayolas. I want it to say:

1 5 LB. CAN OF POWDERED MILK IS WORTH 50¢ IN TRADE
1 5 LB. CAN OF POWDERED EGGS IS WORTH $1.00 IN TRADE
10 #2 CANS OF MACKEREL IS WORTH $1.00 IN TRADE."

And so on. Momma kept her store going. Our customers didn't even have to take their slated provisions home. They'd pick them up from the welfare center downtown and drop them off at the Store. If they didn't want an exchange at the moment they'd put down in one of the big gray ledgers the amount of credit coming to them. We were among the few Negro families not on relief, but Bailey and I were the only children in the town proper that we knew who ate powdered eggs every day and drank the powdered milk.

Our playmates' families exchanged their unwanted food for sugar, coal oil, spices, potted meat, Vienna sausage, peanut butter, soda crackers, toilet soap and even laundry soap. We were always given enough to eat, but we both hated the lumpy milk and mushy eggs, and sometimes we'd stop off at the house of one of the poorer families to get some peanut butter and crackers. Stamps was as slow coming out of the Depression as it had been getting into it. World War II was well along before there was a noticeable change in the economy of that near-forgotten hamlet.

One Christmas we received gifts from our mother and father, who lived separately in a heaven called California, where we were told they could have all the oranges they could eat. And the sun shone all the time. I was sure that wasn't so. I couldn't believe that our mother would laugh and eat oranges in the sunshine without her children. Until that Christmas when we received the gifts I had been confident that they were both dead. I could cry anytime I wanted by picturing my mother (I didn't quite know what she looked like) lying in her coffin. Her hair, which was black, was spread out on a tiny little white pillow and her body was covered with a sheet. The face was brown, like a big O, and since I couldn't fill in the features I printed M O T H E R across the O, and tears would fall down my cheeks like warm milk.

Then came that terrible Christmas with its awful presents when our father, with the vanity I was to find typical, sent his photograph. My gift from Mother was a tea set—a teapot, four cups and saucers and tiny spoons—and a doll with blue eyes and rosy cheeks and yellow hair painted on her head. I didn't know what Bailey received, but after I opened my boxes I went out to the backyard behind the chinaberry tree. The day was cold and the air as clear as water. Frost was still on the bench but I sat down and cried. I looked up and Bailey was coming from the outhouse, wiping his eyes. He had been crying too. I didn't know if he had also told himself they were dead and had been rudely awakened to the truth or whether he was just feeling lonely. The gifts opened the door to questions that neither of us wanted to ask. Why did they send us away? and What did we do so wrong? So Wrong? Why, at three and four, did we have tags put on our arms to be sent by train alone from Long Beach, California, to Stamps, Arkansas, with only the porter to look after us? (Besides, he got off in Arizona.)

Bailey sat down beside me, and that time didn't admonish me not to cry. So I wept and he sniffed a little, but we didn't talk until Momma called us back in the house.

Momma stood in front of the tree that we had decorated with silver ropes and pretty colored balls and said, "You children is the most ungrateful things I ever did see. You think your momma and poppa went to all the trouble to send you these nice play pretties to make you go out in the cold and cry?"

Neither of us said a word. Momma continued, "Sister, I know you tender-hearted, but Bailey Junior, there's no reason for you to set out mewing like a pussy cat, just 'cause you got something from Vivian and Big Bailey." When we still didn't force ourselves to answer, she asked, "You want me to tell Santa Claus to take these things back?" A wretched feeling of being torn engulfed me. I wanted to scream, "Yes. Tell him to take them back." But I didn't move.

Later Bailey and I talked. He said if the things really did come from Mother maybe it meant that she was getting ready to come and get us. Maybe she had just been angry at something we had done, but was forgiving us and would send for us soon. Bailey and I tore the stuffing out of the doll the day after Christmas, but he warned me that I had to keep the tea set in good condition because any day or night she might come riding up.

9

A YEAR LATER our father came to Stamps without warning. It was awful for Bailey and me to encounter the reality one abrupt morning. We, or at any rate I, had built such elaborate fantasies about him and the illusory mother that seeing him in the flesh shredded my inventions like a hard yank on a paper chain. He arrived in front of the Store in a clean gray car (he must have stopped just outside of town to wipe it in preparation for the "grand entrance"). Bailey, who knew such things, said it was a De Soto. His bigness shocked me. His shoulders were so wide I thought he'd have trouble getting in the door. He was taller than anyone I had seen, and if he wasn't fat, which I knew he wasn't, then he was fat-like. His clothes were too small too. They were tighter and woolier than was customary in Stamps. And he was blindingly handsome. Momma cried, "Bailey, my baby. Great God, Bailey." And Uncle Willie stuttered, "Bu-Buh-Bailey." My brother said, "Hot dog and damn. It's him. It's our daddy." And my seven-year-old world humpty-dumptied, never to be put back together again.

His voice rang like a metal dipper hitting a bucket and he spoke English. Proper English, like the school principal, and even better. Our father sprinkled *er*s and even *errer*s in his sentences as liberally as he gave out his twisted-mouth smiles. His lips pulled not down, like Uncle Willie's, but to the side, and his head lay on one side or the other, but never straight on the end of his neck. He had the air of a man who did not believe what he heard or what he himself was saying. He was the first cynic I had met. "So er this is Daddy's er little man? Boy, anybody tell you errer that you er look like me?" He had Bailey in one arm and me in the other. "And Daddy's baby girl. You've errer been good children, er haven't you? Or er I guess I would have er heard about it er from Santa Claus." I was so proud of him it was hard to wait for the gossip to get around that he was in town. Wouldn't the kids be surprised at how handsome our daddy was? And that he loved us enough to come down to Stamps to visit? Everyone could tell from the way he talked and from the car and clothes that he was rich and maybe had a castle out in California. (I later learned that he had been a doorman at Santa Monica's plush Breakers Hotel.) Then the possibility of being compared with him occurred to me, and I didn't want anyone to see him. Maybe he wasn't my real father. Bailey was his son, true enough, but I was an orphan that they picked up to provide Bailey with company.

I was always afraid when I found him watching me, and wished I could grow small like Tiny Tim. Sitting at the table one day, I held the fork in my left hand and pierced a piece of fried chicken. I put the knife through the second tine, as we had been strictly taught, and began to saw against the bone. My father laughed a rich rolling laugh, and I looked up. He imitated me, both elbows going up and down. "Is Daddy's baby going to fly away?" Momma laughed, and Uncle Willie too, and even Bailey snickered a little. Our father was proud of his sense of humor.

For three weeks the Store was filled with people who had gone to school with him or heard about him. The curious and envious milled around and he strutted, throwing *ers* and *errers* all over the place and under the sad eyes of Uncle Willie. Then one day he said he had to get back to California. I was relieved. My world was going to be emptier and dryer, but the agony of having him intrude into every private second would be gone. And the silent threat that had hung in the air since his arrival, the threat of his leaving someday, would be gone. I wouldn't have to wonder whether I loved him or not, or have to answer "Does Daddy's baby want to go to California with Daddy?" Bailey had told him that he wanted to go, but I had kept quiet. Momma was relieved too, although she had had a good time cooking special things for him and showing her California son off to the peasants of Arkansas. But Uncle Willie was suffering under our father's bombastic pressure, and in mother-bird fashion Momma was more concerned with her crippled offspring than the one who could fly away from the nest.

He was going to take us with him! The knowledge buzzed through my days and made me jump unexpectedly like a jack-in-the-box. Each day I found some time to walk to the pond where people went to catch sun perch and striped bass. The hours I chose to go were too early or late for fishermen, so I had the area to myself. I stood on the bank of the green dark water, and my thoughts skidded like the water spiders. Now this way, now that, now the other. Should I go with my father? Should I throw myself into the pond, and not being able to swim, join the body of L.C., the boy who had drowned last summer? Should I beg Momma to let me stay with her? I could tell her that I'd take over Bailey's chores and do my own as well. Did I have the nerve to try life without Bailey? I couldn't decide on any move, so I recited a few Bible verses, and went home.

Momma cut down a few give-aways that had been traded to her by white women's maids and sat long nights in the dining room sewing jumpers and skirts for me. She looked pretty sad, but each time I found her watching me she'd say, as if I had already disobeyed, "You be a good girl now. You hear? Don't you make people think I didn't raise you right. You hear?" She would have been more surprised than I had she taken me in her arms and wept at losing me. Her world was bordered on all sides with work, duty, religion and "her place." I don't think she ever knew that a deep-brooding love hung over everything she touched. In later years I asked her if she loved me and she brushed me off with: "God is love. Just worry about whether you're being a good girl, then He will love you."

I sat in the back of the car, with Dad's leather suitcases, and our cardboard boxes. Although the windows were rolled down, the smell of fried chicken and sweet potatoe pie lay unmoving, and there wasn't enough room to stretch. Whenever he thought about it, Dad asked, "Are you comfortable back there, Daddy's baby?" He never waited to hear my answer, which was "Yes, sir," before he'd resume his conversation with Bailey. He and Bailey told jokes, and Bailey laughed all the time, put out Dad's cigarettes and held one hand on the steering wheel when Dad said, "Come on, boy, help me drive this thing."

After I got tired of passing through the same towns over and over, and seeing the empty-looking houses, small and unfriendly, I closed myself off to everything but the kissing sounds of the tires on the pavement and the steady moan of the motor. I was certainly very vexed with Bailey. There was no doubt that he was trying to butter up Dad; he even started to laugh like him, a Santa Claus, Jr., with his "Ho, ho, ho."

"How are you going to feel seeing your mother? Going to be happy?" he was asking Bailey, but it penetrated the foam I had packed around my senses. Were we going to see Her? I thought we were going to California. I was suddenly terrified. Suppose she laughed at us the way he did? What if she had other children now, whom she kept with her? I said, "I want to go back to Stamps." Dad laughed, "You mean Daddy's baby doesn't want to go to St. Louis to see her mother? She's not going to eat you up, you know."

He turned to Bailey and I looked at the side of his face; he was so unreal to me I felt as if I were watching a doll talk. "Bailey, Junior, ask your sister why she wants to go back to Stamps." He sounded more like a white man than a Negro. Maybe he was the only brown-skinned white man in the world. It would be just my luck that the only one would turn out to be my father. But Bailey was quiet for the first time since we left Stamps. I guess he was thinking too about seeing Mother. How could an eight-year-old contain that much fear? He swallows and holds it behind his tonsils, he tightens his feet and closes the fear between his toes, he contracts his buttock and pushes it up behind the prostate gland.

"Junior, cat's got your tongue? What do you think your mother will say, when I tell her her children didn't want to see her?" The thought that he *would* tell her shook me and Bailey at the same time. He leaned over the back of the seat—"My, it's Mother Dear. You know you want to see Mother Dear. Don't cry." Dad laughed and pitched in his seat and asked himself, I guess, "What will she say to that?"

I stopped crying since there was no chance to get

back to Stamps and Momma. Bailey wasn't going to back me up, I could tell, so I decided to shut up and dry up and wait for whatever seeing Mother Dear was going to bring.

St. Louis was a new kind of hot and a new kind of dirty. My memory had no pictures of the crowded-together soot-covered buildings. For all I knew, we were being driven to Hell and our father was the delivering devil.

Only in strict emergencies did Bailey allow me to speak Pig Latin to him in front of adults, but I had to take the chance that afternoon. We had spun around the same corner, I was sure, about fifty times. I asked Bailey, "Ooday ooyay inkthay isthay is our atherfay, or ooday ooyay inkthay atthay ee-way are eeingbay idkay appednay?" Bailey said, "My, we're in St. Louis, and we're going to see Mother Dear. Don't worry." Dad chuckled and said, "Oohay oodway antway ootay idkay appnay ooyay? Ooday ooyay inkthay ooyay are indlay ergbay il-drenchay?" I thought that my brother and his friends had created Pig Latin. Hearing my father speak it didn't startle me so much as it angered. It was simply another case of the trickiness of adults where children were concerned. Another case in point of the Grownups' Betrayal.

To describe my mother would be to write about a hurricane in its perfect power. Or the climbing, falling colors of a rainbow. We had been received by her mother and had waited on the edge of our seats in the overfurnished living room (Dad talked easily with our grandmother, as whitefolks talk to Blacks, unembarrassed and unapologetic). We were both fearful of Mother's coming and impatient at her delay. It is remarkable how much truth there is in the two expressions: "struck dumb" and "love at first sight." My mother's beauty literally assailed me. Her red lips (Momma said it was a sin to wear lipstick) split to show even white teeth and her fresh-butter color looked see-through clean. Her smile widened her mouth beyond her cheeks beyond her ears and seemingly through the walls to the street outside. I was struck dumb. I knew immediately why she had sent me away. She was too beautiful to have children. I had never seen a woman as pretty as she who was called "Mother." Bailey on his part fell instantly and forever in love. I saw his eyes shining like hers; he had forgotten the loneliness and the nights when we had cried together because we were "unwanted children." He had never left her warm side or shared the icy wind of solitude with me. She was his Mother Dear and I resigned myself to his condition. They were more alike than she and I, or even he and I. They both had physical beauty and personality, so I figured it figured.

Our father left St. Louis a few days later for California, and I was neither glad nor sorry. He was a stranger, and if he chose to leave us with a stranger, it was all of one piece.

10

GRANDMOTHER BAXTER was a quadroon or an octoroon, or in any case she was nearly white. She had been raised by a German family in Cairo, Illinois, and had come to St. Louis at the turn of the century to study nursing. While she was working at Homer G. Phillips Hospital she met and married Grandfather Baxter. She was white (having no features that could even loosely be called Negroid) and he was Black. While she spoke with a throaty German accent until her death, he had the choppy spouting speech of the West Indians.

Their marriage was a happy one. Grandfather had a famous saying that caused great pride in his family: "Bah Jesus, I live for my wife, my children and my dog." He took extreme care to prove that statement true by taking the word of his family even in the face of contradictory evidence.

The Negro section of St. Louis in the mid-thirties had all the finesse of a gold-rush town. Prohibition, gambling and their related vocations were so obviously practiced that it was hard for me to believe that they were against the law. Bailey and I, as newcomers, were quickly told by our schoolmates who the men on the street corners were as we passed. I was sure that they had taken their names from Wild West Books (Hard-hitting Jimmy, Two Gun, Sweet Man, Poker Pete), and to prove me right, they hung around in front of saloons like unhorsed cowboys.

We met the numbers runners, gamblers, lottery takers and whiskey salesmen not only in the loud streets but in our orderly living room as well. They were often there when we returned from school, sitting with hats in their hands, as we had done upon our arrival in the big city. They waited silently for Grandmother Baxter.

Her white skin and the pince-nez that she dramatically took from her nose and let hang free on a chain pinned to her dress were factors that brought her a great deal of respect. Moreover, the reputation of her six mean children and the fact that she was a precinct captain compounded her power and gave her the leverage to deal with even the lowest crook without fear. She had pull with the police department, so the men in their flashy suits and fleshy scars sat with churchlike decorum and waited to ask favors from her. If Grandmother raised the heat off their gambling parlors, or said the word that reduced the bail of a friend waiting in jail, they knew what would be expected of them. Come election, they were to bring in the votes from their neighborhood. She most often got them leniency, and they always brought in the vote.

St. Louis also introduced me to thin-sliced ham (I thought it a delicacy), jelly beans and peanuts mixed, lettuce on sandwich bread, Victrolas and family loyalty. In Arkansas, where we cured our own meat, we ate half-inch slabs of ham for breakfast, but in St. Louis we bought the paper-thin slices in a strange-smelling German store and ate them in sandwiches. If Grandmother never lost her German accent, she also never lost her taste for the thick black German *Brot*, which we bought unsliced. In Stamps, lettuce was used only to make a bed for potato salad or slaw, and peanuts were brought in raw from the field and roasted in the bottom of the oven on cold nights. The rich scents used to fill the house and we were always expected to eat too many. But that was a Stamps custom. In St. Louis, peanuts were bought in paper bags and mixed with jelly beans, which meant that we ate the salt and sugar together and I found them a delicious treat. The best thing the big town had to offer.

When we enrolled in Toussaint L'Ouverture Grammar School, we were struck by the ignorance of our schoolmates and the rudeness of our teachers. Only the vastness of the building impressed us; not even the white school in Stamps was as large.

The students, however, were shockingly backward. Bailey and I did arithmetic at a mature level because of our work in the Store, and we read well because in Stamps there wasn't anything else to do. We were moved up a grade because our teachers thought that we country children would make our classmates feel inferior—and we did. Bailey would not refrain from remarking on our classmates' lack of knowledge. At lunchtime in the large gray concrete playground, he would stand in the center of a crowd of big boys and ask, "Who was Napoleon Bonaparte?" "How many feet make a mile?" It was infighting, Bailey style.

Any of the boys might have been able to beat him with their fists, but if they did, they'd just have had to do it again the next day, and Bailey never held a brief for fighting fair. He taught me that once I got

into a fight I should "grab for the balls right away."
He never answered when I asked, "Suppose I'm
fighting a girl?"

We went to school there a full year, but all I
remember hearing that I hadn't heard before was,
"Making thousands of egg-shaped oughts will im-
prove penmanship."

The teachers were more formal than those we
knew in Stamps, and although they didn't whip
their students with switches, they gave them licks in
the palms of their hands with rulers. In Stamps
teachers were much friendlier, but that was because
they were imported from the Arkansas Negro col-
leges, and since we had no hotels or rooming houses in
town, they had to live with private families. If a
lady teacher took company, or didn't receive any
mail or cried alone in her room at night, by the
weeks' end even the children discussed her morality, her loneliness and her other failings generally. It
would have been near impossible to maintain formality
under a small town's invasions of privacy.

St. Louis teachers, on the other hand, tended to
act very siditty, and talked down to their students
from the lofty heights of education and whitefolks'
enunciation. They, women as well as men, all sounded like my father with their *ers* and *errers*. They
walked with their knees together and talked through
tight lips as if they were as afraid to let the sound
out as they were to inhale the dirty air that the
listener gave off.

We walked to school around walls of bricks and
breathed the coal dust for one discouraging winter.
We learned to say "Yes" and "No" rather than "Yes,
ma'am," and "No, ma'am."

Occasionally Mother, whom we seldom saw in the
house, had us meet her at Louie's. It was a long dark
tavern at the end of the bridge near our school, and
was owned by two Syrian brothers.

We used to come in the back door, and the saw-
dust, stale beer, steam and boiling meat made me

feel as if I'd been eating mothballs. Mother had cut my hair in a bob like hers and straightened it, so my head felt skinned and the back of my neck so bare that I was ashamed to have anyone walk up behind me. Naturally, this kept me turning quickly as if I expected something to happen.

At Louie's we were greeted by Mother's friends as "Bibbie's darling babies" and were given soft drinks and boiled shrimp. While we sat on the stiff wooden booths, Mother would dance alone in front of us to music from the Seeburg. I loved her most at those times. She was like a pretty kite that floated just above my head. If I liked, I could pull it in to me by saying I had to go to the toilet or by starting a fight with Bailey. I never did either, but the power made me tender to her.

The Syrian brothers vied for her attention as she sang the heavy blues that Bailey and I almost understood. They watched her, even when directing their conversation to other customers, and I knew they too were hypnotized by this beautiful lady who talked with her whole body and snapped her fingers louder than anyone in the whole world. We learned the Time Step at Louie's. It is from this basic step that most American Black dances are born. It is a series of taps, jumps and rests, and demands careful listening, feeling and coordination. We were brought before Mother's friends, there in the heavy saloon air, to show our artistry. Bailey learned easily, and has always been the better dancer. But I learned too. I approached the Time Step with the same determination to win that I had approached the time tables with. There was no Uncle Willie or sizzling pot-bellied stove, but there was Mother and her laughing friends, and they amounted to the same thing. We were applauded and given more soft drinks and more shrimp, but it was to be years later before I found the joy and freedom of dancing well.

Mother's brothers, Uncles Tutti, Tom and Ira, were well-known young men about St. Louis. They all had city jobs, which I now understand to have been no mean feat for Negro men. Their jobs and their family set them apart, but they were best known for their unrelenting meanness. Grandfather had told them, "Bah Jesus, if you ever get in jail for stealing or some such foolishness, I'll let you rot. But if you're arrested for fighting, I'll sell the house, lock, stock, and barrel, to get you out!" With that kind of encouragement, backed by explosive tempers, it was no wonder they became fearsome characters. Our youngest uncle, Billy, was not old enough to join in their didoes. One of their more flamboyant escapades has become a proud family legend.

Pat Patterson, a big man, who was himself protected by the shield of a bad reputation, made the mistake of cursing my mother one night when she was out alone. She reported the incident to her brothers. They ordered one of their hangers-on to search the streets for Patterson, and when he was located, to telephone them.

As they waited throughout the afternoon, the living room filled with smoke and the murmurs of plans. From time to time, Grandfather came in from the kitchen and said, "Don't kill him. Mind you, just don't kill him," then went back to his coffee with Grandmother.

They went to the saloon where Patterson sat drinking at a small table. Uncle Tommy stood by the door, Uncle Tutti stationed himself at the toilet door and Uncle Ira, who was the oldest and maybe everyone's ideal, walked over to Patterson. They were all obviously carrying guns.

Uncle Ira said to my mother, "Here, Bibbi. Here's this nigger Patterson. Come over here and beat his ass."

She crashed the man's head with a policeman's billy enough to leave him just this side of death.

There was no police investigation nor social reprobation.

After all, didn't Grandfather champion their wild tempers, and wasn't Grandmother a near-white woman with police pull?

I admit that I was thrilled by their meanness. They beat up whites and Blacks with the same abandon, and liked each other so much that they never needed to learn the art of making outside friends. My mother was the only warm, outgoing personality among her siblings. Grandfather became bedridden during our stay there, and his children spent their free time telling him jokes, gossiping with him and showing their love.

Uncle Tommy, who was gruff and chewed his words like Grandfather, was my favorite. He strung ordinary sentences together and they came out sounding either like the most profane curses or like comical poetry. A natural comedian, he never waited for the laugh that he knew must follow his droll statements. He was never cruel. He was mean.

When we played handball on the side of our house, Uncle Tommy would turn the corner, coming from work. He would pretend at first not to see us, but with the deftness of a cat he would catch the ball and say, "Put your minds where your behinds are, and I'll let you on my team." We children would range around him, but it was only when he reached the steps that he'd wind up his arm and throw the ball over the light post and toward the stars.

He told me often, "Ritie, don't worry 'cause you ain't pretty. Plenty pretty women I seen digging ditches or worse. You smart. I swear to God, I rather you have a good mind than a cute behind."

They bragged often about the binding quality of the Baxter blood. Uncle Tommy said that even the children felt it before they were old enough to be taught. They reminisced over Bailey's teaching me to walk when he was less than three. Displeased at my stumbling motions, he was supposed to have

said, "This is *my* sister. *I* have to teach her to walk."
They also told me how I got the name "My." After
Bailey learned definitely that I was his sister, he
refused to call me Marguerite, but rather addressed
me each time as "Mya Sister," and in later more
articulate years, after the need for brevity had short-
ened the appellation to "My," it was elaborated into
"Maya."

We lived in a big house on Caroline Street with
our grandparents for half the year before Mother
moved us in with her. Moving from the house where
the family was centered meant absolutely nothing to
me. It was simply a small pattern in the grand
design of our lives. If other children didn't move so
much, it just went to show that our lives were fated
to be different from everyone else's in the world.
The new house was no stranger than the other,
except that we were with Mother.

Bailey persisted in calling her Mother Dear until
the circumstance of proximity softened the phrase's
formality to "Muh Dear," and finally to "M'Deah." I
could never put my finger on her realness. She was
so pretty and so quick that even when she had just
awakened, her eyes full of sleep and hair tousled, I
thought she looked just like the Virgin Mary. But
what mother and daughter understand each other,
or even have the sympathy for each other's lack of
understanding?

Mother had prepared a place for us, and we went
to it gratefully. We each had a room with a two-
sheeted bed, plenty to eat and store-bought clothes
to wear. And after all, she didn't have to do it. If we
got on her nerves or if we were disobedient, she
could always send us back to Stamps. The weight of
appreciation and the threat, which was never spoken, of a return to Momma were burdens that
clogged my childish wits into impassivity. I was
called Old Lady and chided for moving and talking
like winter's molasses.

Mother's boyfriend, Mr. Freeman, lived with us,

or we lived with him (I never quite knew which). He was a Southerner, too, and big. But a little flabby. His breasts used to embarrass me when he walked around in his undershirt. They lay on his chest like flat titties.

Even if Mother hadn't been such a pretty woman, light-skinned with straight hair, he was lucky to get her, and he knew it. She was educated, from a well-known family, and after all, wasn't she born in St. Louis? Then she was gay. She laughed all the time and made jokes. He was grateful. I think he must have been many years older than she, but if not, he had the sluggish inferiority of old men married to younger women. He watched her every move and when she left the room, his eyes allowed her reluctantly to go.

11

I HAD DECIDED that St. Louis was a foreign country. I would never get used to the scurrying sounds of flushing toilets, or the packaged foods, or doorbells or the noise of cars and trains and buses that crashed through the walls or slipped under the doors. In my mind I only stayed in St. Louis for a few weeks. As quickly as I understood that I had not reached my home, I sneaked away to Robin Hood's forest and the caves of Alley Oop where all reality was unreal and even that changed every day. I carried the same shield that I had used in Stamps: "I didn't come to stay."

Mother was competent in providing for us. Even if that meant getting someone else to furnish the provisions. Although she was a nurse, she never worked at her profession while we were with her. Mr. Freeman brought in the necessities and she earned extra money cutting poker games in gambling parlors. The straight eight-to-five world simply didn't have enough glamor for her, and it was twenty years later that I first saw her in a nurse's uniform.

Mr. Freeman was a foreman in the Southern Pacific yards and came home late sometimes, after Mother had gone out. He took his dinner off the stove where she had carefully covered it and which she had admonished us not to bother. He ate quietly in the kitchen while Bailey and I read separately and greedily our own Street and Smith pulp magazine. Now that we had spending money, we bought the illustrated paperbacks with their gaudy pictures. When Mother was away, we were put on an honor system. We had to finish our homework, eat dinner and wash the dishes before we could read or listen to *The Lone Ranger*, *Crime Busters* or *The Shadow*.

Mr. Freeman moved gracefully, like a big brown bear, and seldom spoke to us. He simply waited for Mother and put his whole self into the waiting. He never read the paper or patted his foot to radio. He waited. That was all.

If she came home before we went to bed, we saw the man come alive. He would start out of the big chair, like a man coming out of sleep, smiling. I would remember then that a few seconds before, I had heard a car door slam; then Mother's footsteps would signal from the concrete walk. When her key rattled the door, Mr. Freeman would have already asked his habitual question, "Hey, Bibbi, have a good time?"

His query would hang in the air while she sprang over to peck him on the lips. Then she turned to Bailey and me with the lipstick kisses. "Haven't you finished your homework?" If we had and were just reading—"O.K., say your prayers and go to bed." If we hadn't—"Then go to your room and finish ... then say your prayers and go to bed."

Mr. Freeman's smile never grew, it stayed at the same intensity. Sometimes Mother would go over and sit on his lap and the grin on his face looked as if it would stay there forever.

From our rooms we could hear the glasses clink and the radio turned up. I think she must have danced for him on the good nights, because he couldn't dance, but before I fell asleep I often heard feet shuffling to dance rhythms.

I felt very sorry for Mr. Freeman. I felt as sorry for him as I had felt for a litter of helpless pigs born in our backyard sty in Arkansas. We fattened the pigs all year long for the slaughter on the first good frost, and even as I suffered for the cute little wiggly things, I knew how much I was going to enjoy the fresh sausage and hog's headcheese they could give me only with their deaths.

Because of the lurid tales we read and our vivid imaginations and, probably, memories of our brief but hectic lives, Bailey and I were afflicted—he physically and I mentally. He stuttered, and I sweated through horrifying nightmares. He was constantly told to slow down and start again, and on my particularly bad nights my mother would take me in to sleep with her, in the large bed with Mr. Freeman.

Because of a need for stability, children easily become creatures of habit. After the third time in Mother's bed, I thought there was nothing strange about sleeping there.

One morning she got out of bed for an early errand, and I fell asleep again. But I awoke to a pressure, a strange feeling on my left leg. It was too soft to be a hand, and it wasn't the touch of clothes. Whatever it was, I hadn't encountered the sensation in all the years of sleeping with Momma. It didn't move, and I was too startled to. I turned my head a little to the left to see if Mr. Freeman was awake and gone, but his eyes were open and both hands were above the cover. I knew, as if I had always known, it was his "thing" on my leg.

He said, "Just stay right here, Ritie, I ain't gonna hurt you." I wasn't afraid, a little apprehensive, maybe, but not afraid. Of course I knew that lots of people did "it" and they used their "things" to accomplish the deed, but no one I knew had ever done it to anybody. Mr. Freeman pulled me to him, and put his hand between my legs. He didn't hurt, but Momma had drilled into my head: "Keep your legs closed, and don't let nobody see your pocketbook."

"Now, I didn't hurt you. Don't get scared." He threw back the blankets and his "thing" stood up like a brown ear of corn. He took my hand and said, "Feel it." It was mushy and squirmy like the inside of a freshly killed chicken. Then he dragged me on top of his chest with his left arm, and his right hand was moving so fast and his heart was beating so hard that I was afraid that he would die. Ghost stories revealed how people who died wouldn't let go of whatever they were holding. I wondered if Mr. Freeman died holding me how I would ever get free. Would they have to break his arms to get me loose?

Finally he was quiet, and then came the nice part. He held me so softly that I wished he wouldn't ever let me go. I felt at home. From the way he was holding me I knew he'd never let me go or let anything bad ever happen to me. This was probably my real father and we had found each other at last. But then he rolled over, leaving me in a wet place and stood up.

"I gotta talk to you, Ritie." He pulled off his shorts that had fallen to his ankles, and went into the bathroom.

It was true the bed was wet, but I knew I hadn't had an accident. Maybe Mr. Freeman had one while he was holding me. He came back with a glass of water and told me in a sour voice, "Get up. You peed in the bed." He poured water on the wet spot, and it did look like my mattress on many mornings.

Having lived in Southern strictness, I knew when to keep quiet around adults, but I did want to ask him why he said I peed when I was sure he didn't believe that. If he thought I was naughty, would that mean that he would never hold me again? Or admit that he was my father? I had made him ashamed of me.

"Ritie, you love Bailey?" He sat down on the bed and I came close, hoping. "Yes." He was bending down, pulling on his socks, and his back was so large and friendly I wanted to rest my head on it.

"If you ever tell anybody what we did, I'll have to kill Bailey."

What had we done? We? Obviously he didn't mean my peeing in the bed. I didn't understand and didn't dare ask him. It had something to do with his holding me. But there was no chance to ask Bailey either, because that would be telling what we had done. The thought that he might kill Bailey stunned me. After he left the room I thought about telling Mother that I hadn't peed in the bed, but then if she asked me what happened I'd have to tell her about Mr. Freeman holding me, and that wouldn't do.

It was the same old quandary. I had always lived it. There was an army of adults, whose motives and movements I just couldn't understand and who made no effort to understand mine. There was never any question of my disliking Mr. Freeman, I simply didn't understand him either.

For weeks after, he said nothing to me, except the gruff hellos which were given without ever looking in my direction.

This was the first secret I had ever kept from Bailey and sometimes I thought he should be able to read it on my face, but he noticed nothing.

I began to feel lonely for Mr. Freeman and the encasement of his big arms. Before, my world had been Bailey, food, Momma, the Store, reading books and Uncle Willie. Now, for the first time, it included physical contact.

I began to wait for Mr. Freeman to come in from the yards, but when he did, he never noticed me, although I put a lot of feeling into "Good evening, Mr. Freeman."

One evening, when I couldn't concentrate on anything, I went over to him and sat quickly on his lap. He had been waiting for Mother again. Bailey was listening to *The Shadow* and didn't miss me. At first Mr. Freeman sat still, not holding me or anything, then I felt a soft lump under my thigh begin to move. It twitched against me and started to harden. Then he pulled me to his chest. He smelled of coal dust and grease and he was so close I buried my face in his shirt and listened to his heart, it was beating just for me. Only I could hear the thud, only I could feel the jumping on my face. He said, "Sit still, stop squirming." But all the time, he pushed me around on his lap, then suddenly he stood up and I slipped down to the floor. He ran to the bathroom.

For months he stopped speaking to me again. I was hurt and for a time felt lonelier than ever. But then I forgot about him, and even the memory of his holding me precious melted into the general darkness just beyond the great blinkers of childhood.

I read more than ever, and wished my soul that I had been born a boy. Horatio Alger was the greatest writer in the world. His heroes were always good, always won, and were always boys. I could have developed the first two virtues, but becoming a boy was sure to be difficult, if not impossible.

The Sunday funnies influenced me, and although I admired the strong heroes who always conquered in the end, I identified with Tiny Tim. In the toilet, where I used to take the papers, it was tortuous to look for and exclude the unnecessary pages so that I could learn how he would finally outwit his latest adversary. I wept with relief every Sunday as he eluded the evil men and bounded back from each seeming defeat as sweet and gentle as ever. The Katzenjammer kids were fun because they made the adults look stupid. But they were a little too smart-alecky for my taste.

When spring came to St. Louis, I took out my first library card, and since Bailey and I seemed to be growing apart, I spent most of my Saturdays at the library (no interruptions) breathing in the world of penniless shoeshine boys who, with goodness and perseverance, became rich, rich men, and gave baskets of goodies to the poor on holidays. The little princesses who were mistaken for maids, and the long-lost children mistaken for waifs, became more real to me than our house, our mother, our school or Mr. Freeman.

During those months we saw our grandparents and the uncles (our only aunt had gone to California to build her fortune), but they usually asked the same question, "Have you been good children?" for which there was only one answer. Even Bailey wouldn't have dared to answer No.

12

ON A LATE SPRING Saturday, after our chores (nothing like those in Stamps) were done, Bailey and I were going out, he to play baseball and I to the library. Mr. Freeman said to me, after Bailey had gone downstairs, "Ritie, go get some milk for the house."

Mother usually brought milk when she came in, but that morning as Bailey and I straightened the living room her bedroom door had been open, and we knew that she hadn't come home the night before.

He gave me the money and I rushed to the store and back to the house. After putting the milk in the icebox, I turned and had just reached the front door when I heard, "Ritie." He was sitting in the big chair by the radio. "Ritie, come here." I didn't think about the holding time until I got close to him. His pants were open and his "thing" was standing out of his britches by itself.

"No, sir, Mr. Freeman." I started to back away. I didn't want to touch that mushy-hard thing again, and I didn't need him to hold me any more. He grabbed my arm and pulled me between his legs. His face was still and looked kind, but he didn't smile or blink his eyes. Nothing. He did nothing, except reach his left hand around to turn on the radio without even looking at it. Over the noise of music and static, he said, "Now, this ain't gonna hurt you much. You liked it before, didn't you?"

I didn't want to admit that I had in fact liked his holding me or that I had liked his smell or the hard heart-beating, so I said nothing. And his face became like the face of one of those mean natives the Phantom was always having to beat up.

His legs were squeezing my waist. "Pull down your drawers." I hesitated for two reasons: he was holding me too tight to move, and I was sure that any minute my mother or Bailey or the Green Hornet would bust in the door and save me.

"We was just playing before." He released me enough to snatch down my bloomers, and then he dragged me closer to him. Turning the radio up loud, too loud, he said, "If you scream, I'm gonna kill you. And if you tell, I'm gonna kill Bailey." I could tell he meant what he said. I couldn't understand why he wanted to kill my brother. Neither of us had done anything to him. And then.

Then there was the pain. A breaking and entering when even the senses are torn apart. The act of rape on an eight-year-old body is a matter of the needle giving because the camel can't. The child gives, because the body can, and the mind of the violator cannot.

I thought I had died—I woke up in a white-walled world, and it had to be heaven. But Mr. Freeman was there and he was washing me. His hands shook, but he held me upright in the tub and washed my legs. "I didn't mean to hurt you, Ritie. I didn't mean it. But don't you tell . . . Remember, don't you tell a soul."

I felt cool and very clean and just a little tired. "No, sir, Mr. Freeman, I won't tell." I was somewhere above everything. "It's just that I'm so tired I'll just go and lay down a while, please," I whispered to him. I thought if I spoke out loud, he might become frightened and hurt me again. He dried me and handed me my bloomers. "Put these on and go to the library. Your momma ought to be coming home soon. You just act natural."

Walking down the street, I felt the wet on my pants, and my hips seemed to be coming out of their sockets. I couldn't sit long on the hard seats in the library (they had been constructed for children), so I walked by the empty lot where Bailey was playing ball, but he wasn't there. I stood for a while and watched the big boys tear around the dusty diamond and then headed home.

After two blocks, I knew I'd never make it. Not unless I counted every step and stepped on every crack. I had started to burn between my legs more than the time I'd wasted Sloan's Liniment on myself. My legs throbbed, or rather the insides of my thighs throbbed, with the same force that Mr. Freeman's heart had beaten. Thrum . . . step . . . thrum . . . step . . . STEP ON THE CRACK . . . thrum . . . step. I went up the stairs one at a, one at a, one at a time. No one was in the living room, so I went straight to bed, after hiding my red-and-yellow-stained drawers under the mattress.

When Mother came in she said, "Well, young lady, I believe this is the first time I've seen you go to bed without being told. You must be sick."

I wasn't sick, but the pit of my stomach was on fire—how could I tell her that? Bailey came in later and asked me what the matter was. There was nothing to tell him. When Mother called us to eat and I said I wasn't hungry, she laid her cool hand on my forehead and cheeks. "Maybe it's the measles. They say they're going around the neighborhood." After she took my temperature she said, "You have a little fever. You've probably just caught them."

Mr. Freeman took up the whole doorway, "Then Bailey ought not to be in there with her. Unless you want a house full of sick children." She answered over her shoulder, "He may as well have them now as later. Get them over with." She brushed by Mr. Freeman as if he were made of cotton. "Come on, Junior. Get some cool towels and wipe your sister's face."

As Bailey left the room, Mr. Freeman advanced to the bed. He leaned over, his whole face a threat that could have smothered me. "If you tell . . ." And again so softly, I almost didn't hear it—"If you tell." I couldn't summon up the energy to answer him. He had to know that I wasn't going to tell anything. Bailey came in with the towels and Mr. Freeman walked out.

Later Mother made a broth and sat on the edge of the bed to feed me. The liquid went down my throat like bones. My belly and behind were as heavy as cold iron, but it seemed my head had gone away and pure air had replaced it on my shoulders. Bailey read to me from *The Rover Boys* until he got sleepy and went to bed.

That night I kept waking to hear Mother and Mr. Freeman arguing. I couldn't hear what they were saying, but I did hope that she wouldn't make him so mad that he'd hurt her too. I knew he could do it, with his cold face and empty eyes. Their voices came in faster and faster, the high sounds on the heels of the lows. I would have liked to have gone in. Just passed through as if I were going to the toilet. Just show my face and they might stop, but my legs refused to move. I could move the toes and ankles, but the knees had turned to wood.

Maybe I slept, but soon morning was there and

Mother was pretty over my bed. "How're you feeling, baby?"

"Fine, Mother." An instinctive answer. "Where's Bailey?"

She said he was still asleep but that she hadn't slept all night. She had been in my room off and on to see about me. I asked her where Mr. Freeman was, and her face chilled with remembered anger. "He's gone. Moved this morning. I'm going to take your temperature after I put on your Cream of Wheat."

Could I tell her now? The terrible pain assured me that I couldn't. What he did to me, and what I allowed, must have been very bad if already God let me hurt so much. If Mr. Freeman was gone, did that mean Bailey was out of danger? And if so, if I told him, would he still love me?

After Mother took my temperature, she said she was going to bed for a while but to wake her if I felt sicker. She told Bailey to watch my face and arms for spots and when they came up he could paint them with calamine lotion.

That Sunday goes and comes in my memory like a bad connection on an overseas telephone call. Once, Bailey was reading *The Katzenjammer Kids* to me, and then without a pause for sleeping, Mother was looking closely at my face, and soup trickled down my chin and some got into my mouth and I choked. Then there was a doctor who took my temperature and held my wrist.

"Bailey!" I supposed I had screamed, for he materialized suddenly, and I asked him to help me and we'd run away to California or France or Chicago. I knew that I was dying and, in fact, I longed for death, but I didn't want to die anywhere near Mr. Freeman. I knew that even now he wouldn't have allowed death to have me unless he wished it to.

Mother said I should be bathed and the linens had to be changed since I had sweat so much. But when they tried to move me I fought, and even Bailey couldn't hold me. Then she picked me up in her arms and the terror abated for a while. Bailey began to change the bed. As he pulled off the soiled sheets he dislodged the panties I had put under the mattress. They fell at Mother's feet.

13

IN THE HOSPITAL, Bailey told me that I had to tell who did that to me, or the man would hurt another little girl. When I explained that I couldn't tell because the man would kill him, Bailey said knowingly, "He can't kill me. I won't let him." And of course I believed him. Bailey didn't lie to me. So I told him.

Bailey cried at the side of my bed until I started to cry too. Almost fifteen years passed before I saw my brother cry again.

Using the old brain he was born with (those were his words later on that day) he gave his information to Grandmother Baxter, and Mr. Freeman was arrested and was spared the awful wrath of my pistol-whipping uncles.

I would have liked to stay in the hospital the rest of my life. Mother brought flowers and candy. Grandmother came with fruit and my uncles clumped around and around my bed, snorting like wild horses. When they were able to sneak Bailey in, he read to me for hours.

The saying that people who have nothing to do become busybodies is not the only truth. Excitement is a drug, and people whose lives are filled with violence are always wondering where the next "fix" is coming from.

The court was filled. Some people even stood behind the churchlike benches in the rear. Overhead fans moved with the detachment of old men. Grandmother Baxter's clients were there in gay and flippant array. The gamblers in pin-striped suits and their makeup-deep women whispered to me out of blood-red mouths that now I knew as much as they did. I was eight, and grown. Even the nurses in the hospital had told me that now I had nothing to fear. "The worst is over for you," they had said. So I put the words in all the smirking mouths.

I sat with my family (Bailey couldn't come) and they rested still on the seats like solid, cold gray tombstones. Thick and forevermore unmoving.

Poor Mr. Freeman twisted in his chair to look empty threats over to me. He didn't know that he couldn't kill Bailey ... and Bailey didn't lie ... to me.

"What was the defendant wearing?" That was Mr. Freeman's lawyer.

"I don't know."

"You mean to say this man raped you and you don't know what he was wearing?" He snickered as if I had raped Mr. Freeman. "Do you know if you were raped?"

A sound pushed in the air of the court (I was sure it was laughter). I was glad that Mother had let me wear the navy-blue winter coat with brass buttons. Although it was too short and the weather was typical St. Louis hot, the coat was a friend that I hugged to me in the strange and unfriendly place.

"Was that the first time the accused touched you?" The question stopped me. Mr. Freeman had surely done something very wrong, but I was convinced that I had helped him to do it. I didn't want to lie, but the lawyer wouldn't let me think, so I used silence as a retreat.

"Did the accused try to touch you before the time he or rather you say he raped you?"

I couldn't say yes and tell them how he had loved me once for a few minutes and how he had held me close before he thought I had peed in my bed. My uncles would kill me and Grandmother Baxter would stop speaking, as she often did when she was angry. And all those people in the court would stone me as they had stoned the harlot in the Bible. And Mother, who thought I was such a good girl, would be so disappointed. But most important, there was Bailey. I had kept a big secret from him.

"Marguerite, answer the question. Did the accused touch you before the occasion on which you claim he raped you?"

Everyone in the court knew that the answer had to be No. Everyone except Mr. Freeman and me. I looked at his heavy face trying to look as if he would have liked me to say No. I said No.

The lie lumped in my throat and I couldn't get air. How I despised the man for making me lie. Old, mean, nasty thing. Old, black, nasty thing. The tears didn't soothe my heart as they usually did. I screamed, "Ole, mean, dirty thing, you. Dirty old thing." Our lawyer brought me off the stand and to my mother's arms. The fact that I had arrived at my desired destination by lies made it less appealing to me.

Mr. Freeman was given one year and one day, but he never got a chance to do his time. His lawyer (or someone) got him released that very afternoon.

In the living room, where the shades were drawn for coolness, Bailey and I played Monopoly on the floor. I played a bad game because I was thinking how I would be able to tell Bailey how I had lied and, even worse for our relationship, kept a secret from him. Bailey answered the doorbell, because Grandmother was in the kitchen. A tall white policeman asked for Mrs. Baxter. Had they found out about the lie? Maybe the policeman was coming to put me in jail because I had sworn on the Bible that everything I said would be the truth, the whole truth, so help me, God. The man in our living room was taller than the sky and whiter than my image of God. He just didn't have the beard.

"Mrs. Baxter, I thought you ought to know. Freeman's been found dead on the lot behind the slaughterhouse."

Softly, as if she were discussing a church program, she said, "Poor man." She wiped her hands on the dishtowel and just as softly asked, "Do they know who did it?"

The policeman said, "Seems like he was dropped there. Some say he was kicked to death."

Grandmother's color only rose a little. "Tom, thanks for telling me. Poor man. Well, maybe it's better this way. He *was* a mad dog. Would you like a glass of lemonade? Or some beer?"

Although he looked harmless, I knew he was a dreadful angel counting out my many sins.

"No, thanks, Mrs. Baxter. I'm on duty. Gotta be getting back."

"Well, tell your ma that I'll be over when I take up my beer and remind her to save some kraut for me."

And the recording angel was gone. He was gone, and a man was dead because I lied. Where was the balance in that? One lie surely wouldn't be worth a man's life. Bailey could have explained it all to me, but I didn't dare ask him. Obviously I had forfeited my place in heaven forever, and I was as gutless as the doll I had ripped to pieces ages ago. Even Christ Himself turned His back on Satan. Wouldn't He turn His back on me? I could feel the evilness flowing through my body and waiting, pent up, to rush off my tongue if I tried to open my mouth. I clamped my teeth shut, I'd hold it in. If it escaped, wouldn't it flood the world and all the innocent people?

Grandmother Baxter said, "Ritie and Junior, you didn't hear a thing. I never want to hear this situation nor that evil man's name mentioned in my house again. I mean that." She went back into the kitchen to make apple strudel for my celebration.

Even Bailey was frightened. He sat all to himself, looking at a man's death—a kitten looking at a wolf. Not quite understanding it but frightened all the same.

In those moments I decided that although Bailey loved me he couldn't help. I had sold myself to the Devil and there could be no escape. The only thing I could do was to stop talking to people other than Bailey. Instinctively, or somehow, I knew that because I loved him so much I'd never hurt him, but if I talked to anyone else that person might die too. Just my breath, carrying my words out, might poison people and they'd curl up and die like the black fat slugs that only pretended.

I had to stop talking.

I discovered that to achieve perfect personal silence all I had to do was to attach myself leechlike to sound. I began to listen to everything. I probably hoped that after I had heard all the sounds, really heard them and packed them down, deep in my ears, the world would be quiet around me. I walked into rooms where people were laughing, their voices hitting the walls like stones, and I simply stood still—in the midst of the riot of sound. After a minute or two, silence would rush into the room from its hiding place because I had eaten up all the sounds.

In the first weeks my family accepted my behavior as a post-rape, post-hospital affliction. (Neither the term nor the experience was mentioned in Grandmother's house, where Bailey and I were again staying.) They understood that I could talk to Bailey, but to no one else.

Then came the last visit from the visiting nurse, and the doctor said I was healed. That meant that I should be back on the sidewalks playing handball or enjoying the games I had been given when I was sick. When I refused to be the child they knew and accepted me to be, I was called impudent and my muteness sullenness.

For a while I was punished for being so uppity that I wouldn't speak; and then came the thrashings, given by any relative who felt himself offended.

We were on the train going back to Stamps, and this time it was I who had to console Bailey. He cried his heart out down the aisles of the coach, and pressed his little-boy body against the window pane looking for a last glimpse of his Mother Dear.

I have never known if Momma sent for us, or if the St. Louis family just got fed up with my grim presence. There is nothing more appalling than a constantly morose child.

I cared less about the trip than about the fact that Bailey was unhappy, and had no more thought of our destination than if I had simply been heading for the toilet.

14

THE BARRENNESS OF Stamps was exactly what I wanted, without will or consciousness. After St. Louis, with its noise and activity, its trucks and buses, and loud family gatherings, I welcomed the obscure lanes and lonely bungalows set back deep in dirt yards.

The resignation of its inhabitants encouraged me to relax. They showed me a contentment based on the belief that nothing more was coming to them, although a great deal more was due. Their decision to be satisfied with life's inequities was a lesson for me. Entering Stamps, I had the feeling that I was stepping over the border lines of the map and would fall, without fear, right off the end of the world. Nothing more could happen, for in Stamps nothing happened.

Into this cocoon I crept.

For an indeterminate time, nothing was demanded of me or of Bailey. We were, after all, Mrs. Henderson's California grandchildren, and had been away on a glamorous trip way up North to the fabulous St. Louis. Our father had come the year before, driving a big, shiny automobile and speaking the King's English with a big city accent, so all we had to do was lie quiet for months and rake in the profits of our adventures.

Farmers and maids, cooks and handymen, carpenters and all the children in town, made regular pilgrimages to the Store. "Just to see the travelers."

They stood around like cutout cardboard figures and asked, "Well, how is it up North?"

"See any of them big buildings?"

"Ever ride in one of them elevators?"

"Was you scared?"

"Whitefolks any different, like they say?"

Bailey took it upon himself to answer every question, and from a corner of his lively imagination wove a tapestry of entertainment for them that I was sure was as foreign to him as it was to me.

He, as usual, spoke precisely. "They have, in the North, buildings so high that for months, in the winter, you can't see the top floors."

"Tell the truth."

"They've got watermelons twice the size of a cow's head and sweeter than syrup." I distinctly remember his intent face and the fascinated faces of his listeners. "And if you can count the watermelon's seeds, before it's cut open, you can win five zillion dollars and a new car."

Momma, knowing Bailey, warned, "Now Ju, be careful you don't slip up on a not true." (Nice people didn't say "lie.")

"Everybody wears new clothes and have inside toilets. If you fall down in one of them, you get flushed away into the Mississippi River. Some people have iceboxes, only the proper name is Cold Spot or Frigidaire. The snow is so deep you can get buried right outside your door and people won't find you for a year. We made ice cream out of the snow." That was the only fact that I could have supported. During the winter, we had collected a bowl of snow and poured Pet milk over it, and sprinkled it with sugar and called it ice cream.

Momma beamed and Uncle Willie was proud when Bailey regaled the customers with our exploits. We were drawing cards for the Store and objects of the town's adoration. Our journey to magical places alone was a spot of color on the town's drab canvas, and our return made us even more the most enviable of people.

High spots in Stamps were usually negative: droughts, floods, lynchings and deaths.

Bailey played on the country folks' need for diversion. Just after our return he had taken to sarcasm, picked it up as one might pick up a stone, and put it snufflike under his lip. The double entendres, the two-pronged sentences, slid over his tongue to dart rapier-like into anything that happened to be in the way. Our customers, though, generally were so straight thinking and speaking that they were never hurt by his attacks. They didn't comprehend them.

"Bailey Junior sound just like Big Bailey. Got a silver tongue. Just like his daddy."

"I hear tell they don't pick cotton up there. How the people live then?"

Bailey said that the cotton up North was so tall, if ordinary people tried to pick it they'd have to get up on ladders, so the cotton farmers had their cotton picked by machines.

For a while I was the only recipient of Bailey's kindness. It was not that he pitied me but that he felt we were in the same boat for different reasons, and that I could understand his frustration just as he could countenance my withdrawal.

I never knew if Uncle Willie had been told about the incident in St. Louis, but sometimes I caught him watching me with a far-off look in his big eyes. Then he would quickly send me on some errand that would take me out of his presence. When that happened I was both relieved and ashamed. I certainly didn't want a cripple's sympathy (that would have been a case of the blind leading the blind), nor did I want Uncle Willie, whom I loved in my fashion, to think of me as being sinful and dirty. If he thought so, at least I didn't want to know it.

Sounds came to me dully, as if people were speaking through their handkerchiefs or with their hands over their mouths. Colors weren't true either, but rather a vague assortment of shaded pastels that indicated not so much color as faded familiarities. People's names escaped me and I began to worry over my sanity. After all, we had been away less than a year, and customers whose accounts I had formerly remembered without consulting the ledger were now complete strangers.

People, except Momma and Uncle Willie, accepted my unwillingness to talk as a natural outgrowth of a reluctant return to the South. And an indication that I was pining for the high times we had had in the big city. Then, too, I was well known for being "tender-hearted." Southern Negroes used that term to mean sensitive and tended to look upon a person with that affliction as being a little sick or in delicate health. So I was not so much forgiven as I was understood.

15

FOR NEARLY A YEAR, I sopped around the house, the Store, the school and the church, like an old biscuit, dirty and inedible. Then I met, or rather got to know, the lady who threw me my first life line.

Mrs. Bertha Flowers was the aristocrat of Black Stamps. She had the grace of control to appear warm in the coldest weather, and on the Arkansas summer days it seemed she had a private breeze which swirled around, cooling her. She was thin without the taut look of wiry people, and her printed voile dresses and flowered hats were as right for her as denim overalls for a farmer. She was our side's answer to the richest white woman in town.

Her skin was a rich black that would have peeled like a plum if snagged, but then no one would have thought of getting close enough to Mrs. Flowers to ruffle her dress, let along snag her skin. She didn't encourage familiarity. She wore gloves too.

I don't think I ever saw Mrs. Flowers laugh, but she smiled often. A slow widening of her thin black lips to show even, small white teeth, then the slow effortless closing. When she chose to smile on me, I always wanted to thank her. The action was so graceful and inclusively benign.

She was one of the few gentlewomen I have ever known, and has remained throughout my life the measure of what a human being can be.

Momma had a strange relationship with her. Most often when she passed on the road in front of the Store, she spoke to Momma in that soft yet carrying voice, "Good day, Mrs. Henderson." Momma responded with "How you, Sister Flowers?"

Mrs. Flowers didn't belong to our church, nor was she Momma's familiar. Why on earth did she insist on calling her Sister Flowers? Shame made me want to hide my face. Mrs. Flowers deserved better than to be called Sister. Then, Momma left out the verb. Why not ask, "How *are* you, *Mrs.* Flowers?" With the unbalanced passion of the young, I hated her for showing her ignorance to Mrs. Flowers. It didn't occur to me for many years that they were as alike as sisters, separated only by formal education.

Although I was upset, neither of the women was in the least shaken by what I thought an unceremonious greeting. Mrs. Flowers would continue her easy gait up the hill to her little bungalow, and Momma kept on shelling peas or doing whatever had brought her to the front porch.

Occasionally, though, Mrs. Flowers would drift off the road and down to the Store and Momma would say to me, "Sister, you go on and play." As I left I would hear the beginning of an intimate conversation. Momma persistently using the wrong verb, or none at all.

"Brother and Sister Wilcox is sho'ly the meanest—" "Is," Momma? "Is"? Oh, please, not "is," Momma, for two or more. But they talked, and from the side of the building where I waited for the ground to open up and swallow me, I heard the soft-voiced Mrs. Flowers and the textured voice of my grandmother merging and melting. They were interrupted from time to time by giggles that must have come from Mrs. Flowers (Momma never giggled in her life). Then she was gone.

She appealed to me because she was like people I had never met personally. Like women in English novels who walked the moors (whatever they were) with their loyal dogs racing at a respectful distance. Like the women who sat in front of roaring fireplaces, drinking tea incessantly from silver trays full of scones and crumpets. Women who walked over the "heath" and read morocco-bound books and had two last names divided by a hyphen. It would be safe to say that she made me proud to be Negro, just by being herself.

She acted just as refined as whitefolks in the movies and books and she was more beautiful, for none of them could have come near that warm color without looking gray by comparison.

It was fortunate that I never saw her in the company of powhitefolks. For since they tend to think of their whiteness as an evenizer, I'm certain that I would have had to hear her spoken to commonly as Bertha, and my image of her would have been shattered like the unmendable Humpty-Dumpty.

One summer afternoon, sweet-milk fresh in my memory, she stopped at the Store to buy provisions. Another Negro woman of her health and age would have been expected to carry the paper sacks home in one hand, but Momma said, "Sister Flowers, I'll send Bailey up to your house with these things."

She smiled that slow dragging smile; "Thank you, Mrs. Henderson, I'd prefer Marguerite, though." My name was beautiful when she said it. "I've been meaning to talk to her, anyway." They gave each other age-group looks.

Momma said, "Well, that's all right then. Sister, go and change your dress. You going to Sister Flowers's."

The chifforobe was a maze. What on earth did one put on to go to Mrs. Flowers' house? I knew I shouldn't put on a Sunday dress. It might be sacrilegious. Certainly not a house dress, since I was already wearing a fresh one. I chose a school dress, naturally. It was formal without suggesting that going to Mrs. Flowers' house was equivalent to attending church.

I trusted myself back into the Store.

"Now, don't you look nice." I had chosen the right thing, for once.

"Mrs. Henderson, you make most of the children's clothes, don't you?"

"Yes, ma'am. Sure do. Store-bought clothes ain't hardly worth the thread it take to stitch them."

"I'll say you do a lovely job, though, so neat. That dress looks professional."

Momma was enjoying the seldom-received compliments. Since everyone we knew (except Mrs. Flowers, of course) could sew competently, praise was rarely handed out for the commonly practiced craft.

"I try, with the help of the Lord, Sister Flowers, to finish the inside just like I does the outside. Come here, Sister."

I had buttoned up the collar and tied the belt, apronlike, in back. Momma told me to turn around. With one hand she pulled the strings and the belt fell free at both sides of my waist. Then her large hands were at my neck, opening the button loops. I was terrified. What was happening?

"Take it off, Sister." She had her hands on the hem of the dress.

"I don't need to see the inside, Mrs. Henderson, I can tell . . ." But the dress was over my head and my arms were stuck in the sleeves. Momma said, "That'll do. See here, Sister Flowers, I French-seams around the armholes." Through the cloth film, I saw the shadow approach. "That makes it last longer. Children these days would bust out of sheet-metal clothes. They so rough."

"That is a very good job, Mrs. Henderson. You should be proud. You can put your dress back on, Marguerite."

"No ma'am. Pride is a sin. And 'cording to the Good Book, it goeth before a fall."

"That's right. So the Bible says. It's a good thing to keep in mind."

I wouldn't look at either of them. Momma hadn't thought that taking off my dress in front of Mrs. Flowers would kill me stone dead. If I had refused, she would have thought I was trying to be "woman-ish" and might have remembered St. Louis. Mrs. Flowers had known that I would be embarrassed and that was even worse. I picked up the groceries and went out to wait in the hot sunshine. It would be fitting if I got a sunstroke and died before they came outside. Just dropped dead on the slanting porch.

There was a little path beside the rocky road, and Mrs. Flowers walked in front swinging her arms and picking her way over the stones.

She said, without turning her head, to me, "I hear you're doing very good school work, Marguerite, but that it's all written. The teachers report that they have trouble getting you to talk in class." We passed the triangular farm on our left and the path widened to allow us to walk together. I hung back in the separate unasked and unanswerable questions.

"Come and walk along with me, Marguerite." I couldn't have refused even if I wanted to. She pronounced my name so nicely. Or more correctly, she spoke each word with such clarity that I was certain a foreigner who didn't understand English could have understood her.

"Now no one is going to make you talk—possibly no one can. But bear in mind, language is man's way of communicating with his fellow man and it is language alone which separates him from the lower animals." That was a totally new idea to me, and I would need time to think about it.

"Your grandmother says you read a lot. Every chance you get. That's good, but not good enough. Words mean more than what is set down on paper. It takes the human voice to infuse them with the shades of deeper meaning."

I memorized the part about the human voice infusing words. It seemed so valid and poetic.

She said she was going to give me some books and that I not only must read them, I must read them aloud. She suggested that I try to make a sentence sound in as many different ways as possible.

"I'll accept no excuse if you return a book to me that has been badly handled." My imagination boggled at the punishment I would deserve if in fact I did abuse a book of Mrs. Flowers'. Death would be too kind and brief.

The odors in the house surprised me. Somehow I had never connected Mrs. Flowers with food or eating or any other common experience of common people. There must have been an outhouse, too, but my mind never recorded it.

The sweet scent of vanilla had met us as she opened the door.

"I made tea cookies this morning. You see, I had planned to invite you for cookies and lemonade so we could have this little chat. The lemonade is in the icebox."

It followed that Mrs. Flowers would have ice on

an ordinary day, when most families in our town bought ice late on Saturdays only a few times during the summer to be used in the wooden ice-cream freezers.

She took the bags from me and disappeared through the kitchen door. I looked around the room that I had never in my wildest fantasies imagined I would see. Browned photographs leered or threatened from the walls and the white, freshly done curtains pushed against themselves and against the wind. I wanted to gobble up the room entire and take it to Bailey, who would help me analyze and enjoy it.

"Have a seat, Marguerite. Over there by the table." She carried a platter covered with a tea towel. Although she warned that she hadn't tried her hand at baking sweets for some time, I was certain that like everything else about her the cookies would be perfect.

They were flat round wafers, slightly browned on the edges and butter-yellow in the center. With the cold lemonade they were sufficient for childhood's lifelong diet. Remembering my manners, I took nice little lady-like bites off the edges. She said she had made them expressly for me and that she had a few in the kitchen that I could take home to my brother. So I jammed one whole cake in my mouth and the rough crumbs scratched the insides of my jaws, and if I hadn't had to swallow, it would have been a dream come true.

As I ate she began the first of what we later called "my lessons in living." She said that I must always be intolerant of ignorance but understanding of illiteracy. That some people, unable to go to school, were more educated and even more intelligent than college professors. She encouraged me to listen carefully to what country people called mother wit. That in those homely sayings was couched the collective wisdom of generations.

When I finished the cookies she brushed off the

table and brought a thick, small book from the book-case. I had read *A Tale of Two Cities* and found it up to my standards as a romantic novel. She opened the first page and I heard poetry for the first time in my life.

"It was the best of times and the worst of times . . ." Her voice slid in and curved down through and over the words. She was nearly singing. I wanted to look at the pages. Were they the same that I had read? Or were there notes, music, lined on the pages, as in a hymn book? Her sounds began cascading gently. I knew from listening to a thousand preachers that she was nearing the end of her reading, and I hadn't really heard, heard to understand, a single word.

"How do you like that?"

It occurred to me that she expected a response. The sweet vanilla flavor was still on my tongue and her reading was a wonder in my ears. I had to speak.

I said, "Yes, ma'am." It was the least I could do, but it was the most also.

"There's one more thing. Take this book of poems and memorize one for me. Next time you pay me a visit, I want you to recite."

I have tried often to search behind the sophistica-tion of years for the enchantment I so easily found in those gifts. The essence escapes but its aura re-mains. To be allowed, no, invited, into the private lives of strangers, and to share their joys and fears, was a chance to exchange the Southern bitter worm-wood for a cup of mead with Beowulf or a hot cup of tea and milk with Oliver Twist. When I said aloud, "It is a far, far better thing that I do, than I have ever done . . ." tears of love filled my eyes at my selflessness.

On that first day, I ran down the hill and into the road (few cars ever came along it) and had the good sense to stop running before I reached the Store.

I was liked, and what a difference it made. I was respected not as Mrs. Henderson's grandchild or Bailey's sister but for just being Marguerite Johnson.

Childhood's logic never asks to be proved (all conclusions are absolute). I didn't question why Mrs. Flowers had singled me out for attention, nor did it occur to me that Momma might have asked her to give me a little talking to. All I cared about was that she had made tea cookies for *me* and read to *me* from her favorite book. It was enough to prove that she liked me.

Momma and Bailey were waiting inside the Store. He said, "My, what did she give you?" He had seen the books, but I held the paper sack with his cookies in my arms shielded by the poems.

Momma said, "Sister, I know you acted like a little lady. That do my heart good to see settled people take to you all. I'm trying my best, the Lord knows, but these days . . ." Her voice trailed off. "Go on in and change your dress."

In the bedroom it was going to be a joy to see Bailey receive his cookies. I said, "By the way, Bailey, Mrs. Flowers sent you some tea cookies—"

Momma shouted, "What did you say, Sister? You, Sister, what did you say?" Hot anger was crackling in her voice.

Bailey said, "She said Mrs. Flowers sent me some—"

"I ain't talking to you, Ju." I heard the heavy feet walk across the floor toward our bedroom. "Sister, you heard me. What's that you said?" She swelled to fill the doorway.

Bailey said, "Momma." His pacifying voice— "Momma, she—"

"You shut up, Ju. I'm talking to your sister."

I didn't know what sacred cow I had bumped, but it was better to find out than to hang like a thread over an open fire. I repeated, "I said, 'Bailey, by the way, Mrs. Flowers sent you—' "

"That's what I thought you said. Go on and take off your dress. I'm going to get a switch."

At first I thought she was playing. Maybe some heavy joke that would end with "You sure she didn't send me something?" but in a minute she was back in the room with a long, ropy, peach-tree switch, the juice smelling bitter at having been torn loose. She said, "Get down on your knees. Bailey, Junior, you come on, too."

The three of us knelt as she began, "Our Father, you know the tribulations of your humble servant. I have with your help raised two grown boys. Many's the day I thought I wouldn't be able to go on, but you gave me the strength to see my way clear. Now, Lord, look down on this heavy heart today. I'm trying to raise my son's children in the way they should go, but, oh, Lord, the Devil try to hinder me on every hand. I never thought I'd live to hear cursing under this roof, what I try to keep dedicated to the glorification of God. And cursing out of the mouths of babes. But you said, in the last days brother would turn against brother, and children against their parents. That there would be a gnashing of teeth and a rendering of flesh. Father, forgive this child, I beg you, on bended knee."

I was crying loudly now. Momma's voice had risen to a shouting pitch, and I knew that whatever wrong I had committed was extremely serious. She had even left the Store untended to take up my case with God. When she finished we were all crying. She pulled me to her with one hand and hit me only a few times with the switch. The shock of my sin and the emotional release of her prayer had exhausted her.

Momma wouldn't talk right then, but later in the evening I found that my violation lay in using the phrase "by the way." Momma explained that "Jesus was the Way, the Truth and the Light," and anyone who says "by the way" is really saying, "by Jesus," or "by God" and the Lord's name would not be taken in vain in her house.

When Bailey tried to interpret the words with:

"Whitefolks use 'by the way' to mean while we're on the subject," Momma reminded us that "whitefolks' mouths were most in general loose and their words were an abomination before Christ."

16

RECENTLY A WHITE woman from Texas, who would quickly describe herself as a liberal, asked me about my hometown. When I told her that in Stamps my grandmother had owned the only Negro general merchandise store since the turn of the century, she exclaimed, "Why, you were a debutante." Ridiculous and even ludicrous. But Negro girls in small Southern towns, whether poverty-stricken or just munching along on a few of life's necessities, were given as extensive and irrelevant preparations for adulthood as rich white girls shown in magazines. Admittedly the training was not the same. While white girls learned to waltz and sit gracefully with a tea cup balanced on their knees, we were lagging behind, learning the mid-Victorian values with very little money to indulge them. (Come and see Edna Lomax spending the money she made picking cotton on five balls of ecru tatting thread. Her fingers are bound to snag the work and she'll have to repeat the stitches time and time again. But she knows that when she buys the thread.)

We were required to embroider and I had trunkfuls of colorful dishtowels, pillowcases, runners and handkerchiefs to my credit. I mastered the art of crocheting and tatting, and there was a lifetime's supply of dainty doilies that would never be used in sacheted dresser drawers. It went without saying that all girls could iron and wash, but the finer touches around the home, like setting a table with real silver, baking roasts and cooking vegetables without meat, had to be learned elsewhere. Usually at the source of those habits. During my tenth year, a white woman's kitchen became my finishing school.

Mrs. Viola Cullinan was a plump woman who lived in a three-bedroom house somewhere behind the post office. She was singularly unattractive until she smiled, and then the lines around her eyes and mouth which made her look perpetually dirty disappeared, and her face looked like the mask of an impish elf. She usually rested her smile until late afternoon when her women friends dropped in and Miss Glory, the cook, served them cold drinks on the closed-in porch.

The exactness of her house was inhuman. This glass went here and only here. That cup had its place and it was an act of impudent rebellion to place it anywhere else. At twelve o'clock the table was set. At 12:15 Mrs. Cullinan sat down to dinner (whether her husband had arrived or not). At 12:16 Miss Glory brought out the food.

It took me a week to learn the difference between a salad plate, a bread plate and a dessert plate.

Mrs. Cullinan kept up the tradition of her wealthy parents. She was from Virginia. Miss Glory, who was a descendant of slaves that had worked for the Cullinans, told me her history. She had married beneath her (according to Miss Glory). Her husband's family hadn't had their money very long and what they had "didn't 'mount to much."

As ugly as she was, I thought privately, she was lucky to get a husband above or beneath her station. But Miss Glory wouldn't let me say a thing against her mistress. She was very patient with me, however, over the housework. She explained the dishware, silverware and servants' bells.

The large round bowl in which soup was served wasn't a soup bowl, it was a tureen. There were goblets, sherbet glasses, ice-cream glasses, wine glasses, green glass coffee cups with matching saucers, and water glasses. I had a glass to drink from, and it sat with Miss Glory's on a separate shelf from the others. Soup spoons, gravy boat, butter knives, salad forks and carving platter were additions to my vocabulary and in fact almost represented a new language. I was fascinated with the novelty, with the fluttering Mrs. Cullinan and her Alice-in-Wonderland house.

Her husband remains, in my memory, undefined. I lumped him with all the other white men that I had ever seen and tried not to see.

On our way home one evening, Miss Glory told me that Mrs. Cullinan couldn't have children. She said that she was too delicate-boned. It was hard to imagine bones at all under those layers of fat. Miss Glory went on to say that the doctor had taken out all her lady organs. I reasoned that a pig's organs included the lungs, heart and liver, so if Mrs. Cullinan was walking around without those essentials, it explained why she drank alcohol out of unmarked bottles. She was keeping herself embalmed.

When I spoke to Bailey about it, he agreed that I was right, but he also informed me that Mr. Cullinan had two daughters by a colored lady and that I knew them very well. He added that the girls were the spitting image of their father. I was unable to remember what he looked like, although I had just left him a few hours before, but I thought of the Coleman girls. They were very light-skinned and certainly didn't look very much like their mother (no one ever mentioned Mr. Coleman).

My pity for Mrs. Cullinan preceded me the next morning like the Cheshire cat's smile. Those girls, who could have been her daughters, were beautiful. They didn't have to straighten their hair. Even when they were caught in the rain, their braids still hung down straight like tamed snakes. Their mouths were pouty little cupid's bows. Mrs. Cullinan didn't know what she missed. Or maybe she did. Poor Mrs. Cullinan.

For weeks after, I arrived early, left late and tried

very hard to make up for her barrenness. If she had had her own children, she wouldn't have had to ask me to run a thousand errands from her back door to the back door of her friends. Poor old Mrs. Cullinan.

Then one evening Miss Glory told me to serve the ladies on the porch. After I set the tray down and turned toward the kitchen, one of the women asked, "What's your name, girl?" It was the speckled-faced one. Mrs. Cullinan said, "She doesn't talk much. Her name's Margaret."

"Is she dumb?"

"No. As I understand it, she can talk when she wants to but she's usually quiet as a little mouse. Aren't you, Margaret?"

I smiled at her. Poor thing. No organs and couldn't even pronounce my name correctly.

"She's a sweet little thing, though."

"Well, that may be, but the name's too long. I'd never bother myself. I'd call her Mary if I was you."

I fumed into the kitchen. That horrible woman would never have the chance to call me Mary because if I was starving I'd never work for her. I decided I wouldn't pee on her if her heart was on fire. Giggles drifted in off the porch and into Miss Glory's pots. I wondered what they could be laughing about.

Whitefolks were so strange. Could they be talking about me? Everybody knew that they stuck together better than the Negroes did. It was possible that Mrs. Cullinan had friends in St. Louis who heard about a girl from Stamps being in court and wrote to tell her. Maybe she knew about Mr. Freeman.

My lunch was in my mouth a second time and I went outside and relieved myself on the bed of four-o'clocks. Miss Glory thought I might be coming down with something and told me to go on home, that Momma would give me some herb tea, and she'd explain to her mistress.

I realized how foolish I was being before I reached the pond. Of course Mrs. Cullinan didn't know. Otherwise she wouldn't have given me the two nice dresses that Momma cut down, and she certainly wouldn't have called me a "sweet little thing." My stomach felt fine, and I didn't mention anything to Momma.

That evening I decided to write a poem on being white, fat, old and without children. It was going to be a tragic ballad. I would have to watch her carefully to capture the essence of her loneliness and pain.

The very next day, she called me by the wrong name. Miss Glory and I were washing up the lunch dishes when Mrs. Cullinan came to the doorway. "Mary?"

Miss Glory asked, "Who?"

Mrs. Cullinan, sagging a little, knew and I knew. "I want Mary to go down to Mrs. Randall's and take her some soup. She's not been feeling well for a few days."

Miss Glory's face was a wonder to see. "You mean Margaret, ma'am. Her name's Margaret."

"That's too long. She's Mary from now on. Heat that soup from last night and put it in the china tureen and, Mary, I want you to carry it carefully."

Every person I knew had a hellish horror of being "called out of his name." It was a dangerous practice to call a Negro anything that could be loosely construed as insulting because of the centuries of their having been called niggers, jigs, dinges, blackbirds, crows, boots and spooks.

Miss Glory had a fleeting second of feeling sorry for me. Then as she handed me the hot tureen she said, "Don't mind, don't pay that no mind. Sticks and stones may break your bones, but words ... You know, I been working for her for twenty years."

She held the back door open for me. "Twenty years. I wasn't much older than you. My name used to be Hallelujah. That's what Ma named me, but my mistress give me 'Glory,' and it stuck. I likes it better too."

I was in the little path that ran behind the houses when Miss Glory shouted, "It's shorter too."

For a few seconds it was a tossup over whether I would laugh (imagine being named Hallelujah) or cry (imagine letting some white woman rename you for her convenience). My anger saved me from either outburst. I had to quit the job, but the problem was going to be how to do it. Momma wouldn't allow me to quit for just any reason.

"She's a peach. That woman is a real peach." Mrs. Randall's maid was talking as she took the soup from me, and I wondered what her name used to be and what she answered to now.

For a week I looked into Mrs. Cullinan's face as she called me Mary. She ignored my coming late and leaving early. Miss Glory was a little annoyed because I had begun to leave egg yolk on the dishes and wasn't putting much heart in polishing the silver. I hoped that she would complain to our boss, but she didn't.

Then Bailey solved my dilemma. He had me describe the contents of the cupboard and the particular plates she liked best. Her favorite piece was a casserole shaped like a fish and the green glass coffee cups. I kept his instructions in mind, so on the next day when Miss Glory was hanging out clothes and I had again been told to serve the old biddies on the porch, I dropped the empty serving tray. When I heard Mrs. Cullinan scream, "Mary!" I picked up the casserole and two of the green glass cups in readiness. As she rounded the kitchen door I let them fall on the tiled floor.

I could never absolutely describe to Bailey what happened next, because each time I got to the part where she fell on the floor and screwed up her ugly face to cry, we burst out laughing. She actually wobbled around on the floor and picked up shards of the cups and cried, "Oh, Momma. Oh, dear Gawd. It's Momma's china from Virginia. Oh, Momma, I sorry."

Miss Glory came running in from the yard and the women from the porch crowded around. Miss Glory was almost as broken up as her mistress. "You mean to say she broke our Virginia dishes? What we gone do?"

Mrs. Cullinan cried louder, "That clumsy nigger. Clumsy little black nigger."

Old speckled-face leaned down and asked, "Who did it, Viola? Was it Mary? Who did it?"

Everything was happening so fast I can't remember whether her action preceded her words, but I know that Mrs. Cullinan said, "Her name's Margaret, goddamn it, her name's Margaret!" And she threw a wedge of the broken plate at me. It could have been the hysteria which put her aim off, but the flying crockery caught Miss Glory right over her ear and she started screaming.

I left the front door wide open so all the neighbors could hear.

Mrs. Cullinan was right about one thing. My name wasn't Mary.

17

WEEKDAYS REVOLVED on a sameness wheel. They turned into themselves so steadily and inevitably that each seemed to be the original of yesterday's rough draft. Saturdays, however, always broke the mold and dared to be different.

Farmers trekked into town with their children and wives streaming around them. Their board-stiff khaki pants and shirts revealed the painstaking care of a dutiful daughter or wife. They often stopped at the Store to get change for bills so they could give out jangling coins to their children, who shook with their eagerness to get to town. The young kids openly resented their parents' dawdling in the Store and Uncle Willie would call them in and spread among them bits of sweet peanut patties that had been broken in shipping. They gobbled down the candies and were out again, kicking up the powdery dust in the road and worrying if there was going to be time to get to town after all.

Bailey played mumbledypeg with the older boys around the chinaberry tree, and Momma and Uncle Willie listened to the farmers' latest news of the country. I thought of myself as hanging in the Store, a mote imprisoned on a shaft of sunlight. Pushed and pulled by the slightest shift of air, but never falling free into the tempting darkness.

In the warm months, morning began with a quick wash in unheated well water. The suds were dashed on a plot of ground beside the kitchen door. It was called the bait garden (Bailey raised worms). After prayers, breakfast in summer was usually dry cereal and fresh milk. Then to our chores (which on Saturday included weekday jobs)—scrubbing the floors, raking the yards, polishing our shoes for Sunday (Uncle Willie's had to be shined with a biscuit) and attending to the customers who came breathlessly, also in their Saturday hurry.

Looking through the years, I marvel that Saturday was my favorite day in the week. What pleasures could have been squeezed between the fan folds of unending tasks? Children's talent to endure stems from their ignorance of alternatives.

After our retreat from St. Louis, Momma gave us a weekly allowance. Since she seldom dealt with money, other than to take it in and to tithe to the church, I supposed that the weekly ten cents was to tell us that even she realized that a change had come over us, and that our new unfamiliarity caused her to treat us with a strangeness.

I usually gave my money to Bailey, who went to the movies nearly every Saturday. He brought back Street and Smith cowboy books for me.

One Saturday Bailey was late coming back from the Rye-al-toh. Momma had begun heating water for the Saturday-night baths, and all the evening chores were done. Uncle Willie sat in the twilight on the front porch mumbling or maybe singing, and smoking a ready-made. It was quite late. Mothers had called in their children from the group games, and fading sounds of "Yah ... Yah ... you didn't catch me" still hung and floated into the Store.

Uncle Willie said, "Sister, better light the light." On Saturdays we used the electric lights so that last-minute Sunday shoppers could look down the hill and see if the Store was open. Momma hadn't told me to turn them on because she didn't want to believe that night had fallen hard and Bailey was still out in the ungodly dark.

Her apprehension was evident in the hurried movements around the kitchen and in her lonely fearing eyes. The Black woman in the South who raises sons, grandsons and nephews had her heartstrings tied to a hanging noose. Any break from routine may herald for them unbearable news. For this reason, Southern Blacks until the present generation could be counted among America's arch conservatives.

Like most self-pitying people, I had very little pity for my relatives' anxiety. If something indeed had happened to Bailey, Uncle Willie would always have Momma, and Momma had the Store. Then, after all, we weren't their children. But I would be the major loser if Bailey turned up dead. For he was all I claimed, if not all I had.

The bath water was steaming on the cooking stove, but Momma was scrubbing the kitchen table for the umpteenth time.

"Momma," Uncle Willie called and she jumped. "Momma." I waited in the bright lights of the Store, jealous that someone had come along and told these strangers something about my brother and I would be the last to know.

"Momma, why don't you and Sister walk down to meet him?"

To my knowledge Bailey's name hadn't been mentioned for hours, but we all knew whom he meant.

Of course. Why didn't that occur to me? I wanted to be gone. Momma said, "Wait a minute, little lady. Go get your sweater, and bring me my shawl."

It was darker in the road than I'd thought it would be. Momma swung the flashlight's arc over the path and weeds and scary tree trunks. The night suddenly became enemy territory, and I knew that if my brother was lost in this land he was forever lost. He was eleven and very smart, that I granted, but after all he was so small. The Bluebeards and tigers and Rippers could eat him up before he could scream for help.

Momma told me to take the light and she reached for my hand. Her voice came from a high hill above me and in the dark my hand was enclosed in hers. I loved her with a rush. She said nothing—no "Don't worry" or "Don't get tender-hearted." Just the gentle pressure of her rough hand conveyed her own concern and assurance to me.

We passed houses which I knew well by daylight but couldn't recollect in the swarthy gloom.

"Evening, Miz Jenkins." Walking and pulling me along.

"Sister Henderson? Anything wrong?" That was from an outline blacker than the night.

"No, ma'am. Not a thing. Bless the Lord." By the time she finished speaking we had left the worried neighbors far behind.

Mr. Willie Williams' Do Drop Inn was bright with furry red lights in the distance and the pond's fishy smell enveloped us. Momma's hand tightened and let go, and I saw the small figure plodding along, tired and old-mannish. Hands in his pockets and head bent, he walked like a man trudging up the hill behind a coffin.

"Bailey." It jumped out as Momma said, "Ju," and I started to run, but her hand caught mine again and became a vise. I pulled, but she yanked me back to her side. "We'll walk, just like we been walking, young lady." There was no chance to warn Bailey that he was dangerously late, that everybody had been worried and that he should create a good lie or, better, a great one.

Momma said, "Bailey, Junior," and he looked up without surprise. "You know it's night and you just now getting home?"

"Yes, ma'am." He was empty. Where was his alibi?

"What you been doing?"

"Nothing."

"That's all you got to say?"

"Yes, ma'am."

"All right, young man. We'll see when you get home."

She had turned me loose, so I made a grab for Bailey's hand, but he snatched it away. I said, "Hey, Bail," hoping to remind him that I was his sister and his only friend, but he grumbled something like "Leave me alone."

Momma didn't turn on the flashlight on the way back, nor did she answer the questioning Good evenings that floated around us as we passed the darkened houses.

I was confused and frightened. He was going to get a whipping and maybe he had done something terrible. If he couldn't talk to me it must have been serious. But there was no air of spent revelry about him. He just seemed sad. I didn't know what to think.

Uncle Willie said, "Getting too big for your britches, huh? You can't come home. You want to worry your grandmother to death?" Bailey was so far away he was beyond fear. Uncle Willie had a leather belt in his good hand but Bailey didn't notice or didn't care. "I'm going to whip you this time." Our uncle had only whipped us once before and then only with a peach-tree switch, so maybe now he was going to kill my brother. I screamed and grabbed for the belt, but Momma caught me. "Now, don't get uppity, miss, 'less you want some of the same thing. He got a lesson coming to him. You come on and get your bath."

From the kitchen I heard the belt fall down, dry and raspy on naked skin. Uncle Willie was gasping for breath, but Bailey made no sound. I was too afraid to splash water or even to cry and take a chance of drowning out Bailey's pleas for help, but the pleas never came and the whipping was finally over.

I lay awake an eternity, waiting for a sign, a whimper or a whisper, from the next room that he was still alive. Just before I fell exhausted into sleep, I heard Bailey: "Now I lay me down to sleep, I pray the Lord my soul to keep, if I should die before I wake, I pray the Lord my soul to take."

My last memory of that night was the question, Why is he saying the baby prayer? We had been saying the "Our Father, which art in heaven" for years.

For days the Store was a strange country, and we were all newly arrived immigrants. Bailey didn't talk, smile or apologize. His eyes were so vacant, it seemed his soul had flown away, and at meals I tried to give him the best pieces of meat and the largest portion of dessert, but he turned them down.

Then one evening at the pig pen he said without warning, "I saw Mother Dear."

If he said it, it was bound to be the truth. He wouldn't lie to me. I don't think I asked him where or when.

"In the movies." He laid his head on the wooden railing. "It wasn't really her. It was a woman named Kay Francis. She's a white movie star who looks just like Mother Dear."

There was no difficulty believing that a white movie star looked like our mother and that Bailey had seen her. He told me that the movies were changed each week, but when another picture came to Stamps starring Kay Francis he would tell me and we'd go together. He even promised to sit with me.

He had stayed late on the previous Saturday to see the film over again. I understood, and understood too why he couldn't tell Momma or Uncle Willie. She was our mother and belonged to us. She was never mentioned to anyone because we simply didn't have enough of her to share.

We had to wait nearly two months before Kay Francis returned to Stamps. Bailey's mood had lightened considerably, but he lived in a state of expectation and it made him more nervous than he was usually. When he told me that the movie would be shown, we went into our best behavior and were the exemplary children that Grandmother deserved and wished to think us.

It was a gay light comedy, and Kay Francis wore long-sleeved white silk shirts with big cuff links. Her bedroom was all satin and flowers in vases, and her maid, who was Black, went around saying "Lawsy, missy" all the time. There was a Negro chauffeur too, who rolled his eyes and scratched his head, and I wondered how on earth an idiot like that could be trusted with her beautiful cars.

The whitefolks downstairs laughed every few minutes, throwing the discarded snicker up to the Negroes in the buzzards' roost. The sound would jag around in our air for an indecisive second before the balcony's occupants accepted it and sent their own guffaws to riot with it against the walls of the theater.

I laughed, too, but not at the hateful jokes made on my people. I laughed because, except that she was white, the big movie star looked just like my mother. Except that she lived in a big mansion with a thousand servants, she lived just like my mother. And it was funny to think of the whitefolks' not knowing that the woman they were adoring could be my mother's twin, except that she was white and my mother was prettier. Much prettier.

The movie star made me happy. It was extraordinary good fortune to be able to save up one's money and go see one's mother whenever one wanted to. I bounced out of the theater as if I'd been given an unexpected present. But Bailey was cast down again. (I had to beg him not to stay for the next show.) On the way home he stopped at the railroad track and waited for the night freight train. Just before it reached the crossing, he tore out and ran across the tracks.

I was left on the other side in hysteria. Maybe the giant wheels were grinding his bones into a bloody mush. Maybe he tried to catch a boxcar and got flung into the pond and drowned. Or even worse, maybe he caught the train and was forever gone.

When the train passed he pushed himself away from the pole where he had been leaning, berated me for making all that noise and said, "Let's go home."

One year later he did catch a freight, but because of his youth and the inscrutable ways of fate, he didn't find California and his Mother Dear—he got stranded in Baton Rouge, Louisiana, for two weeks.

18

ANOTHER DAY WAS OVER. In the soft dark the cotton truck spilled the pickers out and roared out of the yard with a sound like a giant's fart. The workers stepped around in circles for a few seconds as if they had found themselves unexpectedly in an unfamiliar place. Their minds sagged.

In the Store the men's faces were the most painful to watch, but I seemed to have no choice. When they tried to smile to carry off their tiredness as if it was nothing, the body did nothing to help the mind's attempt at disguise. Their shoulders drooped even as they laughed, and when they put their hands on their hips in a show of jauntiness, the palms slipped the thighs as if the pants were waxed.

"Evening, Sister Henderson. Well, back where we started, huh?"

"Yes, sir, Brother Stewart. Back where you started, bless the Lord." Momma could not take the smallest achievement for granted. People whose history and future were threatened each day by extinction considered that it was only by divine intervention that they were able to live at all. I find it interesting that the meanest life, the poorest existence, is attributed to God's will, but as human beings become more affluent, as their living standard and style begin to ascend the material scale, God descends the scale of responsibility at a commensurate speed.

"That's just who get the credit. Yes, ma'am. The blessed Lord." Their overalls and shirts seemed to be torn on purpose and the cotton lint and dust in their hair gave them the appearance of people who had turned gray in the past few hours.

The women's feet had swollen to fill the discarded men's shoes they wore, and they washed their arms at the well to dislodge dirt and splinters that had accrued to them as part of the day's pickings.

I thought them all hateful to have allowed themselves to be worked like oxen, and even more shameful to try to pretend that things were not as bad as they were. When they leaned too hard on the partly glass candy counter, I wanted to tell them shortly to stand up and "assume the posture of a man," but Momma would have beaten me if I'd opened my mouth. She ignored the creaks of the counter under their weight and moved around filling their orders and keeping up a conversation. "Going to put your dinner on, Sister Williams?" Bailey and I helped Momma, while Uncle Willie sat on the porch and heard the day's account.

"Praise the Lord, no, ma'am. Got enough left over

from last night to do us. We going home and get cleaned up to go to the revival meeting."

Go to church in that cloud of weariness? Not go home and lay those tortured bones in a feather bed? The idea came to me that my people may be a race of masochists and that not only was it our fate to live the poorest, roughest life but that we liked it like that.

"I know what you mean, Sister Williams. Got to feed the soul just like you feed the body. I'm taking the children, too, the Lord willing. Good Book say, 'Raise a child in the way he should go and he will not depart from it.'"

"That's what it say. Sure is what it say."

The cloth tent had been set on the flatlands in the middle of a field near the railroad tracks. The earth was carpeted with a silky layer of dried grass and cotton stalks. Collapsible chairs were poked into the still-soft ground and a large wooden cross was hung from the center beam at the rear of the tent. Electric lights had been strung from behind the pulpit to the entrance flap and continued outside on poles made of rough two-by-fours.

Approached in the dark the swaying bulbs looked lonely and purposeless. Not as if they were there to provide light or anything meaningful. And the tent, that blurry bright three-dimensional A, was so foreign to the cotton field, that it might just get up and fly away before my eyes.

People, suddenly visible in the lamplight, streamed toward the temporary church. The adults' voices relayed the serious intent of their mission. Greetings were exchanged, hushed.

"Evening, sister, how you?"

"Bless the Lord, just trying to make it in."

Their minds were concentrated on the coming meeting, soul to soul, with God. This was no time to indulge in human concerns or personal questions.

"The good Lord give me another day, and I'm

thankful." Nothing personal in that. The credit was God's, and there was no illusion about the Central Position's shifting or becoming less than Itself.

Teenagers enjoyed revivals as much as adults. They used the night outside meetings to play at courting. The impermanence of a collapsible church added to the frivolity, and their eyes flashed and winked and the girls giggled little silver drops in the dusk while the boys postured and swaggered and pretended not to notice. The nearly grown girls wore skirts as tight as the custom allowed and the young men slicked their hair down with Moroline Hairdressing and water.

To small children, though, the idea of praising God in a tent was confusing, to say the least. It seemed somehow blasphemous. The lights hanging slack overhead, the soft ground underneath and the canvas wall that faintly blew in and out, like cheeks puffed with air, made for the feeling of a country fair. The nudgings and jerks and winks of the bigger children surely didn't belong in a church. But the tension of the elders—their expectation, which weighted like a thick blanket over the crowd—was the most perplexing of all.

Would the gentle Jesus care to enter into that transitory setting? The altar wobbled and threatened to overturn and the collection table sat at a rakish angle. One leg had yielded itself to the loose dirt. Would God the Father allow His only Son to mix with this crowd of cotton pickers and maids, washerwomen and handymen? I knew He sent His spirit on Sundays to the church, but after all that was a church and the people had had all day Saturday to shuffle off the cloak of work and the skin of despair.

Everyone attended the revival meetings. Members of the hoity-toity Mount Zion Baptist Church mingled with the intellectual members of the African Methodist Episcopal and African Methodist Episcopal Zion, and the plain working people of the Christian

Methodist Episcopal. These gatherings provided the one time in the year when all of those good village people associated with the followers of the Church of God in Christ. The latter were looked upon with some suspicion because they were so loud and raucous in their services. Their explanation that "the Good Book say, 'Make a joyful noise unto the Lord, and be exceedingly glad'" did not in the least minimize the condescension of their fellow Christians. Their church was far from the others, but they could be heard on Sunday, a half mile away, singing and dancing until they sometimes fell down in a dead faint. Members of the other churches wondered if the Holy Rollers were going to heaven after all their shouting. The suggestion was that they were having their heaven right here on earth.

This was their annual revival.

Mrs. Duncan, a little woman with a bird face, started the service. "I know I'm a witness for my Lord ... I know I'm a witness for my Lord, I know I'm a witness ..."

Her voice, a skinny finger, stabbed high up in the air and the church responded. From somewhere down front came the jangling sound of a tambourine. Two beats on "know," two beats on "I'm a" and two beats on the end of "witness."

Other voices joined the near shriek of Mrs. Duncan. They crowded around and tenderized the tone. Handclaps snapped in the roof and solidified the beat. When the song reached its peak in sound and passion, a tall, thin man who had been kneeling behind the altar all the while stood up and sang with the audience for a few bars. He stretched out his long arms and grasped the platform. It took some time for the singers to come off their level of exaltation, but the minister stood resolute until the song unwound like a child's playtoy and lay quieted in the aisles.

"Amen." He looked at the audience.

"Yes, sir, amen." Nearly everyone seconded him.

"I say, Let the church say 'Amen.'"

Everyone said, "Amen."

"Thank the Lord. Thank the Lord."

"That's right, thank the Lord. Yes, Lord. Amen."

"We will have prayer, led by Brother Bishop."

Another tall, brown-skinned man wearing square glasses walked up to the altar from the front row. The minister knelt at the right and Brother Bishop at the left.

"Our Father"—he was singing—"You who took my feet out the mire and clay—"

The church moaned, "Amen."

"You who saved my soul. One day. Look, sweet Jesus. Look down, on these your suffering children—"

The church begged, "Look down, Lord."

"Build us up where we're torn down . . . Bless the sick and the afflicted . . ."

It was the usual prayer. Only his voice gave it something new. After every two words he gasped and dragged the air over his vocal chords, making a sound like an inverted grunt. "You who"—grunt—"saved my"—gasp—"soul one"—inhalation—"day"—humph.

Then the congregation, led again by Mrs. Duncan, flew into "Precious Lord, take my hand, lead me on, let me stand." It was sung at a faster clip than the usual one in the C.M.E. Church, but at that tempo it worked. There was a joy about the tune that changed the meaning of its sad lyrics. "When the darkness appears, and the night draweth near and my life is almost gone . . ." There seemed to be an abandon which suggested that with all those things it should be a time for great rejoicing.

The serious shouters had already made themselves known, and their fans (cardboard advertisements from Texarkana's largest Negro funeral home) and lacy white handkerchiefs waved high in the air. In their dark hands they looked like small kites without the wooden frames.

The tall minister stood again at the altar. He waited for the song and the revelry to die.

He said, "Amen. Glory."

The church skidded off the song slowly. "Amen. Glory."

He still waited, as the last notes remained in the air, staircased on top of each other. "At the river I stand—" "I stand, guide my feet—" "Guide my feet, take my hand." Sung like the last circle in a round. Then quiet descended.

The Scripture reading was from Matthew, twenty-fifth chapter, thirtieth verse through the forty-sixth.

His text for the sermon was "The least of these."

After reading the verses to the accompaniment of a few Amens he said, "First Corinthians tells me, 'Even if I have the tongue of men and of angels and have not charity, I am as nothing. Even if I give all my clothes to the poor and have not charity, I am as nothing. Even if I give my body to be burned and have not charity it availeth me nothing. Burned, I say, and have not charity, it availeth nothing.' I have to ask myself, what is this thing called Charity? If good deeds are not charity—"

The church gave in quickly. "That's right, Lord."

"—if giving my flesh and blood is not charity?"

"Yes, Lord."

"I have to ask myself what is this charity they talking so much about."

I had never heard a preacher jump into the muscle of his sermon so quickly. Already the humming pitch had risen in the church, and those who knew had popped their eyes in anticipation of the coming excitement. Momma sat tree-trunk still, but she had balled her handkerchief in her hand and only the corner, which I had embroidered, stuck out.

"As I understand it, charity vaunteth not itself. Is not puffed up." He blew himself up with a deep breath to give us the picture of what Charity was not. "Charity don't go around saying 'I give you food and I give you clothes and by rights you ought to thank me.'"

The congregation knew whom he was talking about and voiced agreement with his analysis. "Tell the truth, Lord."

"Charity don't say, 'Because I give you a job, you got to bend your knee to me.'" The church was rocking with each phrase. "It don't say, 'Because I pays you what you due, you got to call me master.' It don't ask me to humble myself and belittle myself. That ain't what Charity is."

Down front to the right, Mr. and Mrs. Stewart, who only a few hours earlier had crumbled in our front yard, defeated by the cotton rows, now sat on the edges of their rickety-rackety chairs. Their faces shone with the delight of their souls. The mean whitefolks was going to get their comeuppance. Wasn't that what the minister said, and wasn't he quoting from the words of God Himself? They had been refreshed with the hope of revenge and the promise of justice.

"Aaagh. Raagh. I said ... Charity. Woooooo, a Charity. It don't want nothing for itself. It don't want to be bossman ... Waah ... It don't want to be headman ... Waah ... It don't want to be foreman ... Waah ... It ... I'm talking about Charity ... It don't want ... Oh Lord ... help me tonight ... It don't want to be bowed to and scraped at ..."

America's historic bowers and scrapers shifted easily and happily in the makeshift church. Reassured that although they might be the lowest of the low they were at least not uncharitable, and "in that great Gettin' Up Morning, Jesus was going to separate the sheep (them) from the goats (the whitefolks)."

"Charity is simple." The church agreed, vocally.

"Charity is poor." That was us he was talking about.

"Charity is plain." I thought, that's about right. Plain and simple.

"Charity is ... Oh, Oh, Oh. Cha-ri-ty. Where are you? Wooo ... Charity ... Hump."

One chair gave way and the sound of splintering wood split the air in the rear of the church.

"I call you and you don't answer. Woooh, oh Charity."

Another holler went up in front of me, and a large woman flopped over, her arms above her head like a candidate for baptism. The emotional release was contagious. Little screams burst around the room like Fourth of July firecrackers.

The minister's voice was a pendulum. Swinging left and down and right and down and left and—"How can you claim to be my brother, and hate me? Is that Charity? How can you claim to be my sister and despise me? Is that supposed to be Charity? How can you claim to be my friend and misuse and wrongfully abuse me? Is that Charity? Oh, my children, I stopped by here—"

The church swung on the end of his phrases. Punctuating. Confirming. "Stop by here, Lord."

"—to tell you, to open your heart and let Charity reign. Forgive your enemies for His sake. Show the Charity that Jesus was speaking of to this sick old world. It has need of the charitable giver." His voice was falling and the explosions became fewer and quieter.

"And now I repeat the words of the Apostle Paul, and 'now abideth faith, hope and charity, these three; but the greatest of these is charity.' "

The congregation lowed with satisfaction. Even if they were society's pariahs, they were going to be angels in a marble white heaven and sit on the right hand of Jesus, the Son of God. The Lord loved the poor and hated those cast high in the world. Hadn't He Himself said it would be easier for a camel to go through the eye of a needle than for a rich man to enter heaven? They were assured that they were going to be the only inhabitants of that land of milk and honey, except of course a few whitefolks like

John Brown who history books said was crazy anyway. All the Negroes had to do generally, and those at the revival especially, was bear up under this life of toil and cares, because a blessed home awaited them in the far-off bye and bye.

"Bye and bye, when the morning come, when all the saints of God's are gathering home, we will tell the story of how we overcome and we'll understand it better bye and bye."

A few people who had fainted were being revived on the side aisles when the evangelist opened the doors of the church. Over the sounds of "Thank you, Jesus," he started a long-meter hymn:

> "I came to Jesus, as I was,
> worried, wounded and sad,
> I found in Him a resting place,
> And He has made me glad."

The old ladies took up the hymn and shared it in tight harmony. The humming crowd began to sound like tired bees, restless and anxious to get home.

"All those under the sound of my voice who have no spiritual home, whose hearts are burdened and heavy-ladened, let them come. Come before it's too late. I don't ask you to join the Church of God in Christ. No. I'm a servant of God, and in this revival, we are out to bring straying souls to Him. So if you join this evening, just say which church you want to be affiliated with, and we will turn you over to a representative of that church body. Will one deacon of the following churches come forward?"

That was revolutionary action. No one had ever heard of a minister taking in members for another church. It was our first look at Charity among preachers. Men from the A.M.E., A.M.E.Z., Baptist and C.M.E. churches went down front and assumed stances a few feet apart. Converted sinners flowed down the aisles to shake hands with the evangelist and stayed at his side or were directed to one of the men in line. Over twenty people were saved that night.

There was nearly as much commotion over the saving of the sinners as there had been during the gratifying melodic sermon.

The Mothers of the Church, old ladies with white lace disks pinned to their thinning hair, had a service all their own. They walked around the new converts singing,

> "Before this time another year,
>   I may be gone,
>   In some lonesome graveyard,
>   Oh, Lord, how long?"

When the collection was taken up and the last hymn given to the praise of God, the evangelist asked that everyone in his presence rededicate his soul to God and his life's work to Charity. Then we were dismissed.

Outside and on the way home, the people played in their magic, as children poke in mud pies, reluctant to tell themselves that the game was over.

"The Lord touched him tonight, didn't He?"

"Surely did. Touched him with a mighty fire."

"Bless the Lord. I'm glad I'm saved."

"That's the truth. It make a whole lot of difference."

"I wish them people I works for could of heard that sermon. They don't know what they letting theyselves in for."

"Bible say, 'He who can hear, let him hear. He who can't, shame on 'em.'"

They basked in the righteousness of the poor and the exclusiveness of the downtrodden. Let the whitefolks have their money and power and segregation and sarcasm and big houses and schools and lawns like carpets, and books, and mostly—mostly—let them have their whiteness. It was better to be meek and lowly, spat upon and abused for this little time than to spend eternity frying in the fires of hell. No one would have admitted that the Christian and charitable people were happy to think of their oppressors' turning forever on the Devil's spit over the flames of fire and brimstone.

But that was what the Bible said and it didn't make mistakes. "Ain't it said somewhere in there that 'before one word of this changes, heaven and earth shall fall away?' Folks going to get what they deserved."

When the main crowd of worshipers reached the short bridge spanning the pond, the ragged sound of honky-tonk music assailed them. A barrelhouse blues was being shouted over the stamping of feet on a wooden floor. Miss Grace, the good-time woman, had her usual Saturday-night customers. The big white house blazed with lights and noise. The people inside had forsaken their own distress for a little while.

Passing near the din, the godly people dropped their heads and conversation ceased. Reality began its tedious crawl back into their reasoning. After all, they were needy and hungry and despised and dispossessed, and sinners the world over were in the driver's seat. How long, merciful Father? How long?

A stranger to the music could not have made a distinction between the songs sung a few minutes before and those being danced to in the gay house by the railroad tracks. All asked the same questions. How long, oh God? How long?

19

THE LAST INCH of space was filled, yet people continued to wedge themselves along the walls of the Store. Uncle Willie had turned the radio up to its last notch so that youngsters on the porch wouldn't miss a word. Women sat on kitchen chairs, dining-room chairs, stools and upturned wooden boxes. Small children and babies perched on every lap available and men leaned on the shelves or on each other.

The apprehensive mood was shot through with shafts of gaiety, as a black sky is streaked with lightning.

"I ain't worried 'bout this fight. Joe's gonna whip that cracker like it's open season."

"He gone whip him till that white boy call him Momma."

At last the talking was finished and the string-along songs about razor blades were over and the fight began.

"A quick jab to the head." In the Store the crowd grunted. "A left to the head and a right and another left." One of the listeners cackled like a hen and was quieted.

"They're in a clench, Louis is trying to fight his way out."

Some bitter comedian on the porch said, "That white man don't mind hugging that niggah now, I betcha."

"The referee is moving in to break them up, but Louis finally pushed the contender away and it's an uppercut to the chin. The contender is hanging on, now he's backing away. Louis catches him with a short left to the jaw."

A tide of murmuring assent poured out the doors and into the yard.

"Another left and another left. Louis is saving that mighty right ..." The mutter in the Store had grown into a baby roar and it was pierced by the clang of a bell and the announcer's "That's the bell for round three, ladies and gentlemen."

As I pushed my way into the Store I wondered if the announcer gave any thought to the fact that he was addressing as "ladies and gentlemen" all the Negroes around the world who sat sweating and praying, glued to their "master's voice."

There were only a few calls for R. C. Colas, Dr. Peppers, and Hire's root beer. The real festivities would begin after the fight. Then even the old

Christian ladies who taught their children and tried themselves to practice turning the other cheek would buy soft drinks, and if the Brown Bomber's victory was a particularly bloody one they would order peanut patties and Baby Ruths also.

Bailey and I lay the coins on top of the cash register. Uncle Willie didn't allow us to ring up sales during a fight. It was too noisy and might shake up the atmosphere. When the gong rang for the next round we pushed through the near-sacred quiet to the herd of children outside.

"He's got Louis against the ropes and now it's a left to the body and a right to the ribs. Another right to the body, it looks like it was low . . . Yes, ladies and gentlemen, the referee is signaling but the contender keeps raining the blows on Louis. It's another to the body, and it looks like Louis is going down."

My race groaned. It was our people falling. It was another lynching, yet another Black man hanging on a tree. One more woman ambushed and raped. A Black boy whipped and maimed. It was hounds on the trail of a man running through slimy swamps. It was a white woman slapping her maid for being forgetful.

The men in the Store stood away from the walls and at attention. Women greedily clutched the babes on their laps while on the porch the shufflings and smiles, flirtings and pinching of a few minutes before were gone. This might be the end of the world. If Joe lost we were back in slavery and beyond help. It would all be true, the accusations that we were lower types of human beings. Only a little higher than the apes. True that we were stupid and ugly and lazy and dirty and, unlucky and worst of all, that God Himself hated us and ordained us to be hewers of wood and drawers of water, forever and ever, world without end.

We didn't breathe. We didn't hope. We waited.

"He's off the ropes, ladies and gentlemen. He's

moving towards the center of the ring." There was no time to be relieved. The worst might still happen.

"And now it looks like Joe is mad. He's caught Carnera with a left hook to the head and a right to the head. It's a left jab to the body and another left to the head. There's a left cross and a right to the head. The contender's right eye is bleeding and he can't seem to keep his block up. Louis is penetrating every block. The referee is moving in, but Louis sends a left to the body and it's the uppercut to the chin and the contender is dropping. He's on the canvas, ladies and gentlemen."

Babies slid to the floor as women stood up and men leaned toward the radio.

"Here's the referee. He's counting. One, two, three, four, five, six, seven . . . Is the contender trying to get up again?"

All the men in the store shouted, "NO."

"—eight, nine, ten." There were a few sounds from the audience, but they seemed to be holding themselves in against tremendous pressure.

"The fight is all over, ladies and gentlemen. Let's get the microphone over to the referee . . . Here he is. He's got the Brown Bomber's hand, he's holding it up . . . Here he is . . ."

Then the voice, husky and familiar, came to wash over us—"The winnah, and still heavyweight champeen of the world . . . Joe Louis."

Champion of the world. A Black boy. Some Black mother's son. He was the strongest man in the world. People drank Coca-Colas like ambrosia and ate candy bars like Christmas. Some of the men went behind the Store and poured white lightning in their soft-drink bottles, and a few of the bigger boys followed them. Those who were not chased away came back blowing their breath in front of themselves like proud smokers.

It would take an hour or more before the people would leave the Store and head for home. Those who lived too far had made arrangements to stay in town. It wouldn't do for a Black man and his family to be caught on a lonely country road on a night when Joe Louis had proved that we were the strongest people in the world.

20

> "Acka Backa, Sody Cracka
> Acka Backa, Boo
> Acka Backa, Sody Cracka
> I'm in love with you."

THE SOUNDS OF tag beat through the trees while the top branches waved in contrapuntal rhythms. I lay on a moment of green grass and telescoped the children's game to my vision. The girls ran about wild, now here, now there, never here, never was, they seemed to have no more direction than a splattered egg. But it was a shared if seldom voiced knowledge that all movements fitted, and worked according to a larger plan. I raised a platform for my mind's eye and marveled down on the outcome of "Acka Backa." The gay picnic dresses dashed, stopped and darted like beautiful dragonflies over a dark pool. The boys, black whips in the sunlight, popped behind the trees where their girls had fled, half hidden and throbbing in the shadows.

The summer picnic fish fry in the clearing by the pond was the biggest outdoor event of the year. Everyone was there. All churches were represented, as well as the social groups (Elks, Eastern Star, Masons, Knights of Columbus, Daughters of Pythias), professional people (Negro teachers from Lafayette County) and all the excited children.

Musicians brought cigar-box guitars, harmonicas, juice harps, combs wrapped in tissue paper and even bathtub basses.

The amount and variety of foods would have

found approval on the menu of a Roman epicure. Pans of fried chicken, covered with dishtowels, sat under benches next to a mountain of potato salad crammed with hard-boiled eggs. Whole rust-red sticks of bologna were clothed in cheese-cloth. Homemade pickles and chow-chow, and baked country hams, aromatic with cloves and pineapples, vied for prominence. Our steady customers had ordered cold watermelons, so Bailey and I chugged the striped-green fruit into the Coca-Cola box and filled all the tubs with ice as well as the big black wash pot that Momma used to boil her laundry. Now they too lay sweating in the happy afternoon air.

The summer picnic gave ladies a chance to show off their baking hands. On the barbecue pit, chickens and spareribs sputtered in their own fat and a sauce whose recipe was guarded in the family like a scandalous affair. However, in the ecumenical light of the summer picnic every true baking artist could reveal her prize to the delight and criticism of the town. Orange sponge cakes and dark brown mounds dripping Hershey's chocolate stood layer to layer with ice-white coconuts and light brown caramels. Pound cakes sagged with their buttery weight and small children could no more resist licking the icings than their mothers could avoid slapping the sticky fingers.

Proven fishermen and weekend amateurs sat on the trunks of trees at the pond. They pulled the struggling bass and the silver perch from the swift water. A rotating crew of young girls scaled and cleaned the catch and busy women in starched aprons salted and rolled the fish in corn meal, then dropped them in Dutch ovens trembling with boiling fat.

On one corner of the clearing a gospel group was rehearsing. Their harmony, packed as tight as sardines, floated over the music of the county singers and melted into the songs of the small children's ring games.

"Boys, don'chew let that ball fall on none of my cakes, you do and it'll be me on you."

"Yes, ma'am," and nothing changed. The boys continued hitting the tennis ball with pailings snatched from a fence and running holes in the ground, colliding with everyone.

I had wanted to bring something to read, but Momma said if I didn't want to play with the other children I could make myself useful by cleaning fish or bringing water from the nearest well or wood for the barbecue.

I wandered into a retreat by accident. Signs with arrows around the barbecue pit pointed MEN, WOMEN, CHILDREN toward fading lanes, grown over since last year. Feeling ages old and very wise at ten, I couldn't allow myself to be found by small children squatting behind a tree. Neither did I have the nerve to follow the arrow pointing the way for WOMEN. If any grownup had caught me there, it was possible that she'd think I was being "womanish" and would report me to Momma, and I knew what I could expect from her. So when the urge hit me to relieve myself, I headed toward another direction. Once through the wall of sycamore trees I found myself in a clearing ten times smaller than the picnic area, and cool and quiet. After my business was taken care of, I found a seat between two protruding roots of a black walnut tree and leaned back on its trunk. Heaven would be like that for the deserving. Maybe California too. Looking straight up at the uneven circle of sky, I began to sense that I might be falling into a blue cloud, far away. The children's voices and the thick odor of food cooking over open fires were the hooks I grabbed just in time to save myself.

Grass squeaked and I jumped at being found. Louise Kendricks walked into my grove. I didn't know that she too was escaping the gay spirit. We were the same age and she and her mother lived in a neat little bungalow behind the school. Her cousins, who were in our age group, were wealthier and fairer, but I had secretly believed Louise to be the prettiest female in Stamps, next to Mrs. Flowers.

"What you doing sitting here by yourself, Marguerite?" She didn't accuse, she asked for information. I said that I was watching the sky. She asked, "What for?" There was obviously no answer to a question like that, so I didn't make up one. Louise reminded me of Jane Eyre. Her mother lived in reduced circumstances, but she was genteel, and though she worked as a maid I decided she should be called a governess and did so to Bailey and myself. (Who could teach a romantic dreamy ten-year-old to call a spade a spade?) Mrs. Kendricks could not have been very old, but to me all people over eighteen were adults and there could be no degree given or taken. They had to be catered to and pampered with politeness, then they had to stay in the same category of lookalike, soundalike and beingalike. Louise was a lonely girl, although she had plenty of playmates and was a ready partner for any ring game in the schoolyard.

Her face, which was long and dark chocolate brown, had a thin sheet of sadness over it, as light but as permanent as the viewing gauze on a coffin. And her eyes, which I thought her best feature, shifted quickly as if what they sought had just a second before eluded her.

She had come near and the spotted light through the trees fell on her face and braids in running splotches. I had never noticed before, but she looked exactly like Bailey. Her hair was "good"—more straight than kinky—and her features had the regularity of objects placed by a careful hand.

She looked up—"Well, you can't see much sky from here." Then she sat down, an arm away from me. Finding two exposed roots, she laid thin wrists on them as if she had been in an easy chair. Slowly she leaned back against the tree. I closed my eyes and thought of the necessity of finding another place and the unlikehood of there being another with all the qualifications that this one had. There was a little peal of a scream and before I could open my eyes Louise had grabbed my hand. "I was falling"— she shook her long braids—"I was falling in the sky."

I liked her for being able to fall in the sky and admit it. I suggested, "Let's try together. But we have to sit up straight on the count of five." Louise asked, "Want to hold hands? Just in case?" I did. If one of us did happen to fall, the other could pull her out.

After a few near tumbles into eternity (both of us knew what it was), we laughed at having played with death and destruction and escaped.

Louise said, "Let's look at that old sky while we're spinning." We took each other's hands in the center of the clearing and began turning around. Very slowly at first. We raised our chins and looked straight at the seductive patch of blue. Faster, just a little faster, then faster, faster yet. Yes, help, we were falling. Then eternity won, after all. We couldn't stop spinning or falling until I was jerked out of her grasp by greedy gravity and thrown to my fate below—no, above, not below. I found myself safe and dizzy at the foot of the sycamore tree. Louise had ended on her knees at the other side of the grove.

This was surely the time to laugh. We lost but we hadn't lost anything. First we were giggling and crawling drunkenly toward each other and then we were laughing out loud uproariously. We slapped each other on the back and shoulders and laughed some more. We had made a fool or a liar out of something, and didn't that just beat all?

In daring to challenge the unknown with me, she became my first friend. We spent tedious hours teaching ourselves the Tut language. You (Yak oh you) know (kack nug oh wug) what (wack hash a tut). Since all the other children spoke Pig Latin, we were superior because Tut was hard to speak and even harder to understand. At last I began to comprehend what girls giggled about. Louise would rattle off a few sentences to me in the unintelligible Tut language and would laugh. Naturally I laughed too. Snickered, really, understanding nothing. I don't think she understood half of what she was saying herself, but, after all, girls have to giggle, and after being a woman for three years I was about to become a girl.

In school one day, a girl whom I barely knew and had scarcely spoken to brought me a note. The intricate fold indicated that it was a love note. I was sure she had the wrong person, but she insisted. Picking the paper loose, I confessed to myself that I was frightened. Suppose it was somebody being funny? Suppose the paper would show a hideous beast and the word YOU written over it. Children did that sometimes just because they claimed I was stuck-up. Fortunately I had got permission to go to the toilet—an outside job—and in the reeking gloom I read:

Dear Friend, M.J.

Times are hard and friends are few
I take great pleasure in writing you
Will you be my Valentine?

Tommy Valdon

I pulled my mind apart. Who? Who was Tommy Valdon? Finally a face dragged itself from my memory. He was the nice-looking brown-skinned boy who lived across the pond. As soon as I had pinned him down, I began to wonder, Why? Why me? Was it a joke? But if Tommy was the boy I remembered he was a very sober person and a good student. Well, then, it wasn't a joke. All right, what evil dirty things did he have in mind? My questions fell over themselves, an army in retreat. Haste, dig for cover. Protect your flanks. Don't let the enemy close the gap between you. What did a Valentine do, anyway?

Starting to throw the paper in the foul-smelling hole, I thought of Louise. I could show it to her. I folded the paper back in the original creases, and went back to class. There was no time during the lunch period since I had to run to the Store and wait on customers. The note was in my sock and every time Momma looked at me, I feared that her church gaze might have turned into X-ray vision and she could not only see the note and read its message but would interpret it as well. I felt myself slipping down a sheer cliff of guilt, and a second time I nearly destroyed the note but there was no opportunity. The take-up bell rang and Bailey raced me to school, so the note was forgotten. But serious business is serious, and it had to be attended to. After classes I waited for Louise. She was talking to a group of girls, laughing. But when I gave her our signal (two waves of the left hand) she said good-bye to them and joined me in the road. I didn't give her the chance to ask what was on my mind (her favorite question); I simply gave her the note. Recognizing the fold she stopped smiling. We were in deep waters. She opened the letter and read it aloud twice. "Well, what do you think?"

I said, "What do I think? That's what I'm asking you? What is there to think?"

"Looks like he wants you to be his valentine."

"Louise, I can read. But what does it mean?"

"Oh, you know. His valentine. His love."

There was that hateful word again. That treacherous word that yawned up at you like a volcano.

"Well, I won't. Most decidedly I won't. Not ever again."

"Have you been his valentine before? What do you mean never again?"

I couldn't lie to my friend and I wasn't about to freshen old ghosts.

"Well, don't answer him then, and that's the end of it." I was a little relieved that she thought it could be gotten rid of so quickly. I tore the note in half and gave her a part. Walking down the hill we minced the paper in a thousand shreds and gave it to the wind.

Two days later a monitor came into my classroom. She spoke quietly to Miss Williams, our teacher. Miss Williams said, "Class, I believe you remember that tomorrow is Valentine's Day, so named for St. Valentine, the martyr, who died around A.D. 270 in Rome. The day is observed by exchanging tokens of affection, and cards. The eighth-grade children have completed theirs and the monitor is acting as mailman. You will be given cardboard, ribbon and red tissue paper during the last period today so that you may make your gifts. Glue and scissors are here at the work table. Now, stand when your name is called."

She had been shuffling the colored envelopes and calling names for some time before I noticed. I had been thinking of yesterday's plain invitation and the expeditious way Louise and I took care of it.

We who were being called to receive valentines were only slightly more embarrassed than those who sat and watched as Miss Williams opened each envelope. "Helen Gray." Helen Gray, a tall, dull girl from Louisville, flinched. "Dear Valentine"— Miss Williams began reading the badly rhymed childish drivel. I seethed with shame and anticipation and yet had time to be offended at the silly poetry that I could have bettered in my sleep.

"Margue-you-reete Ann Johnson. My goodness, this looks more like a letter than a valentine. 'Dear Friend, I wrote you a letter and saw you tear it up with your friend Miss L. I don't believe you meant to hurt my feelings so whether you answer or not you will always be my valentine. T.V.' "

"Class"—Miss Williams smirked and continued lazily without giving us permission to sit down—"although you are only in the seventh grade, I'm sure you wouldn't be so presumptuous as to sign a letter with an initial. But here is a boy in the eighth grade, about to graduate—blah, blah, blooey, blah. You may collect your valentines and these letters on your way out."

It was a nice letter and Tommy had beautiful penmanship. I was sorry I tore up the first. His statement that whether I answered him or not would not influence his affection reassured me. He couldn't be after you-know-what if he talked like that. I told Louise that the next time he came to the Store I was going to say something extra nice to him. Unfortunately the situation was so wonderful to me that each time I saw Tommy I melted in delicious giggles and was unable to form a coherent sentence. After a while he stopped including me in his general glances.

21

BAILEY STUCK BRANCHES in the ground behind the house and covered them with a worn-through blanket, making a tent. It was to be his Captain Marvel hideaway. There he initiated girls into the mysteries of sex. One by one, he took the impressed, the curious, the adventurous into the gray shadows, after explaining that they were going to play Momma and Poppa. I was assigned the role of Baby and lookout. The girls were commanded to pull up their dresses and then he lay on top and wiggled his hips.

I sometimes had to lift the flap (our signal that an adult was approaching) and so I saw their pathetic struggles even as they talked about school and the movies.

He had been playing the game for about six months before he met Joyce. She was a country girl about four years older than Bailey (he wasn't quite eleven when they met) whose parents had died and she along with her brothers and sisters had been parceled out to relatives. Joyce had come to Stamps to live with a widowed aunt who was even poorer than the poorest person in town. Joyce was quite advanced physically for her age. Her breasts were not the hard little knots of other girls her age; they filled out the tops of her skimpy little dresses. She walked stiffly, as if she were carrying a load of wood between her legs. I thought of her as being coarse, but Bailey said she was cute and that he wanted to play house with her.

In the special way of women, Joyce knew she had made a conquest, and managed to hang around the Store in the late afternoons and all day Saturdays. She ran errands for Momma when we were busy in the Store and sweated profusely. Often when she came in after running down the hill, her cotton dress would cling to her thin body and Bailey would glue his eyes on her until her clothes dried.

Momma gave her small gifts of food to take to her aunt, and on Saturdays Uncle Willie would sometimes give her a dime for "show fare."

During Passover week we weren't allowed to go to the movies (Momma said we all must sacrifice to purify our souls), and Bailey and Joyce decided that the three of us would play house. As usual, I was to be Baby.

He strung the tent and Joyce crawled in first. Bailey told me to sit outside and play with my doll baby, and he went in and the flap closed.

"Well, ain't you going to open your trousers?" Joyce's voice was muffled.

"No. You just pull up your dress."

There were rustling sounds from the tent and the sides pooched out as if they were trying to stand up.

Bailey asked, "What are you doing?"

"Pulling off my drawers."

"What for?"

"We can't do it with my drawers on."

"Why not?"

"How are you going to get to it?"

Silence. My poor brother didn't know what she meant. I knew. I lifted the flap and said, "Joyce, don't you do that to my brother." She nearly screamed, but she kept her voice low, "Margaret, you close that door." Bailey added, "Yes. Close it. You're supposed to be playing with our doll baby." I thought he would go to the hospital if he let her do that to him, so I warned him, "Bailey, if you let her do that to you, you'll be sorry." But he threatened that if I didn't close the door he wouldn't speak to me for a month, so I let the end of the blanket fall and sat down on the grass in front of the tent.

Joyce poked her head out and said in a sugary, white-woman-in-the-movies voice, "Baby, you go get some wood. Daddy and I going to light a fire, then I'm going to make you some cake." Then her voice changed as if she was going to hit me. "Go. Git."

Bailey told me after that Joyce had hairs on her thing and that she had gotten them from "doing it" with so many boys. She even had hair under her arms. Both of them. He was very proud of her accomplishments.

As their love affair progressed, his stealing from the Store increased. We had always taken candy and a few nickels and of course the sour pickles, but Bailey, now called upon to feed Joyce's ravening hunger, took cans of sardines and greasy Polish sausage and cheese and even the expensive cans of pink salmon that our family could seldom afford to eat.

Joyce's willingness to do odd jobs slackened about this time. She complained that she wasn't feeling all that well. But since she now had a few coins, she still hung around the Store eating Planter's peanuts and drinking Dr. Pepper.

Momma ran her off a few times. "Ain't you said you wasn't feeling well, Joyce? Hadn't you better get home and let your aunty do something for you?"

"Yes, ma'am." Then reluctantly she was off the porch, her stiff-legged walk carrrying her up the hill and out of sight.

I think she was Bailey's first love outside the family. For him, she was the mother who let him get as close as he dreamed, the sister who wasn't moody and withdrawing, and teary and tender-hearted. All he had to do was keep the food coming in and she kept the affection flowing. It made no difference to him that she was almost a woman, or possibly it was just that difference which made her so appealing.

She was around for a few months, and as she had appeared, out of limbo, so she disappeared into nothingness. There was no gossip about her, no clues to her leaving or her whereabouts. I noticed the change in Bailey before I discovered that she was gone. He lost his interest in everything. He mulled around and it would be safe to say "he paled." Momma noticed and said that he was feeling poorly because of the change in seasons (we were nearing fall), so she went to the woods for certain leaves, made him a tea and forced him to drink it after a heaping spoonful of sulfur and molasses. The fact that he didn't fight it, didn't try to talk his way out of taking the medicine, showed without a glimmer of doubt he was very sick.

If I had disliked Joyce while she had Bailey in her grasp, I hated her for leaving. I missed the tolerance she had brought to him (he had nearly given up sarcasm and playing jokes on the country people) and he had taken to telling me his secrets again. But now that she was gone he rivaled me in being uncommunicative. He closed in upon himself like a pond swallowing a stone. There was no evidence that he had ever opened up, and when I mentioned her he responded with "Joyce who?"

Months later, when Momma was waiting on Joyce's aunt, she said, "Yes ma'am, Mrs. Goodman, life's just one thing right after the other."

Mrs. Goodman was leaning on the red Coca-Cola

box. "That's the blessed truth, Sister Henderson." She sipped the expensive drink.

"Things change so fast, it make your head swim." That was Momma's way of opening up a conversation. I stayed mouse-quiet so that I'd be able to hear the gossip and take it to Bailey.

"Now, you take little Joyce. She used to be around the Store all the time. Then she went up just like smoke. We ain't seed hide nor hair of her in months."

"No'm. I shamed to tell you . . . what took her off." She settled in on a kitchen chair. Momma spied me in the shadows. "Sister, the Lord don't like little jugs with big ears. You ain't got something to do, I'll find something for you."

The truth had to float to me through the kitchen door.

"I ain't got much, Sister Henderson, but I give that child all I had."

Momma said she bound that was true. She wouldn't say "bet."

"And after all I did, she run off with one of those railroad porters. She was loose just like her mammy before her. You know how they say 'blood will tell'?"

Momma asked, "How did the snake catch her?"

"Well, now, understand me, Sister Henderson, I don't hold this against you, I knows you a God-fearing woman. But it seems like she met him here."

Momma was flustered. Such goings on at the Store? She asked, "At the Store?"

"Yes, ma'am. 'Member when that bunch of Elks come over for their baseball game?" (Momma must have remembered. I did.) "Well, as it turned out, he was one of them. She left me a teenincy note. Said people in Stamps thought they were better than she was, and that she hadn't only made one friend, and that was your grandson. Said she was moving to Dallas, Texas, and gone marry that railroad porter."

Momma said, "Do, Lord."

Mrs. Goodman said, "You know, Sister Henderson, she wasn't with me long enough for me to get the real habit of her, but still I miss her. She was sweet when she wanted to be." Momma consoled her with, "Well, we got to keep our mind on the words of the Book. It say, 'The Lord giveth and the Lord taketh away.'"

Mrs. Goodman chimed in and they finished the phrase together, "Blessed be the name of the Lord."

I don't know how long Bailey had known about Joyce, but later in the evening when I tried to bring her name into our conversation, he said, "Joyce? She's got somebody to do it to her all the time now." And that was the last time her name was mentioned.

22

THE WIND BLEW over the roof and ruffled the shingles. It whistled sharp under the closed door. The chimney made fearful sounds of protest as it was invaded by the urgent gusts.

A mile away ole Kansas City Kate (the train much admired but too important to stop in Stamps) crashed through the middle of town, blew its *wooo-wee* warnings, and continued to an unknown glamorous destination without looking back.

There was going to be a storm and it was a perfect night for rereading *Jane Eyre*. Bailey had finished his chores and was already behind the stove with Mark Twain. It was my turn to close the Store, and my book, half read, lay on the candy counter. Since the weather was going to be bad I was sure Uncle Willie would agree, in fact, encourage me to close early (save electricity) and join the family in Momma's bedroom, which functioned as our sitting room. Few people would be out in weather that threatened a tornado (for though the wind blew,

the sky was as clear and still as a summer morning).
Momma agreed that I might as well close, and I went
out on the porch, closed the shutters, slipped the
wooden bar over the door and turned off the light.

Pots rattled in the kitchen where Momma was
frying corn cakes to go with vegetable soup for
supper, and the homey sounds and scents cushioned
me as I read of Jane Eyre in the cold English
mansion of a colder English gentleman. Uncle Willie
was engrossed in the *Almanac*, his nightly reading,
and my brother was far away on a raft on the
Mississippi.

I was the first to hear the rattle on the back door.
A rattle and knock, a knock and rattle. But suspect-
ing that it might have been the mad wife in the
tower, I didn't credit it. Then Uncle Willie heard it
and summoned Bailey back from Huck Finn to un-
latch the bolt.

Through the open door the moonshine fell into
the room in a cold radiance to rival our meager lamplight. We all waited—I with a dread expectancy—
for no human being was there. The wind alone
came in, struggling with the weak flame in the
coal-oil lamp. Pushing and bunting about the family
warmth of our pot-bellied stove. Uncle Willie
thought it must have been the storm and told Bailey
to close the door. But just before he secured the raw
wooden slab a voice drifted through the crack; it
wheezed, "Sister Henderson? Brother Willie?"

Bailey nearly closed the door again, but Uncle
Willie asked, "Who is it?" and Mr. George Taylor's
pinched brown face swam out of the gray and into
view. He assured himself that we hadn't gone to bed,
and was welcomed in. When Momma saw him she
invited him to stay for supper and told me to stick
some sweet potatoes in the ashes to stretch the
evening meal. Poor Brother Taylor had been taking
meals all over town, ever since he buried his wife in
the summer. Maybe due to the fact that I was in my
romanticist period, or because children have a built-

in survival apparatus, I feared he was interested in marrying Momma and moving in with us.

Uncle Willie cradled the *Almanac* in his divided lap. "You welcome here anytime, Brother Taylor, anytime, but this is a bad night. It say right here"—with his crippled hand he rapped the *Almanac*—"that November twelfth, a storm going to be moving over Stamps out of the east. A rough night." Mr. Taylor remained exactly in the same position he had taken when he arrived, like a person too cold to readjust his body even to get closer to the fire. His neck was bent and the red light played over the polished skin of his hairless head. But his eyes bound me with a unique attraction. They sat deep in his little face and completely dominated the other features with a roundness which seemed to be outlined in dark pencil, giving him an owlish appearance. And when he sensed my regarding him so steadily his head hardly moved but his eyes swirled and landed on me. If his look had contained contempt or patronage, or any of the vulgar emotions revealed by adults in confrontation with children, I would have easily gone back to my book, but his eyes gave off a watery nothing—a nothingness which was completely unbearable. I saw a glassiness, observed before only in new marbles or a bottle top embedded in a block of ice. His glance moved so swiftly from me it was nearly possible to imagine that I had in fact imagined the interchange.

"But, as I say, you welcome. We can always make a place under this roof." Uncle Willie didn't seem to notice that Mr. Taylor was oblivious to everything he said. Momma brought the soup into the room, took the kettle off the heater and placed the steaming pot on the fire. Uncle Willie continued, "Momma, I told Brother Taylor he is welcome here anytime." Momma said, "That's right, Brother Taylor. You not supposed to sit around that lonely house feeling sorry for yourself. The Lord giveth and the Lord taketh away."

I'm not sure whether it was Momma's presence or the bubbling soup on the stove which influenced him, but Mr. Taylor appeared to have livened up considerably. He shook his shoulders as if shaking off a tiresome touch, and attempted a smile that failed. "Sister Henderson, I sure appreciate ... I mean, I don't know what I'd do if it wasn't for everybody ... I mean, you don't know what it's worth to me to be able to ... Well, I mean I'm thankful." At each pause, he pecked his head over his chest like a turtle coming out of its shell, but his eyes didn't move.

Momma, always self-conscious at public displays of emotions not traceable to a religious source, told me to come with her and we'd bring the bread and bowls. She carried the food and I trailed after her, bringing the kerosene lamp. The new light set the room in an eerie, harsh perspective. Bailey still sat, doubled over his book, a Black hunchbacked gnome. A finger forerunning his eyes along the page. Uncle Willie and Mr. Taylor were frozen like people in a book on the history of the American Negro.

"Now, come on, Brother Taylor." Momma was pressing a bowl of soup on him. "You may not be hungry, but take this for nourishment." Her voice had the tender concern of a healthy person speaking to an invalid, and her plain statement rang thrillingly true: "I'm thankful." Bailey came out of his absorption and went to wash his hands.

"Willie, say the blessing." Momma set Bailey's bowl down and bowed her head. During grace, Bailey stood in the doorway, a figure of obedience, but I knew his mind was on Tom Sawyer and Jim as mine would have been on Jane Eyre and Mr. Rochester, but for the glittering eyes of wizened old Mr. Taylor.

Our guest dutifully took a few spoonfuls of soup and bit a semicircle in the bread, then put his bowl on the floor. Something in the fire held his attention as we ate noisily.

Noticing his withdrawal, Momma said, "It don't do for you to take on so, I know you all was together a long time—"

Uncle Willie said, "Forty years."

"—but it's been around six months since she's gone to her rest ... and you got to keep faith. He never gives us more than we can bear." The statement heartened Mr. Taylor. He picked up his bowl again and raked his spoon through the thick soup.

Momma saw that she had made some contact, so she went on, "You had a whole lot of good years. Got to be grateful for them. Only thing is, it's a pity you all didn't have some children."

If my head had been down I would have missed Mr. Taylor's metamorphosis. It was not a change that came by steps but rather, it seemed to me, of a sudden. His bowl was on the floor with a thud, and his body leaned toward Momma from the hips. However, his face was the most striking feature of all. The brown expanse seemed to darken with life, as if an inner agitation played under his thin skin. The mouth, opened to show the long teeth, was a dark room furnished with a few white chairs.

"Children." He gum-balled the word around in his empty mouth. "Yes, sir, children." Bailey (and I), used to be addressed so, looked at him expectantly.

"That's what she want." His eyes were vital, and straining to jump from the imprisoning sockets. "That's what she said. Children."

The air was weighted and thick. A bigger house had been set on our roof and was imperceptibly pushing us into the ground.

Momma asked, in her nice-folks voice, "What who said, Brother Taylor?" She knew the answer. We all knew the answer.

"Florida." His little wrinkled hands were making fists, then straightening, then making fists again. "She said it just last night."

Bailey and I looked at each other and I hunched my chair closer to him. "Said 'I want some children.' "

When he pitched his already high voice to what he considered a feminine level, or at any rate to his wife's, Miz Florida's, level, it streaked across the room, zigzagging like lightning.

Uncle Willie had stopped eating and was regarding him with something like pity. "Maybe you was dreaming, Brother Taylor. Could have been a dream."

Momma came in placatingly. "That's right. You know, the children was reading me something th'other day. Say folks dream about whatever was on their mind when they went to sleep."

Mr. Taylor jerked himself up. "It wasn't not no dream. I was as wide awake as I am this very minute." He was angry and the tension increased his little mask of strength.

"I'll tell you what happened."

Oh, Lord, a ghost story. I hated and dreaded the long winter nights when late customers came to the Store to sit around the heater roasting peanuts and trying to best each other in telling lurid tales of ghosts and hants, banshees and juju, voodoo and other anti-life stories. But a real one, that happened to a real person, and last night. It was going to be intolerable. I got up and walked to the window.

Mrs. Florida Taylor's funeral in June came on the heels of our final exams. Bailey and Louise and I had done very well and were pleased with ourselves and each other. The summer stretched golden in front of us with promises of picnics and fish frys, blackberry hunts and croquet games till dark. It would have taken a personal loss to penetrate my sense of well-being. I had met and loved the Brontë sisters, and had replaced Kipling's "If" with "Invictus." My friendship with Louise was solidified over jacks, hopscotch and confessions, deep and dark, exchanged often after many a "Cross your heart you won't tell?" I never talked about St. Louis to her, and had generally come to believe that the nightmare with its attendant guilt and fear hadn't really happened to me. It happened to a nasty little girl, years and years before, who had no chain on me at all.

At first the news that Mrs. Taylor was dead did not strike me as a particularly newsy bit of information. As children do, I thought that since she was very old she had only one thing to do, and that was to die. She was a pleasant enough woman, with her steps made mincing by age and her little hands like gentle claws that liked to touch young skin. Each time she came to the Store, I was forced to go up to her, while she raked her yellow nails down my cheeks. "You sure got a pretty complexion." It was a rare compliment in a world of very few such words of praise, so it balanced being touched by the dry fingers.

"You going to the funeral, Sister." Momma wasn't asking a question.

Momma said, "You going 'cause Sister Taylor thought so much of you she left you her yellow brooch." (She wouldn't say "gold," because it wasn't.) "She told Brother Taylor, 'I want Sis Henderson's grandbaby to have my gold brooch.' So you'll have to go."

I had followed a few coffins up the hill from the church to the cemetery, but because Momma said I was tender-hearted I had never been forced to sit through a funeral service. At eleven years old, death is more unreal than frightening. It seemed a waste of a good afternoon to sit in church for a silly old brooch, which was not only not gold but was too old for me to wear. But if Momma said I had to go it was certain that I would be there.

The mourners on the front benches sat in a blue-serge, black-crepe-dress gloom. A funeral hymn made its way around the church tediously but successfully. It eased into the heart of every gay thought, into the care of each happy memory. Shattering the light and hopeful: "On the other side of Jordan, there is a peace for the weary, there is a peace for me." The inevitable destination of all living things seemed but a short step away. I had never considered before that dying, death, dead, passed away, were words and phrases that might be even faintly connected with me.

But on that onerous day, oppressed beyond relief, my own mortality was borne in upon me on sluggish tides of doom.

No sooner had the mournful song run its course than the minister took to the altar and delivered a sermon that in my state gave little comfort. Its subject was, "Thou art my good and faithful servant with whom I am well pleased." His voice enweaved itself through the somber vapors left by the dirge. In a monotonous tone he warned the listeners that "this day might be your last," and the best insurance against dying a sinner was to "make yourself right with God" so that on the fateful day He would say, "Thou art my good and faithful servant with whom I am well pleased."

After he had put the fear of the cold grave under our skins, he began to speak of Mrs. Taylor, "A godly woman, who gave to the poor, visited the sick, tithed to the church and in general lived a life of goodliness." At this point he began to talk directly to the coffin, which I had noticed upon my arrival and had studiously avoided thereafter.

"I hungered and you gave me to eat. I was thirsty and you gave me to drink. I was sick and you visited me. In prison, and you left me not. Inasmuch as you have done it unto the least of one of these, you have done it unto Me." He bounded off the dais and approached the velvet gray box. With an imperious gesture, he snatched the gray cloth off the open flap and gazed downward into the mystery.

"Sleep on, thy graceful soul, till Christ calls you to come forth into His bright heaven."

He continued speaking directly to the dead woman, and I half wished she would rise up and answer him, offended by the coarseness of his approach. A scream burst from Mr. Taylor. He stood up suddenly and lengthened his arms toward the minister, the coffin and his wife's corpse. For a long minute he hovered, his back to the church as the instructive words kept falling around the room, rich with promise, full with warnings. Momma and other ladies caught him in time to bring him back to the bench, where he quickly folded upon himself like a Br'er Rabbit rag doll.

Mr. Taylor and the high church officials were the first to file around the bier to wave farewell to the departed and get a glimpse of what lay in store for all men. Then on heavy feet, made more ponderous by the guilt of the living viewing the dead, the adult church marched up to the coffin and back to their seats. Their faces, which showed apprehension before reaching the coffin, revealed, on the way down the opposite aisle, a final confirmation of their fears. Watching them was a little like peeping through a window when the shade is not drawn flush. Although I didn't try, it was impossible not to record their roles in the drama.

And then a black-dressed usher stuck her hand out woodenly toward the children's rows. There was the shifty rustling of unreadiness but finally a boy of fourteen led us off and I dared not hang back, as much as I hated the idea of seeing Mrs. Taylor. Up the aisle, the moans and screams merged with the sickening smell of woolen black clothes worn in summer weather and green leaves wilting over yellow flowers. I couldn't distinguish whether I was smelling the clutching sound of misery or hearing the cloying odor of death.

It would have been easier to see her through the gauze, but instead I looked down on the stark face that seemed suddenly so empty and evil. It knew secrets that I never wanted to share. The cheeks had fallen back to the ears and a solicitous mortician had put lipstick on the black mouth. The scent of decay was sweet and clasping. It groped for life with a hunger both greedy and hateful. But it was hypnotic. I wanted to be off but my shoes had glued themselves to the floor and I had to hold on to the sides of the coffin to remain standing. The unexpected halt in the moving line caused the children to press upon each other, and whispers of no small intent reached my ears.

"Move along, Sister, move along." It was Momma. Her voice tugged at my will and someone pushed from the rear, so I was freed.

Instantly I surrendered myself to the grimness of death. The change it had been able to effect in Mrs. Taylor showed that its strength could not be resisted. Her high-pitched voice, which parted the air in the Store, was forever stilled, and the plump brown face had been deflated and patted flat like a cow's ordurous dropping.

The coffin was carried on a horse-drawn wagon to the cemetery, and all the way I communed with death's angels, questioning their choice of time, place and person.

For the first time the burial ceremony had meaning for me.

"Ashes to ashes and dust to dust." It was certain that Mrs. Taylor was returning to the earth from whence she came. In fact, upon considering, I concluded that she had looked like a mud baby, lying on the white satin of her velvet coffin. A mud baby, molded into form by creative children on a rainy day, soon to run back into the loose earth.

The memory of the grim ceremony had been so real to me that I was surprised to look up and see Momma and Uncle Willie eating by the stove. They were neither anxious nor hesitant, as if they knew a man has to say what he has to say. But I didn't want to hear any of it, and the wind, allying itself with me, threatened the chinaberry tree outside the back door.

"Last night, after I said my prayers, I lay down on the bed. Well, you know it's the same bed she died on." Oh, if he'd shut up. Momma said, "Sister, sit down and eat your soup. Cold night like this you need something hot in your stomach. Go on, Brother Taylor. Please." I sat down as near Bailey as possible.

"Well, something told me to open my eyes."

"What kind of something?" Momma asked, not laying down her spoon.

"Yes, sir," Uncle Willie explained, "there can be a good something and there can be a bad something."

"Well, I wasn't sure, so I figured better open 'em, 'cause it could have been, well, either one. I did, and the first thing, I saw little baby angel. It was just as fat as a butterball, and laughing, eyes blue, blue, blue."

Uncle Willie asked, "A baby angel?"

"Yes, sir, and it was laughing right in my face. Then I heard this long moan, 'Agh-h-h-.' Well, as you say, Sister Henderson, we been together over forty years. I know Florida's voice. I wasn't scared right then. I called 'Florida?' Then that angel laughed harder and the moan got louder."

I set my bowl down and got closer to Bailey. Mrs. Taylor had been a very pleasant woman, smiling all the time and patient. The only thing that jarred and bothered me when she came in the Store was her voice. Like near-deaf people, she screamed, half not hearing what she was saying and partly hoping her listeners would reply in kind. That was when she was living. The thought of that voice coming out of the grave and all the way down the hill from the cemetery and hanging over my head was enough to straighten my hair.

"Yes, sir." He was looking at the stove and the red glow fell on his face. It seemed as if he had a fire going inside his head. "First I called, 'Florida, Florida. What do you want?' And that devilish angel kept on laughing to beat the band." Mr. Taylor tried to laugh and only succeeded in looking frightened. " 'I

want some . . .' That's when she said 'I want some.' "
He made his voice sound like the wind, if the wind
had bronchial pneumonia. He wheezed, " 'I want some
chi-il-dren.' "

Bailey and I met halfway on the drafty floor.

Momma said, "Now, Brother Taylor, could be you
was dreaming. You know, they say whatever you
goes to bed with on your mind . . ."

"No, ma'am, Sister Henderson, I was as wide
awake as I am right now."

"Did she let you see her?" Uncle Willie had a
dreamy look on his face.

"No, Willie, all I seed was that fat little white
baby angel. But wasn't no mistaking that voice . . . 'I
want some children.' "

The cold wind had frozen my feet and my spine,
and Mr. Taylor's impersonation had chilled my blood.

Momma said, "Sister, go bring the long fork to
take the potatoes out."

"Ma'am?" Surely she didn't mean the long fork that
hung on the wall behind the kitchen stove—a scary
million miles away.

"I said, go get the fork. The potatoes are burning."

I unwound my legs from the gripping fear and
almost tripped onto the stove. Momma said, "That
child would stumble over the pattern in a rug. Go
on, Brother Taylor, did she say any more?"

I didn't want to hear it if she did, but I wasn't
eager to leave the lighted room where my family sat
around the friendly fire.

"Well, she said 'Aaah' a few more times and then
that angel started to walk off the ceiling. I tell you I
was purt' near scared stiff."

I had reached the no man's ocean of darkness. No
great decision was called for. I knew it would be
torturous to go through the thick blackness of Uncle
Willie's bedroom, but it would be easier than staying
around to hear the ghoulish story. Also, I couldn't
afford to aggravate Momma. When she was dis-

pleased she made me sleep on the edge of the bed
and that night I knew I needed to be close to her.

One foot into the darkness and the sense of detachment from reality nearly made me panic. The
idea came to me that I might never get out into the
light again. Quickly I found the door leading back to
the familiar, but as I opened it the awful story
reached out and tried to grab my ears. I closed the
door.

Naturally, I believed in hants and ghosts and
"thangs." Having been raised by a super-religious
Southern Negro grandmother, it would have been
abnormal had I not been superstitious.

The trip to the kitchen and back could not have
taken more than two minutes, yet in that time I
tramped through swampy cemeteries, climbed over
dusty gravestones and eluded litters of night-black
cats.

Back in the family circle, I remarked to myself
how like a cyclopean eye was the belly of the red-hot
stove.

"It reminded me of the time when my daddy
died. You know we're very close." Mr. Taylor had
hypnotized himself into the eerie world of horrors.

I broke into his reminiscences. "Momma, here's
the fork." Bailey had lain down on his side behind
the stove and his eyes were shining. He was more
fascinated with Mr. Taylor's morbid interest in his
story than with the tale itself.

Momma put her hand on my arm and said, "You
shaking, Sister. What's the matter?" My skin still
rippled from the experience of fear.

Uncle Willie laughed and said, "Maybe she was
scared to go in the kitchen."

His high little laugh didn't fool me. Everyone was
uneasy at being beckoned into the unknown.

"No sir, I ain't never seen nothing so clear as that
little angel baby." His jaws were scissoring mechani-
cally on the already mushy sweet potatoes. "Just

laughing, like a house on fire. What you reckon it mean, Sister Henderson?"

Momma had reared back in her rocking chair, a half smile on her face, "If you sure you wasn't dreaming, Brother Taylor . . ."

"I was as wide awake as I am"—he was becoming angry again—"as I am right now."

"Well, then, maybe it means—"

"I ought to know when I'm asleep and when I'm awake."

"—maybe it mean Sister Florida wants you to work with the children in the church."

"One thing I always used to tell Florida, people won't let you get your words in edgewise—"

"Could be she's trying to tell you—"

"I ain't crazy, you know. My mind's just as good as it was."

"—to take a Sunday school class—"

"Thirty years ago. If I say I was awake when I saw that little fat angel, then people ought to—"

"Sunday school need more teachers. Lord knows that's so."

"—believe me when I say so."

Their remarks and responses were like a Ping-Pong game with each volley clearing the net and flying back to the opposition. The sense of what they were saying became lost, and only the exercise remained. The exchange was conducted with the certainty of a measured hoedown and had the jerkiness of Monday's wash snapping in the wind—now cracking east, then west, with only the intent to whip the dampness out of the cloth.

Within a few minutes the intoxication of doom had fled, as if it had never been, and Momma was encouraging Mr. Taylor to take in one of the Jenkins boys to help him with his farm. Uncle Willie was nodding at the fire, and Bailey had escaped back to the calm adventures of Huckleberry Finn. The change in the room was remarkable. Shadows which had lengthened and darkened over the bed in the corner had disappeared or revealed themselves as dark images of familiar chairs and such. The light which dashed on the ceiling steadied, and imitated rabbits rather than lions, and donkeys instead of ghouls.

I laid a pallet for Mr. Taylor in Uncle Willie's room and crawled under Momma, who I knew for the first time was so good and righteous she could command the fretful spirits, as Jesus had commanded the sea. "Peace, be still."

23

THE CHILDREN IN Stamps trembled visibly with anticipation. Some adults were excited too, but to be certain the whole young population had come down with graduation epidemic. Large classes were graduating from both the grammar school and the high school. Even those who were years removed from their own day of glorious release were anxious to help with preparations as a kind of dry run. The junior students who were moving into the vacating classes' chairs were tradition-bound to show their talents for leadership and management. They strutted through the school and around the campus exerting pressure on the lower grades. Their authority was so new that occasionally if they pressed a little too hard it had to be overlooked. After all, next term was coming, and it never hurt a sixth grader to have a play sister in the eighth grade, or a tenth-year student to be able to call a twelfth grader Bubba. So all was endured in a spirit of shared understanding. But the graduating classes themselves were the nobility. Like travelers with exotic destinations on their minds, the graduates were remarkably forgetful. They came to school without their books, or tablets or even pencils. Volunteers fell over themselves to secure replacements for the missing equipment. When accepted, the willing workers might or might not be thanked, and it was of no importance to the pregraduation rites. Even teachers were respectful of the now quiet and aging seniors, and tended to speak to them, if not as equals, as beings only slightly lower than themselves. After tests were returned and grades given, the student body, which acted like an extended family, knew who did well, who excelled, and what piteous ones had failed.

Unlike the white high school, Lafayette County Training School distinguished itself by having neither lawn, nor hedges, nor tennis court, nor climbing ivy. Its two buildings (main classrooms, the grade school and home economics) were set on a dirt hill with no fence to limit either its boundaries or those of bordering farms. There was a large expanse to the left of the school which was used alternately as a baseball diamond or a basketball court. Rusty hoops on the swaying poles represented the permanent recreational equipment, although bats and balls could be borrowed from the P. E. teacher if the borrower was qualified and if the diamond wasn't occupied.

Over this rocky area relieved by a few shady tall persimmon trees the graduating class walked. The girls often held hands and no longer bothered to speak to the lower students. There was a sadness about them, as if this old world was not their home and they were bound for higher ground. The boys, on the other hand, had become more friendly, more outgoing. A decided change from the closed attitude they projected while studying for finals. Now they seemed not ready to give up the old school, the familiar paths and classrooms. Only a small percentage would be continuing on to college—one of the South's A & M (agricultural and mechanical) schools, which trained Negro youths to be carpenters, farmers, handymen, masons, maids, cooks and baby nurses. Their future rode heavily on their shoulders, and blinded them to the collective joy that had pervaded the lives of the boys and girls in the grammar school graduating class.

Parents who could afford it had ordered new shoes and ready-made clothes for themselves from Sears and Roebuck or Montgomery Ward. They also engaged the best seamstresses to make the floating graduating dresses and to cut down secondhand pants which would be pressed to a military slickness for the important event.

Oh, it was important, all right. Whitefolks would attend the ceremony, and two or three would speak of God and home, and the Southern way of life, and Mrs. Parsons, the principal's wife, would play the graduation march while the lower-grade graduates paraded down the aisles and took their seats below the platform. The high school seniors would wait in empty classrooms to make their dramatic entrance.

In the Store I was the person of the moment. The birthday girl. The center. Bailey had graduated the year before, although to do so he had had to forfeit all pleasures to make up for his time lost in Baton Rouge.

My class was wearing butter-yellow piqué dresses, and Momma launched out on mine. She smocked the yoke into tiny crisscrossing puckers, then shirred the rest of the bodice. Her dark fingers ducked in and out of the lemony cloth as she embroidered raised daisies around the hem. Before she considered herself finished she had added a crocheted cuff on the puff sleeves, and a pointy crocheted collar.

I was going to be lovely. A walking model of all the various styles of fine hand sewing and it didn't worry me that I was only twelve years old and merely graduating from the eighth grade. Besides, many teachers in Arkansas Negro schools had only that diploma and were licensed to impart wisdom.

The days had become longer and more noticeable. The faded beige of former times had been replaced with strong and sure colors. I began to see my classmates' clothes, their skin tones, and the dust that waved off pussy willows. Clouds that lazed across the sky were objects of great concern to me. Their shiftier shapes might have held a message that in my new happiness and with a little bit of time I'd soon decipher. During that period I looked at the arch of heaven so religiously my neck kept a steady ache. I had taken to smiling more often, and my jaws hurt from the unaccustomed activity. Between the two physical sore spots, I suppose I could have been uncomfortable, but that was not the case. As a member of the winning team (the graduating class of 1940) I had outdistanced unpleasant sensations by miles. I was headed for the freedom of open fields.

Youth and social approval allied themselves with me and we trammeled memories of slights and insults. The wind of our swift passage remodeled my features. Lost tears were pounded to mud and then to dust. Years of withdrawal were brushed aside and left behind, as hanging ropes of parasitic moss.

My work alone had awarded me a top place and I was going to be one of the first called in the graduating ceremonies. On the classroom blackboard, as well as on the bulletin board in the auditorium, there were blue stars and white stars and red stars. No absences, no tardinesses, and my academic work was among the best of the year. I could say the preamble to the Constitution even faster than Bailey. We timed ourselves often: "Wethepeopleof-theUnitedStatesinordertoformamoreperfectunion . . ." I had memorized the Presidents of the United States from Washington to Roosevelt in chronological as well as alphabetical order.

My hair pleased me too. Gradually the black mass had lengthened and thickened, so that it kept at last to its braided pattern, and I didn't have to yank my scalp off when I tried to comb it.

Louise and I had rehearsed the exercises until we tired out ourselves. Henry Reed was class valedictorian. He was a small, very black boy with hooded eyes, a long, broad nose and an oddly shaped head. I had admired him for years because each term he and I vied for the best grades in our class. Most often he bested me, but instead of being disappointed I was pleased that we shared top places between us. Like many Southern Black children, he lived with his grandmother, who was as strict as Momma and as kind as she knew how to be. He was courteous, respectful and soft-spoken to elders, but on the playground he chose to play the roughest games. I admired him. Anyone, I reckoned, sufficiently afraid or sufficiently dull could be polite. But to be able to operate at a top level with both adults and children was admirable.

His valedictory speech was entitled "To Be or Not to Be." The rigid tenth-grade teacher had helped him write it. He'd been working on the dramatic stresses for months.

The weeks until graduation were filled with heady activities. A group of small children were to be presented in a play about buttercups and daisies and bunny rabbits. They could be heard throughout the building practicing their hops and their little songs that sounded like silver bells. The older girls (non-graduates, of course) were assigned the task of making refreshments for the night's festivities. A tangy scent of ginger, cinnamon, nutmeg and chocolate wafted around the home economics building as the budding cooks made samples for themselves and their teachers.

In every corner of the workshop, axes and saws split fresh timber as the woodshop boys made sets and stage scenery. Only the graduates were left out of the general bustle. We were free to sit in the library at the back of the building or look in quite detachedly, naturally, on the measures being taken for our event.

Even the minister preached on graduation the Sunday before. His subject was, "Let your light so shine that men will see your good works and praise your Father, Who is in Heaven." Although the sermon was purported to be addressed to us, he used the occasion to speak to backsliders, gamblers and general ne'er-do-wells. But since he had called our names at the beginning of the service we were mollified.

Among Negroes the tradition was to give presents to children going only from one grade to another. How much more important this was when the person was graduating at the top of the class. Uncle Willie and Momma had sent away for a Mickey Mouse watch like Bailey's. Louise gave me four embroidered handkerchiefs. (I gave her three crocheted doilies.) Mrs. Sneed, the minister's wife, made me an underskirt to wear for graduation, and nearly every customer gave me a nickel or maybe even a dime with the instruction "Keep on moving to higher ground," or some such encouragement.

Amazingly the great day finally dawned and I was out of bed before I knew it. I threw open the back door to see it more clearly, but Momma said, "Sister, come away from that door and put your robe on."

I hoped the memory of that morning would never leave me. Sunlight was itself still young, and the day had none of the insistence maturity would bring it in a few hours. In my robe and barefoot in the backyard, under cover of going to see about my new beans, I gave myself up to the gentle warmth and thanked God that no matter what evil I had done in my life He had allowed me to live to see this day. Somewhere in my fatalism I had expected to die, accidentally, and never have the chance to walk up the stairs in the auditorium and gracefully receive my hard-earned diploma. Out of God's merciful bosom I had won reprieve.

Bailey came out in his robe and gave me a box wrapped in Christmas paper. He said he had saved his money for months to pay for it. It felt like a box of chocolates, but I knew Bailey wouldn't save money to buy candy when we had all we could want under our noses.

He was as proud of the gift as I. It was a soft-leather-bound copy of a collection of poems by Edgar Allan Poe, or, as Bailey and I called him, "Eap." I turned to "Annabel Lee" and we walked up and down the garden rows, the cool dirt between our toes, reciting the beautifully sad lines.

Momma made a Sunday breakfast although it was only Friday. After we finished the blessing, I opened my eyes to find the watch on my plate. It was a dream of a day. Everything went smoothly and to my credit. I didn't have to be reminded or scolded for anything. Near evening I was too jittery to attend to chores, so Bailey volunteered to do all before his bath.

Days before, we had made a sign for the Store, and as we turned out the lights Momma hung the cardboard over the doorknob. It read clearly: CLOSED. GRADUATION.

My dress fitted perfectly and everyone said that I looked like a sunbeam in it. On the hill, going toward the school, Bailey walked behind with Uncle Willie, who muttered, "Go on, Ju." He wanted him to walk ahead with us because it embarrassed him to have to walk so slowly. Bailey said he'd let the ladies walk together, and the men would bring up the rear. We all laughed, nicely.

Little children dashed by out of the dark like fireflies. Their crepe-paper dresses and butterfly wings were not made for running and we heard more than one rip, dryly, and the regretful "uh uh" that followed.

The school blazed without gaiety. The windows seemed cold and unfriendly from the lower hill. A sense of ill-fated timing crept over me, and if Momma hadn't reached for my hand I would have drifted back to Bailey and Uncle Willie, and possibly beyond. She made a few slow jokes about my feet getting cold, and tugged me along to the now-strange building.

Around the front steps, assurance came back. There were my fellow "greats," the graduating class. Hair brushed back, legs oiled, new dresses and pressed pleats, fresh pocket handkerchiefs and little handbags, all homesewn. Oh, we were up to snuff, all right. I joined my comrades and didn't even see my family go in to find seats in the crowded auditorium.

The school band struck up a march and all classes filed in as had been rehearsed. We stood in front of our seats, as assigned, and on a signal from the choir director, we sat. No sooner had this been accomplished than the band started to play the national anthem. We rose again and sang the song, after which we recited the pledge of allegiance. We remained standing for a brief minute before the choir director and the principal signaled to us, rather desperately I thought, to take our seats. The command was so unusual that our carefully rehearsed and smooth-running machine was thrown off. For a full minute we fumbled for our chairs and bumped into each other awkwardly. Habits change or solidify under pressure, so in our state of nervous tension we had been ready to follow our usual assembly pattern: the American national anthem, then the pledge of allegiance, then the song every Black person I knew called the Negro National Anthem. All done in the same key, with the same passion and most often standing on the same foot.

Finding my seat at last, I was overcome with a presentiment of worse things to come. Something unrehearsed, unplanned, was going to happen, and we were going to be made to look bad. I distinctly remember being explicit in the choice of pronoun. It was "we," the graduating class, the unit, that concerned me then.

The principal welcomed "parents and friends" and asked the Baptist minister to lead us in prayer. His invocation was brief and punchy, and for a second I thought we were getting back on the high road to right action. When the principal came back to the dais, however, his voice had changed. Sounds always affected me profoundly and the principal's voice was one of my favorites. During assembly it melted and lowed weakly into the audience. It had not been in my plan to listen to him, but my curiosity was piqued and I straightened up to give him my attention.

He was talking about Booker T. Washington, our "late great leader," who said we can be as close as the fingers on the hand, etc. ... Then he said a few vague things about friendship and the friendship of kindly people to those less fortunate than themselves. With that his voice nearly faded, thin, away. Like a river diminishing to a stream and then to a trickle. But he cleared his throat and said, "Our speaker tonight, who is also our friend, came from Texarkana to deliver the commencement address, but due to the irregularity of the train schedule, he's going to, as they say, 'speak and run.' " He said that we understood and wanted the man to know that we were most grateful for the time he was able to give us and then something about how we were willing always to adjust to another's program, and without more ado—"I give you Mr. Edward Donleavy."

Not one but two white men came through the door offstage. The shorter one walked to the speaker's platform, and the tall one moved over to the center seat and sat down. But that was our principal's seat, and already occupied. The dislodged gentleman bounced around for a long breath or two before the Baptist minister gave him his chair, then with more dignity than the situation deserved, the minister walked off the stage.

Donleavy looked at the audience once (on reflection, I'm sure that he wanted only to reassure himself that we were really there), adjusted his glasses and began to read from a sheaf of papers.

He was glad "to be here and to see the work going on just as it was in the other schools."

At the first "Amen" from the audience I willed the offender to immediate death by choking on the word. But Amens and Yes, sir's began to fall around the room like rain through a ragged umbrella.

He told us of the wonderful changes we children in Stamps had in store. The Central School (naturally, the white school was Central) had already been granted improvements that would be in use in the fall. A well-known artist was coming from Little Rock to teach art to them. They were going to have the newest microscopes and chemistry equipment for their laboratory. Mr. Donleavy didn't leave us long in the dark over who made these improvements available to Central High. Nor were we to be ignored in the general betterment scheme he had in mind.

He said that he had pointed out to people at a very high level that one of the first-line football tacklers at Arkansas Agricultural and Mechanical College had graduated from good old Lafayette County Training School. Here fewer Amen's were heard. Those few that did break through lay dully in the air with the heaviness of habit.

He went on to praise us. He went on to say how he had bragged that "one of the best basketball players at Fisk sank his first ball right here at Lafayette County Training School."

The white kids were going to have a chance to become Galileos and Madame Curies and Edisons and Gauguins, and our boys (the girls weren't even in on it) would try to be Jesse Owenses and Joe Louises.

Owens and the Brown Bomber were great heroes in our world, but what school official in the white-goddom of Little Rock had the right to decide that those two men must be our only heroes? Who decided that for Henry Reed to become a scientist he had to work like George Washington Carver, as a bootblack, to buy a lousy microscope? Bailey was obviously always going to be too small to be an athlete, so which concrete angel glued to what country seat had decided that if my brother wanted to become a lawyer he had to first pay penance for his skin by picking cotton and hoeing corn and studying correspondence books at night for twenty years?

The man's dead words fell like bricks around the auditorium and too many settled in my belly. Constrained by hard-learned manners I couldn't look behind me, but to my left and right the proud graduating class of 1940 had dropped their heads. Every girl in my row had found something new to do with her handkerchief. Some folded the tiny squares into love knots, some into triangles, but most were wadding them, then pressing them flat on their yellow laps.

On the dais, the ancient tragedy was being replayed. Professor Parsons sat, a sculptor's reject, rigid. His large, heavy body seemed devoid of will or willingness, and his eyes said he was no longer with us. The other teachers examined the flag (which was draped stage right) or their notes, or the windows which opened on our now-famous playing diamond.

Graduation, the hush-hush magic time of frills and gifts and congratulations and diplomas, was finished for me before my name was called. The accomplishment was nothing. The meticulous maps, drawn in three colors of ink, learning and spelling decasyllabic words, memorizing the whole of *The Rape of Lucrece*—it was for nothing. Donleavy had exposed us.

We were maids and farmers, handymen and washerwomen, and anything higher that we aspired to was farcical and presumptuous.

Then I wished that Gabriel Prosser and Nat Turner had killed all whitefolks in their beds and that Abraham Lincoln had been assassinated before the signing of the Emancipation Proclamation, and that Harriet Tubman had been killed by that blow on her head and Christopher Columbus had drowned in the *Santa María*.

It was awful to be Negro and have no control over my life. It was brutal to be young and already trained to sit quietly and listen to charges brought against my color with no chance of defense. We should all be dead. I thought I should like to see us all dead, one on top of the other. A pyramid of flesh with the whitefolks on the bottom, as the broad base, then the Indians with their silly tomahawks and teepees and wigwams and treaties, the Negroes with their mops and recipes and cotton sacks and spirituals sticking out of their mouths. The Dutch children should all stumble in their wooden shoes and break their necks. The French should choke to death on the Louisiana Purchase (1803) while silk-worms ate all the Chinese with their stupid pigtails. As a species, we were an abomination. All of us.

Donleavy was running for election, and assured our parents that if he won we could count on having the only colored paved playing field in that part of Arkansas. Also—he never looked up to acknowledge the grunts of acceptance—also, we were bound to get some new equipment for the home economics building and the workshop.

He finished, and since there was no need to give any more than the most perfunctory thank-you's, he nodded to the men on the stage, and the tall white man who was never introduced joined him at the door. They left with the attitude that now they were off to something really important. (The graduation ceremonies at Lafayette County Training School had been a mere preliminary.)

The ugliness they left was palpable. An uninvited guest who wouldn't leave. The choir was summoned and sang a modern arrangement of "Onward, Christian Soldiers," with new words pertaining to graduates seeking their place in the world. But it didn't work.

Elouise, the daughter of the Baptist minister, recited "Invictus," and I could have cried at the impertinence of "I am the master of my fate, I am the captain of my soul."

My name had lost its ring of familiarity and I had to be nudged to go and receive my diploma. All my preparations had fled. I neither marched up to the stage like a conquering Amazon, nor did I look in the audience for Bailey's nod of approval. Marguerite Johnson, I heard the name again, my honors were read, there were noises in the audience of appreciation, and I took my place on the stage as rehearsed.

I thought about colors I hated: ecru, puce, lavender, beige and black.

There was shuffling and rustling around me, then Henry Reed was giving his valedictory address, "To Be or Not to Be." Hadn't he heard the whitefolks? We couldn't *be*, so the question was a waste of time. Henry's voice came out clear and strong. I feared to look at him. Hadn't he got the message? There was no "nobler in the mind" for Negroes because the world didn't think we had minds, and they let us know it. "Outrageous fortune"? Now, that was a joke. When the ceremony was over I had to tell Henry Reed some things. That is, if I still cared. Not "rub," Henry, "erase." "Ah, there's the erase." Us.

Henry had been a good student in elocution. His voice rose on tides of promise and fell on waves of warnings. The English teacher had helped him to create a sermon winging through Hamlet's soliloquy. To be a man, a doer, a builder, a leader, or to be a tool, an unfunny joke, a crusher of funky toadstools. I marveled that Henry could go through with the speech as if we had a choice.

I had been listening and silently rebutting each sentence with my eyes closed; then there was a hush, which in an audience warns that something unplanned is happening. I looked up and saw Henry Reed, the conservative, the proper, the A student, turn his back to the audience and turn to us (the proud graduating class of 1940) and sing, nearly speaking,

> "Lift ev'ry voice and sing
> Till earth and heaven ring
> Ring with the harmonies of Liberty . . ."

It was the poem written by James Weldon Johnson. It was the music composed by J. Rosamond Johnson. It was the Negro national anthem. Out of habit we were singing it.

Our mothers and fathers stood in the dark hall and joined the hymn of encouragement. A kindergarten teacher led the small children onto the stage and the buttercups and daisies and bunny rabbits marked time and tried to follow:

> "Stony the road we trod
> Bitter the chastening rod
> Felt in the days when hope, unborn, had died.
> Yet with a steady beat
> Have not our weary feet
> Come to the place for which our fathers sighed?"

Every child I knew had learned that song with his ABC's and along with "Jesus Loves Me This I Know." But I personally had never heard it before. Never heard the words, despite the thousands of times I had sung them. Never thought they had anything to do with me.

On the other hand, the words of Patrick Henry had made such an impression on me that I had been able to stretch myself tall and trembling and say, "I

---

know not what course others may take, but as for me, give me liberty or give me death."

And now I heard, really for the first time:

"We have come over a way that with tears
has been watered,
We have come, treading our path through
the blood of the slaughtered."

While echoes of the song shivered in the air, Henry Reed bowed his head, said "Thank you," and returned to his place in the line. The tears that slipped down many faces were not wiped away in shame.

We were on top again. As always, again. We survived. The depths had been icy and dark, but now a bright sun spoke to our souls. I was no longer simply a member of the proud graduating class of 1940; I was a proud member of the wonderful, beautiful Negro race.

Oh, Black known and unknown poets, how often have your auctioned pains sustained us? Who will compute the lonely nights made less lonely by your songs, or by the empty pots made less tragic by your tales?

If we were a people much given to revealing secrets, we might raise monuments and sacrifice to the memories of our poets, but slavery cured us of that weakness. It may be enough, however, to have it said that we survive in exact relationship to the dedication of our poets (include preachers, musicians and blues singers).

24

THE ANGEL OF the candy counter had found me out at last, and was exacting excruciating penance for all the stolen Milky Ways, Mounds, Mr. Goodbars and Hersheys with Almonds. I had two cavities that were rotten to the gums. The pain was beyond the bailiwick of crushed aspirins or oil of cloves. Only one thing could help me, so I prayed earnestly that I'd be allowed to sit under the house and have the building collapse on my left jaw. Since there was no Negro dentist in Stamps, nor doctor either, for that matter, Momma had dealt with previous toothaches by pulling them out (a string tied to the tooth with the other end looped over her fist), pain killers and prayer. In this particular instance the medicine had proved ineffective; there wasn't enough enamel left to hook a string on, and the prayers were being ignored because the Balancing Angel was blocking their passage.

I lived a few days and nights in blinding pain, not so much toying with as seriously considering the idea of jumping in the well, and Momma decided I had to be taken to a dentist. The nearest Negro dentist was in Texarkana, twenty-five miles away, and I was certain that I'd be dead long before we reached half the distance. Momma said we'd go to Dr. Lincoln, right in Stamps, and he'd take care of me. She said he owed her a favor.

I knew that there were a number of whitefolks in town that owed her favors. Bailey and I had seen the books which showed how she had lent money to Blacks and whites alike during the Depression, and most still owed her. But I couldn't aptly remember seeing Dr. Lincoln's name, nor had I ever heard of a Negro's going to him as a patient. However, Momma said we were going, and put water on the stove for our baths. I had never been to a doctor, so she told me that after the bath (which would make my mouth feel better) I had to put on freshly starched and ironed underclothes from inside out. The ache failed to respond to the bath, and I knew then that the pain was more serious than that which anyone had ever suffered.

Before we left the Store, she ordered me to brush

my teeth and then wash my mouth with Listerine. The idea of even opening my clamped jaws increased the pain, but upon her explanation that when you go to a doctor you have to clean yourself all over, but most especially the part that's to be examined, I screwed up my courage and unlocked my teeth. The cool air in my mouth and the jarring of my molars dislodged what little remained of my reason. I had frozen to the pain, my family nearly had to tie me down to take the toothbrush away. It was no small effort to get me started on the road to the dentist. Momma spoke to all the passers-by, but didn't stop to chat. She explained over her shoulder that we were going to the doctor and she'd "pass the time of day" on our way home.

Until we reached the pond the pain was my world, an aura that haloed me for three feet around. Crossing the bridge into whitefolks' country, pieces of sanity pushed themselves forward. I had to stop moaning and start walking straight. The white towel, which was drawn under my chin and tied over my head, had to be arranged. If one was dying, it had to be done in style if the dying took place in whitefolks' part of town.

On the other side of the bridge the ache seemed to lessen as if a whitebreeze blew off the whitefolks and cushioned everything in their neighborhood—including my jaw. The gravel road was smoother, the stones smaller and the tree branches hung down around the path and nearly covered us. If the pain didn't diminish then, the familiar yet strange sights hypnotized me into believing that it had.

But my head continued to throb with the measured insistence of a bass drum, and how could a toothache pass the calaboose, hear the songs of the prisoners, their blues and laughter, and not be changed? How could one or two or even a mouthful of angry tooth roots meet a wagonload of powhitetrash children, endure their idiotic snobbery and not feel less important?

Behind the building which housed the dentist's office ran a small path used by servants and those tradespeople who catered to the butcher and Stamps' one restaurant. Momma and I followed that lane to the backstairs of Dentist Lincoln's office. The sun was bright and gave the day a hard reality as we climbed up the steps to the second floor.

Momma knocked on the back door and a young white girl opened it to show surprise at seeing us there. Momma said she wanted to see Dentist Lincoln and to tell him Annie was there. The girl closed the door firmly. Now the humiliation of hearing Momma describe herself as if she had no last name to the young white girl was equal to the physical pain. It seemed terribly unfair to have a toothache and a headache and have to bear at the same time the heavy burden of Blackness.

It was always possible that the teeth would quiet down and maybe drop out of their own accord. Momma said we would wait. We leaned in the harsh sunlight on the shaky railings of the dentist's back porch for over an hour.

He opened the door and looked at Momma. "Well, Annie, what can I do for you?"

He didn't see the towel around my jaw or notice my swollen face.

Momma said, "Dentist Lincoln. It's my grandbaby here. She got two rotten teeth that's giving her a fit."

She waited for him to acknowledge the truth of her statement. He made no comment, orally or facially.

"She had this toothache purt' near four days now, and today I said, 'Young lady, you going to the Dentist.' "

"Annie?"

"Yes, sir, Dentist Lincoln."

He was choosing words the way people hunt for shells. "Annie, you know I don't treat nigra, colored people."

"I know, Dentist Lincoln. But this here is just my

little grandbaby, and she ain't gone be no trouble to you . . ."

"Annie, everybody has a policy. In this world you have to have a policy. Now, my policy is I don't treat colored people."

The sun had baked the oil out of Momma's skin and melted the Vaseline in her hair. She shone greasily as she leaned out of the dentist's shadow.

"Seem like to me, Dentist Lincoln, you might look after her, she ain't nothing but a little mite. And seems like maybe you owe me a favor or two."

He reddened slightly. "Favor or no favor. The money has all been repaid to you and that's the end of it. Sorry, Annie." He had his hand on the doorknob. "Sorry." His voice was a bit kinder on the second "Sorry," as if he really was.

Momma said, "I wouldn't press on you like this for myself but I can't take No. Not for my grandbaby. When you come to borrow my money you didn't have to beg. You asked me, and I lent it. Now, it wasn't my policy. I ain't no moneylender, but you stood to lose this building and I tried to help you out."

"It's been paid, and raising your voice won't make me change my mind. My policy . . ." He let go of the door and stepped nearer Momma. The three of us were crowded on the small landing. "Annie, my policy is I'd rather stick my hand in a dog's mouth than in a nigger's."

He had never once looked at me. He turned his back and went through the door into the cool beyond. Momma backed up inside herself for a few minutes. I forgot everything except her face which was almost a new one to me. She leaned over and took the doorknob, and in her everyday soft voice she said, "Sister, go on downstairs. Wait for me. I'll be there directly."

Under the most common of circumstances I knew it did no good to argue with Momma. So I walked down the steep stairs, afraid to look back and afraid not to do so. I turned as the door slammed, and she was gone.

Momma walked in that room as if she owned it. She shoved that silly nurse aside with one hand and strode into the dentist's office. He was sitting in his chair, sharpening his mean instruments and putting extra sting into his medicines. Her eyes were blazing like live coals and her arms had doubled themselves in length. He looked up at her just before she caught him by the collar of his white jacket.

"Stand up when you see a lady, you contemptuous scoundrel." *Her tongue had thinned and the words rolled off well enunciated. Enunciated and sharp like little claps of thunder.*

The dentist had no choice but to stand at R.O.T.C. attention. His head dropped after a minute and his voice was humble. "Yes, ma'am, Mrs. Henderson."

"You knave, do you think you acted like a gentleman, speaking to me like that in front of my granddaughter?" She didn't shake him, although she had the power. She simply held him upright.

"No, ma'am, Mrs. Henderson."

"No, ma'am, Mrs. Henderson, what?" Then she did give him the tiniest of shakes, but because of her strength the action set his head and arms to shaking loose on the ends of his body. He stuttered much worse than Uncle Willie. "No, ma'am. Mrs. Henderson, I'm sorry."

With just an edge of her disgust showing, Momma slung him back in his dentist's chair. "Sorry is as sorry does, and you're about the sorriest dentist I ever laid my eyes on." (She could afford to slip into the vernacular because she had such eloquent command of English.)

"I didn't ask you to apologize in front of Marguerite, because I don't want her to know my power, but I order you, now and herewith. Leave Stamps by sundown."

"Mrs. Henderson, I can't get my equipment ..." He was shaking terribly now.

"Now, that brings me to my second order. You will never again practice dentistry. Never! When you get settled in your next place, you will be a vegetarian caring for dogs with the mange, cats with the cholera and cows with the epizootic. Is that clear?"

The saliva ran down his chin and his eyes filled with tears. *"Yes, ma'am. Thank you for not killing me. Thank you, Mrs. Henderson."*

Momma pulled herself back from being ten feet tall with eight-foot arms and said, "You're welcome for nothing, you varlet, I wouldn't waste a killing on the likes of you."

On her way out she waved her handkerchief at the nurse and turned her into a crocus sack of chicken feed.

Momma looked tired when she came down the stairs, but who wouldn't be tired if they had gone through what she had. She came close to me and adjusted the towel under my jaw (I had forgotten the toothache; I only knew that she made her hands gentle in order not to awaken the pain). She took my hand. Her voice never changed. "Come on, Sister."

I reckoned we were going home where she would concoct a brew to eliminate the pain and maybe give me new teeth too. New teeth that would grow overnight out of my gums. She led me toward the drugstore, which was in the opposite direction from the Store. "I'm taking you to Dentist Baker in Texarkana."

I was glad after all that that I had bathed and put on Mum and Cashmere Bouquet talcum powder. It was a wonderful surprise. My toothache had quieted to solemn pain, Momma had obliterated the evil white man, and we were going on a trip to Texarkana, just the two of us.

On the Greyhound she took an inside seat in the back, and I sat beside her. I was so proud of being her granddaughter and sure that some of her magic must have come down to me. She asked if I was scared. I only shook my head and leaned over on her cool brown upper arm. There was no chance that a dentist, especially a Negro dentist, would dare hurt me then. Not with Momma there. The trip was uneventful, except that she put her arm around me, which was very unusual for Momma to do.

The dentist showed me the medicine and the needle before he deadened my gums, but if he hadn't I wouldn't have worried. Momma stood right behind him. Her arms were folded and she checked on everything he did. The teeth were extracted and she bought me an ice cream cone from the side window of a drug counter. The trip back to Stamps was quiet, except that I had to spit into a very small empty snuff can which she had gotten for me and it was difficult with the bus humping and jerking on our country roads.

At home, I was given a warm salt solution, and when I washed out my mouth I showed Bailey the empty holes, where the clotted blood sat like filling in a pie crust. He said I was quite brave, and that was my cue to reveal our confrontation with the peckerwood dentist and Momma's incredible powers.

I had to admit that I didn't hear the conversation, but what else could she have said than what I said she said? What else done? He agreed with my analysis in a lukewarm way, and I happily (after all, I'd been sick) flounced into the Store. Momma was preparing our evening meal and Uncle Willie leaned on the door sill. She gave her version.

"Dentist Lincoln got right uppity. Said he'd rather put his hand in a dog's mouth. And when I reminded him of the favor, he brushed it off like a piece of lint. Well, I sent Sister downstairs and went inside. I hadn't never been in his office before, but I found the door to where he takes out teeth, and him and the nurse was in there thick as thieves. I just stood there till he caught sight of me." Crash bang the pots on the stove. "He jumped just like he was sitting on a pin. He said, 'Annie, I done tole you, I ain't gonna mess around in no niggah's mouth.' I said, 'Somebody's got to do it then,' and he said, 'Take her to Texarkana to the colored dentist' and that's when I said, 'If you paid me my money I could afford to take her.' He said, 'It's all been paid.' I tole him everything but the interest had been paid. He said, ' 'Twasn't no interest.' I said, ' 'Tis now. I'll take ten dollars as payment in full.' You know, Willie, it wasn't no right thing to do, 'cause I lent that money without thinking about it.

"He tole that little snippity nurse of his'n to give me ten dollars and make me sign a 'paid in full' receipt. She gave it to me and I signed the papers. Even though by rights he was paid up before, I figger, he gonna be that kind of nasty, he gonna have to pay for it."

Momma and her son laughed and laughed over the white man's evilness and her retributive sin.

I preferred, much preferred, my version.

25

KNOWING MOMMA, I knew that I never knew Momma. Her African-bush secretiveness and suspiciousness had been compounded by slavery and confirmed by centuries of promises made and promises broken. We have a saying among Black Americans which describes Momma's caution. "If you ask a Negro where he's been, he'll tell you where he's going." To understand this important information, it is necessary to know who uses this tactic and on whom it works. If an unaware person is told a part of the truth (it is imperative that the answer embody truth), he is satisfied that his query has been answered. If an aware person (one who himself uses the stratagem) is given an answer which is truthful but bears only slightly if at all on the question, he knows that the information he seeks is of a private nature and will not be handed to him willingly. Thus direct denial, lying and the revelation of personal affairs are avoided.

Momma told us one day that she was taking us to California. She explained that we were growing up, that we needed to be with our parents, that Uncle Willie was, after all, crippled, that she was getting old. All true, and yet none of those truths satisfied our need for The Truth. The Store and the rooms in back became a going-away factory. Momma sat at the sewing machine all hours, making and remaking clothes for use in California. Neighbors brought out of their trunks pieces of material that had been packed away for decades in blankets of mothballs (I'm certain I was the only girl in California who went to school in water-marked moiré skirts and yellowed satin blouses, satin-back crepe dresses and crepe de Chine underwear).

Whatever the real reason, The Truth, for taking us to California, I shall always think it lay mostly in an incident in which Bailey had the leading part. Bailey had picked up the habit of imitating Claude Rains, Herbert Marshall and George McCready. I didn't think it at all strange that a thirteen-year-old boy in the unreconstructed Southern town of Stamps spoke with an Englishy accent. His heroes included D'Artagnan and the Count of Monte Cristo and he affected what he thought were their swashbuckling gallantries.

On an afternoon a few weeks before Momma revealed her plan to take us West, Bailey came into the Store shaking. His little face was no longer black but a dirty, colorless gray. As was our habit upon entering the Store, he walked behind the candy counter and leaned on the cash register. Uncle Willie had sent him on an errand to whitefolks' town and he wanted an explanation for Bailey's tardiness. After a brief moment our uncle could see that something was wrong, and feeling unable to cope, he called Momma from the kitchen.

"What's the matter, Bailey Junior?"

He said nothing. I knew when I saw him that it would be useless to ask anything while he was in that state. It meant that he had seen or heard of something so ugly or frightening that he was paralyzed as a result. He explained when we were smaller that when things were very bad his soul just crawled behind his heart and curled up and went to sleep. When it awoke, the fearful thing had gone away. Ever since we read *The Fall of the House of Usher*, we had made a pact that neither of us would allow the other to be buried without making "absolutely, positively sure" (his favorite phrase) that the person was dead. I also had to swear that when his soul was sleeping I would never try to wake it, for the shock might make it go to sleep forever. So I let him be, and after a while Momma had to let him alone too.

I waited on customers, and walked around him or leaned over him and, as I suspected, he didn't respond. When the spell wore off he asked Uncle Willie what colored people had done to white people in the first place. Uncle Willie, who never was one for explaining things because he took after Momma, said little except that "colored people hadn't even bothered a hair on whitefolks' heads." Momma added that some people said that whitefolks had come over to Africa (she made it sound like a hidden valley on the moon) and stole the colored people and made them slaves, but nobody really believed it was true. No way to explain what happened "blows and scores" ago, but right now they had the upper hand. Their time wasn't long, though. Didn't Moses lead the children of Israel out of the bloody hands of Pharaoh and into the Promised Land? Didn't the Lord protect the Hebrew children in the fiery furnace and didn't my Lord deliver Daniel? We only had to wait on the Lord.

Bailey said he saw a man, a colored man, whom nobody had delivered. He was dead. (If the news hadn't been so important, we would have been visited with one of Momma's outbursts and prayers. Bailey was nearly blaspheming.) He said, "The man was dead and rotten. Not stinking but rotten."

Momma ordered, "Ju, watch your tongue."

Uncle Willie asked, "Who, who was it?"

Bailey was just tall enough to clear his face over the cash register. He said, "When I passed the calaboose, some men had just fished him out of the pond. He was wrapped in a sheet, all rolled up like a mummy, then a white man walked over and pulled the sheet off. The man was on his back but the white man stuck his foot under the sheet and rolled him over on the stomach."

He turned to me. "My, he had no color at all. He was bloated like a ball." (We had had a running argument for months. Bailey said there was no such thing as colorlessness, and I argued that if there was color there also had to be an opposite and now he was admitting that it was possible. But I didn't feel good about my win.) "The colored men backed off and I did too, but the white man stood there, looking down, and grinned. Uncle Willie, why do they hate us so much?"

Uncle Willie muttered, "They don't really hate us. They don't know us. How can they hate us? They mostly scared."

Momma asked if Bailey had recognized the man, but he was caught in the happening and the event.

"Mr. Bubba told me I was too young to see something like that and I oughta hightail it home, but I had to stay. Then the white man called us closer. He said, 'O.K., you boys, stretch him out in the calaboose and when the Sheriff comes along he'll notify his people. This here's one nigger nobody got to worry about no more. He ain't going nowhere else.' Then the men picked up corners of the sheet, but since nobody wanted to get close to the man they held the very ends and he nearly rolled out on the ground. The white man called me to come and help too."

Momma exploded. "Who was it?" She made herself clear. "Who was the white man?"

Bailey couldn't let go of the horror. "I picked up a side of the sheet and walked right in the calaboose with the men. I walked in the calaboose carrying a rotten dead Negro." His voice was ancient with shock. He was literally bug-eyed.

"The white man played like he was going to lock us all up in there, but Mr. Bubba said, 'Ow, Mr. Jim. We didn't do it. We ain't done nothing wrong.' Then the white man laughed and said we boys couldn't take a joke, and opened the door." He breathed his relief. "Whew, I was glad to get out of there. The calaboose, and the prisoners screaming they didn't want no dead nigger in there with them. That he'd stink up the place. They called the white man 'Boss.' They said, 'Boss, surely we ain't done nothing bad enough for you to put another nigger in here with us, and a dead one at that.' Then they laughed. They all laughed like there was something funny."

Bailey was talking so fast he forgot to stutter, he forgot to scratch his head and clean his fingernails with his teeth. He was away in a mystery, locked in the enigma that young Southern Black boys start to unravel, start to *try* to unravel, from seven years old to death. The humorless puzzle of inequality and hate. His experience raised the question of worth and values, of aggressive inferiority and aggressive arrogance. Could Uncle Willie, a Black man, Southern, crippled moreover, hope to answer the questions, both asked` and unuttered? Would Momma, who knew the ways of the whites and the wiles of the Blacks, try to answer her grandson, whose very life depended on his not truly understanding the enigma? Most assuredly not.

They both responded characteristically. Uncle Willie said something like he didn't know what the world was coming to, and Momma prayed, "God rest his soul, poor man." I'm sure she began piecing together the details of our California trip that night.

Our transportation was Momma's major concern for some weeks. She had arranged with a railroad employee to provide her with a pass in exchange for groceries. The pass allowed a reduction in her fare only, and even that had to be approved, so we were made to abide in a kind of limbo until white people we would never see, in offices we would never visit, signed and stamped and mailed the pass back to Momma. My fare had to be paid in "ready cash." That sudden drain on the nickel-plated cash register lopsided our financial stability. Momma decided Bailey couldn't accompany us, since we had to use the pass during a set time, but that he would follow within a month or so when outstanding bills were paid. Although our mother now lived in San Francisco, Momma must have felt it wiser to go first to Los Angeles where our father was. She dictated letters to me, advising them both that we were on our way.

And we were on our way, but unable to say when. Our clothes were washed, ironed and packed, so for an immobile time we wore those things not good enough to glow under the California sun. Neighbors, who understood the complications of travel, said goodbye a million times.

"Well, if I don't see you before your ticket comes through, Sister Henderson, have a good trip and hurry back home." A widowed friend of Momma's had agreed to look after (cook, wash, clean and provide company for) Uncle Willie, and after thousands of arrested departures, at last we left Stamps.

My sorrow at leaving was confined to a gloom at separating from Bailey for a month (we had never been parted), the imagined loneliness of Uncle Willie (he put on a good face, though at thirty-five he'd never been separated from his mother) and the

loss of Louise, my first friend. I wouldn't miss Mrs.
Flowers, for she had given me her secret word
which called forth a djinn who was to serve me all
my life: books.

26

THE INTENSITY WITH which young people live demands that they "blank out" as often as possible. I
didn't actually think about facing Mother until the
last day of our journey. I was "going to California."
To oranges and sunshine and movie stars and earth-
quakes and (finally I realized) to Mother. My old
guilt came back to me like a much-missed friend. I
wondered if Mr. Freeman's name would be mentioned, or if I would be expected to say something
about the situation myself. I certainly couldn't ask
Momma, and Bailey was a zillion miles away.

The agony of wonder made the fuzzy seats hard,
soured the boiled eggs, and when I looked at Momma she seemed too big and too black and very
old-fashioned. Everything I saw shuttered against
me. The little towns, where nobody waved, and the
other passengers in the train, with whom I had
achieved an almost kinfolk relationship, disappeared
into a common strangeness.

I was as unprepared to meet my mother as a
sinner is reluctant to meet his Maker. And all too
soon she stood before me, smaller than memory
would have her but more glorious than any recall.
She wore a light-tan suede suit, shoes to match and
a mannish hat with a feather in the band, and she
patted my face with gloved hands. Except for the
lipsticked mouth, white teeth and shining black
eyes, she might have just emerged from a dip in a
beige bath. My picture of Mother and Momma em-
bracing on the train platform has been darkly retained through the coating of the then embarrass-

ment and the now maturity. Mother was a blithe chick nuzzling around the large, solid dark hen. The sounds they made had a rich inner harmony. Momma's deep, slow voice lay under my mother's rapid peeps and chirps like stones under rushing water.

The younger woman kissed and laughed and rushed about collecting our coats and getting our luggage carted off. She easily took care of the details that would have demanded half of a country person's day. I was struck again by the wonder of her, and for the length of my trance, the greedy uneasinesses were held at bay.

We moved into an apartment, and I slept on a sofa that miraculously transformed itself at night into a large comfortable bed. Mother stayed in Los Angeles long enough to get us settled, then she returned to San Francisco to arrange living accommodations for her abruptly enlarged family.

Momma and Bailey (he joined us a month after our arrival) and I lived in Los Angeles about six months while our permanent living arrangements were being concluded. Daddy Bailey visited occasionally, bringing shopping bags of fruit. He shone like a Sun God, benignly warming and brightening his dark subjects.

Since I was enchanted with the creation of my own world, years had to pass before I reflected on Momma's remarkable adjustment to that foreign life. An old Southern Negro woman who had lived her life under the left breast of her community learned to deal with white landlords, Mexican neighbors and Negro strangers. She shopped in supermarkets larger than the town she came from. She dealt with accents that must have struck jarringly on her ears. She, who had never been more than fifty miles from her birthplace, learned to traverse the maze of Spanish-named streets in that enigma that is Los Angeles.

She made the same kinds of friends she had always had. On late Sunday afternoons before evening church services, old women who were carbon copies of herself came to the apartment to share leftovers from the Sunday meal and religious talk of a Bright Hereafter.

When the arrangements for our move north were completed, she broke the shattering news that she was going back to Arkansas. She had done her job. She was needed by Uncle Willie. We had our own parents at last. At least we were in the same state.

There were foggy days of unknowing for Bailey and me. It was all well and good to say we would be with our parents, but after all, who were they? Would they be more severe with our didoes than she? That would be bad. Or more lax? Which would be even worse. Would we learn to speak that fast language? I doubted that, and I doubted even more that I would ever find out what they laughed about so loudly and so often.

I would have been willing to return to Stamps even without Bailey. But Momma left for Arkansas without me with her solid air packed around her like cotton.

Mother drove us toward San Francisco over the big white highway that would not have surprised me had it never ended. She talked incessantly and pointed out places of interest. As we passed Capistrano she sang a popular song that I'd heard on the radio: "When the swallows come back to Capistrano."

She strung humorous stories along the road like a bright wash and tried to captivate us. But her being, and her being our mother, had done the job so successfully that it was a little distracting to see her throwing good energy after good.

The big car was obedient under her one-hand driving, and she pulled on her Lucky Strike so hard that her cheeks were sucked in to make valleys in her face. Nothing could have been more magical than to have found her at last, and have her solely to ourselves in the closed world of a moving car.

Although we were both enraptured, neither Bailey nor I was unaware of her nervousness. The knowledge that we had the power to upset that goddess made us look at each other conspiratorially and smile. It also made her human.

We spent a few dingy months in an Oakland apartment which had a bathtub in the kitchen and was near enough to the Southern Pacific Mole to shake at the arrival and departure of every train. In many ways it was St. Louis revisited—along with Uncles Tommy and Billy—and Grandmother Baxter of the pince-nez and strict carriage was again In Residence, though the mighty Baxter clan had fallen into hard times after the death of Grandfather Baxter some years earlier.

We went to school and no family member questioned the output or quality of our work. We went to a playground which sported a basketball court, a football field and Ping Pong tables under awnings. On Sundays instead of going to church we went to the movies.

I slept with Grandmother Baxter, who was afflicted with chronic bronchitis and smoked heavily. During the day she stubbed out half-finished cigarettes and put them in an ashtray beside her bed. At night when she woke up coughing she fumbled in the dark for a butt (she called them "Willies") and after a blaze of light she smoked the strengthened tobacco until her irritated throat was deadened with nicotine. For the first weeks of sleeping with her, the shaking bed and scent of tobacco woke me, but I readily became used to it and slept peacefully through the night.

One evening after going to bed normally, I awoke to another kind of shaking. In the blunted light through the window shade I saw my mother kneeling by my bed. She brought her face close to my ear.

"Ritie," she whispered, "Ritie. Come, but be very quiet." Then she quietly rose and left the room.

Dutifully and in a haze of ponderment I followed. Through the half-open kitchen door the light showed Bailey's pajamaed legs dangling from the covered bathtub. The clock on the dining-room table said 2:30. I had never been up at that hour.

I looked Bailey a question and he returned a sheepish gaze. I knew immediately that there was nothing to fear. Then I ran my mind through the catalogue of important dates. It wasn't anybody's birthday, or April Fool's Day, or Halloween, but it was something.

Mother closed the kitchen door and told me to sit beside Bailey. She put her hands on her hips and said we had been invited to a party.

Was that enough to wake us in the middle of the night! Neither of us said anything.

She continued, "I am giving a party and you are my honored and only guests."

She opened the oven and took out a pan of her crispy brown biscuits and showed us a pot of milk chocolate on the back of the stove. There was nothing for it but to laugh at our beautiful and wild mother. When Bailey and I started laughing, she joined in, except that she kept her finger in front of her mouth to try to quiet us.

We were served formally, and she apologized for having no orchestra to play for us but said she'd sing as a substitute. She sang and did the Time Step and the Snake Hips and the Suzy Q. What child can resist a mother who laughs freely and often, especially if the child's wit is mature enough to catch the sense of the joke?

Mother's beauty made her powerful and her power made her unflinchingly honest. When we asked her what she did, what her job was, she walked us to Oakland's Seventh Street, where dusty bars and smoke shops sat in the laps of storefront churches. She pointed out Raincoat's Pinochle Parlor and Slim Jenkins' pretentious saloon. Some nights she played pinochle for money or ran a poker game at Mother Smith's or stopped at Slim's for a few drinks. She told us that she had never cheated anybody and wasn't making any preparations to do so. Her work was as honest as the job held by fat Mrs. Walker (a maid), who lived next door to us, and "a damn sight better paid." She wouldn't bust suds for anybody nor be anyone's kitchen bitch. The good Lord gave her a mind and she intended to use it to support her mother and her children. She didn't need to add "And have a little fun along the way."

In the street people were genuinely happy to see her. "Hey, baby. What's the news?"

"Everything's steady, baby, steady."

"How you doing, pretty?"

"I can't win, 'cause of the shape I'm in." (Said with a laugh that belied the content.)

"You all right, momma?"

"Aw, they tell me the whitefolks still in the lead." (Said as if that was not quite the whole truth.)

She supported us efficiently with humor and imagination. Occasionally we were taken to Chinese restaurants or Italian pizza parlors. We were introduced to Hungarian goulash and Irish stew. Through food we learned that there were other people in the world.

With all her jollity, Vivian Baxter had no mercy. There was a saying in Oakland at the time which, if she didn't say it herself, explained her attitude. The saying was, "Sympathy is next to shit in the dictionary, and I can't even read." Her temper had not diminished with the passing of time, and when a passionate nature is not eased with moments of compassion, melodrama is likely to take the stage. In each outburst of anger my mother was *fair*. She had the impartiality of nature, with the same lack of indulgence or clemency.

Before we arrived from Arkansas, an incident took place that left the main actors in jail and in the hospital. Mother had a business partner (who may have been a little more than that) with whom she ran a restaurant cum gambling casino. The partner was not shouldering his portion of the responsibility, according to Mother, and when she confronted him he became haughty and domineering, and he unforgivably called her a bitch. Now, everyone knew that although she cursed as freely as she laughed, no one cursed around her, and certainly no one cursed her. Maybe for the sake of business arrangements she restrained a spontaneous reaction. She told her partner, "I'm going to be one bitch, and I've already been that one." In a foolhardy gesture the man relieved himself of still another "bitch"—and Mother shot him. She had anticipated some trouble when she determined to speak to him and so had taken the precaution to slip a little .32 in her big skirt pocket.

Shot once, the partner stumbled toward her, instead of away, and she said that since she had intended to shoot him (notice: shoot, not kill) she had no reason to run away, so she shot him a second time. It must have been a maddening situation for them. To her, each shot seemed to impel him forward, the reverse of her desire; and for him, the closer he got to her, the more she shot him. She stood her ground until he reached her and flung both arms around her neck, dragging her to the floor. She later said the police had to untwine him before he could be taken to the ambulance. And on the following day, when she was released on bail, she looked in a mirror and "had black eyes down to here." In throwing his arms around her, he must have struck her. She bruised easily.

The partner lived, though shot twice, and although the partnership was dissolved they retained admiration for each other. He had been shot, true, but in her fairness she had warned him. And he had had the strength to give her two black eyes and then live. Admirable qualities.

World War II started on a Sunday afternoon when I was on my way to the movies. People in the streets shouted, "We're at war. We've declared war on Japan."

I ran all the way home. Not too sure I wouldn't be bombed before I reached Bailey and Mother. Grandmother Baxter calmed my anxiety by explaining that America would not be bombed, not as long as Franklin Delano Roosevelt was President. He was, after all, a politician's politician and he knew what he was doing.

Soon after, Mother married Daddy Clidell, who turned out to be the first father I would know. He was a successful businessman, and he and Mother moved us to San Francisco. Uncle Tommy, Uncle Billy and Grandmother Baxter remained in the big house in Oakland.

27

IN THE EARLY months of World War II, San Francisco's Fillmore district, or the Western Addition, experienced a visible revolution. On the surface it appeared to be totally peaceful and almost a refutation of the term "revolution." The Yakamoto Sea Food Market quietly became Sammy's Shoe Shine Parlor and Smoke Shop. Yashigira's Hardware metamorphosed into La Salon de Beauté owned by Miss Clorinda Jackson. The Japanese shops which sold products to Nisei customers were taken over by enterprising Negro businessmen, and in less than a year became permanent homes away from home for the newly arrived Southern Blacks. Where the odors of tempura, raw fish and *cha* had dominated, the aroma of chitlings, greens and ham hocks now prevailed.

The Asian population dwindled before my eyes. I was unable to tell the Japanese from the Chinese and as yet found no real difference in the national origin of such sounds as Ching and Chan or Moto and Kano.

As the Japanese disappeared, soundlessly and without protest, the Negroes entered with their loud jukeboxes, their just-released animosities and the relief of escape from Southern bonds. The Japanese area became San Francisco's Harlem in a matter of months.

A person unaware of all the factors that make up oppression might have expected sympathy or even support from the Negro newcomers for the dislodged Japanese. Especially in view of the fact that they (the Blacks) had themselves undergone concentration-camp living for centuries in slavery's plantations and later in sharecroppers' cabins. But the sensations of common relationship were missing.

The Black newcomer had been recruited on the desiccated farm lands of Georgia and Mississippi by war-plant labor scouts. The chance to live in two- or three-story apartment buildings (which became instant slums), and to earn two- and even three-figured weekly checks, was blinding. For the first time he could think of himself as a Boss, a Spender. He was able to pay other people to work for him, i.e. the dry cleaners, taxi drivers, waitresses, etc. The shipyards and ammunition plants brought to booming life by the war let him know that he was needed and even appreciated. A completely alien yet very pleasant position for him to experience. Who could expect this man to share his new and dizzying importance with concern for a race that he had never known to exist?

Another reason for his indifference to the Japanese removal was more subtle but was more profoundly felt. The Japanese were not whitefolks. Their eyes, language and customs belied the white skin and proved to their dark successors that since they didn't have to be feared, neither did they have

to be considered. All this was decided uncon-
sciously.

No member of my family and none of the family
friends ever mentioned the absent Japanese. It was as
if they had never owned or lived in the houses we
inhabited. On Post Street, where our house was, the
hill skidded slowly down to Fillmore, the market
heart of our district. In the two short blocks before it
reached its destination, the street housed two day-
and-night restaurants, two pool halls, four Chinese
restaurants, two gambling houses, plus diners, shoeshine shops, beauty salons, barber shops and at least
four churches. To fully grasp the never-ending activity in San Francisco's Negro neighborhood during
the war, one need only know that the two blocks
described were side streets that were duplicated
many times over in the eight- to ten-square-block
area.

The air of collective displacement, the impermanence of life in wartime and the gauche personalities of the more recent arrivals tended to dissipate
my own sense of not belonging. In San Francisco,
for the first time, I perceived myself as part of
something. Not that I identified with the newcomers, nor with the rare Black descendants of native San Franciscans, nor with the whites or even
the Asians, but rather with the times and the city. I
understood the arrogance of the young sailors who
marched the streets in marauding gangs, approaching every girl as if she were at best a prostitute and at worst an Axis agent bent on making the
U.S.A. lose the war. The undertone of fear that San
Francisco would be bombed which was abetted by
weekly air raid warnings, and civil defense drills in
school, heightened my sense of belonging. Hadn't I,
always, but ever and ever, thought that life was just
one great risk for the living?

Then the city acted in wartime like an intelligent
woman under siege. She gave what she couldn't
with safety withhold, and secured those things

which lay in her reach. The city became for me the ideal of what I wanted to be as a grownup. Friendly but never gushing, cool but not frigid or distant, distinguished without the awful stiffness.

To San Franciscans "the City That Knows How" was the Bay, the fog, Sir Francis Drake Hotel, Top o' the Mark, Chinatown, the Sunset District and so on and so forth and so white. To me, a thirteen-year-old Black girl, stalled by the South and Southern Black life style, the city was a state of beauty and a state of freedom. The fog wasn't simply the steamy vapors off the bay caught and penned in by hills, but a soft breath of anonymity that shrouded and cushioned the bashful traveler. I became dauntless and free of fears, intoxicated by the physical fact of San Francisco. Safe in my protecting arrogance, I was certain that no one loved her as impartially as I. I walked around the Mark Hopkins and gazed at the Top o' the Mark, but (maybe sour grapes) was more impressed by the view of Oakland from the hill than by the tiered building or its fur-draped visitors. For weeks, after the city and I came to terms about my belonging, I haunted the points of interest and found them empty and un-San Francisco. The naval officers with their well-dressed wives and clean white babies inhabited another time-space dimension than I. The well-kept old women in chauffeured cars and blond girls in buckskin shoes and cashmere sweaters might have been San Franciscans, but they were at most gilt on the frame of my portrait of the city.

Pride and Prejudice stalked in tandem the beautiful hills. Native San Franciscans, possessive of the city, had to cope with an influx, not of awed respectful tourists but of raucous unsophisticated provincials. They were also forced to live with skin-deep guilt brought on by the treatment of their former Nisei schoolmates.

Southern white illiterates brought their biases intact to the West from the hills of Arkansas and the swamps of Georgia. The Black ex-farmers had not left their distrust and fear of whites which history had taught them in distressful lessons. These two groups were obliged to work side by side in the war plants, and their animosities festered and opened like boils on the face of the city.

San Franciscans would have sworn on the Golden Gate Bridge that racism was missing from the heart of their air-conditioned city. But they would have been sadly mistaken.

A story went the rounds about a San Franciscan white matron who refused to sit beside a Negro civilian on the streetcar, even after he made room for her on the seat. Her explanation was that she would not sit beside a draft dodger who was a Negro as well. She added that the least he could do was fight for his country the way her son was fighting on Iwo Jima. The story said that the man pulled his body away from the window to show an armless sleeve. He said quietly and with great dignity, "Then ask your son to look around for my arm, which I left over there."

28

ALTHOUGH MY GRADES were very good (I had been put up two semesters on my arrival from Stamps), I found myself unable to settle down in the high school. It was an institution for girls near my house, and the young ladies were faster, brasher, meaner and more prejudiced than any I had met at Lafayette County Training School. Many of the Negro girls were, like me, straight from the South, but they had known or claimed to have known the bright lights of Big D (Dallas) or T Town (Tulsa, Oklahoma), and their language bore up their claims. They strutted with an aura of invincibility, and along with some of the Mexican students who put knives in their tall pompadours they absolutely intimidated the white girls and those Black and Mexican students who had no shield of fearlessness. Fortunately I was transferred to George Washington High School.

The beautiful buildings sat on a moderate hill in the white residential district, some sixty blocks from the Negro neighborhood. For the first semester, I was one of three Black students in the school, and in that rarefied atmosphere I came to love my people more. Mornings as the streetcar traversed my ghetto I experienced a mixture of dread and trauma. I knew that all too soon we would be out of my familiar setting, and Blacks who were on the streetcar when I got on would all be gone and I alone would face the forty blocks of neat streets, smooth lawns, white houses and rich children.

In the evenings on the way home the sensations were joy, anticipation and relief at the first sign which said BARBECUE or DO DROP INN or HOME COOKING or at the first brown faces on the streets. I recognized that I was again in my country.

In the school itself I was disappointed to find that I was not the most brilliant or even nearly the most brilliant student. The white kids had better vocabularies than I and, what was more appalling, less fear in the classrooms. They never hesitated to hold up their hands in response to a teacher's question; even when they were wrong they were wrong aggressively, while I had to be certain about all my facts before I dared to call attention to myself.

George Washington High School was the first real school I attended. My entire stay there might have been time lost if it hadn't been for the unique personality of a brilliant teacher. Miss Kirwin was that rare educator who was in love with information. I will always believe that her love of teaching came not so much from her liking for students but from her desire to make sure that some of the things she knew would find repositories so that they could be shared again.

She and her maiden sister worked in the San Francisco city school system for over twenty years. My Miss Kirwin, who was a tall, florid, buxom lady with battleship-gray hair, taught civics and current events. At the end of a term in her class our books were as clean and the pages as stiff as they had been when they were issued to us. Miss Kirwin's students were never or very rarely called upon to open textbooks.

She greeted each class with "Good day, ladies and gentlemen." I had never heard an adult speak with such respect to teenagers. (Adults usually believe that a show of honor diminishes their authority.) "In today's *Chronicle* there was an article on the mining industry in the Carolinas [or some such distant subject]. I am certain that all of you have read the article. I would like someone to elaborate on the subject for me."

After the first two weeks in her class, I, along with all the other excited students, read the San Francisco papers, *Time* magazine, *Life* and everything else available to me. Miss Kirwin proved Bailey right. He had told me once that "all knowledge is spendable currency, depending on the market."

There were no favorite students. No teacher's pets. If a student pleased her during a particular period, he could not count on special treatment in the next day's class, and that was as true the other way around. Each day she faced us with a clean slate and acted as if ours were clean as well. Reserved and firm in her opinions, she spent no time in indulging the frivolous.

She was stimulating instead of intimidating. Where some of the other teachers went out of their way to be nice to me—to be a "liberal" with me—and others ignored me completely, Miss Kirwin never seemed to notice that I was Black and therefore different. I was Miss Johnson and if I had the answer to a question she posed I was never given any more than the word "Correct," which was what she said to every other student with the correct answer.

Years later when I returned to San Francisco I made visits to her classroom. She always remembered that I was Miss Johnson, who had a good mind and should be doing something with it. I was never encouraged on those visits to loiter or linger about her desk. She acted as if I must have had other visits to make. I often wondered if she knew she was the only teacher I remembered.

I never knew why I was given a scholarship to the California Labor School. It was a college for adults, and many years later I found that it was on the House Un-American Activities list of subversive organizations. At fourteen I accepted a scholarship and got one for the next year as well. In the evening classes I took drama and dance, along with white and Black grownups. I had chosen drama simply because I liked Hamlet's soliloquy beginning, "To be, or not to be." I had never seen a play and did not connect movies with the theater. In fact, the only times I had heard the soliloquy had been when I had melodramatically recited to myself. In front of a mirror.

It was hard to curb my love for the exaggerated gesture and the emotive voice. When Bailey and I read poems together, he sounded like a fierce Basil Rathbone and I like a maddened Bette Davis. At the California Labor School a forceful and perceptive teacher quickly and unceremoniously separated me from melodrama.

She made me do six months of pantomime.

Bailey and Mother encouraged me to take dance, and he privately told me that the exercise would make my legs big and widen my hips. I needed no greater inducement.

My shyness at moving clad in black tights around a large empty room did not last long. Of course, at first, I thought everyone would be staring at my cucumber-shaped body with its knobs for knees, knobs for elbows and, alas, knobs for breasts. But they really did not notice me, and when the teacher floated across the floor and finished in an arabesque my fancy was taken. I would learn to move like that. I would learn to, in her words, "occupy space." My days angled off Miss Kirwin's class, dinner with Bailey and Mother, and drama and dance.

The allegiances I owed at this time in my life would have made very strange bedfellows: Momma with her solemn determination, Mrs. Flowers and her books, Bailey with his love, my mother and her gaiety, Miss Kirwin and her information, my evening classes of drama and dance.

29

OUR HOUSE WAS a fourteen-room typical San Franciscan post-Earthquake affair. We had a succession of roomers, bringing and taking their different accents, and personalities and foods. Shipyard workers clanked up the stairs (we all slept on the second floor except Mother and Daddy Clidell) in their steel-tipped boots and metal hats, and gave way to much-powdered prostitutes, who giggled through their make-up and hung their wigs on the doorknobs. One couple (they were college graduates) held long adult conversations with me in the big kitchen downstairs, until the husband went off to war. Then the wife who had been so charming and ready to smile changed into a silent shadow that played infrequently along the walls. An older couple lived with us for a year or so. They owned a restaurant and had no personality to enchant or interest a teenager, except that the husband was called Uncle Jim, and the wife Aunt Boy. I never figured that out.

The quality of strength lined with tenderness is an unbeatable combination, as are intelligence and necessity when unblunted by formal education. I was prepared to accept Daddy Clidell as one more faceless name added to Mother's roster of conquests. I had trained myself so successfully through the years to display interest, or at least attention, while my mind skipped free on other subjects that I could have lived in his house without ever seeing him and without his becoming the wiser. But his character beckoned and elicited admiration. He was a simple man who had no inferiority complex about his lack of education and, even more amazing, no superiority complex because he had succeeded despite that lack. He would say often, "I been to school three years in my life. In Slaten, Texas, times was hard, and I had to help my daddy on the farm."

No recriminations lay hidden under the plain statement, nor was there boasting when he said, "If I'm living a little better now, it's because I treats everybody right."

He owned apartment buildings and, later, pool halls, and was famous for being that rarity "a man of honor." He didn't suffer, as many "honest men" do, from the detestable righteousness that diminishes their virtue. He knew cards and men's hearts. So during the age when Mother was exposing us to certain facts of life, like personal hygiene, proper posture, table manners, good restaurants and tipping practices, Daddy Clidell taught me to play poker, blackjack, tonk and high, low, Jick, Jack and the Game. He wore expensively tailored suits and a large yellow diamond stickpin. Except for the jewelry, he was a conservative dresser and carried himself with the unconscious pomp of a man of secure means. Unexpectedly, I resembled him, and when he, Mother and I walked down the street his friends often said, "Clidell, that's sure your daughter. Ain't no way you can deny her."

Proud laughter followed those declarations, for he

had never had children. Because of his late-arriving but intense paternal sense, I was introduced to the most colorful characters in the Black underground. One afternoon, I was invited into our smoke-filled dining room to make the acquaintance of Stonewall Jimmy, Just Black, Cool Clyde, Tight Coat and Red Leg. Daddy Clidell explained to me that they were the most successful con men in the world, and they were going to tell me about some games so that I would never be "anybody's mark."

To begin, one man warned me, "There ain't never been a mark yet that didn't want something for nothing." Then they took turns showing me their tricks, how they chose their victims (marks) from the wealthy bigoted whites and in every case how they used the victims' prejudice against them.

Some of the tales were funny, a few were pathetic, but all were amusing or gratifying to me, for the Black man, the con man who could act the most stupid, won out every time over the powerful, arrogant white.

I remember Mr. Red Leg's story like a favorite melody.

"Anything that works against you can also work for you once you understand the Principle of Reverse.

"There was a cracker in Tulsa who bilked so many Negroes he could set up a Negro Bilking Company. Naturally he got to thinking, Black Skin means Damn Fool. Just Black and I went to Tulsa to check him out. Come to find out, he's a perfect mark. His momma must have been scared in an Indian massacre in Africa. He hated Negroes only a little more than he despised Indians. And he was greedy.

"Black and I studied him and decided he was worth setting up against the store. That means we were ready to put out a few thousand dollars in preparation. We pulled in a white boy from New York, a good con artist, and had him open an office in Tulsa. He was supposed to be a Northern real

estate agent trying to buy up valuable land in Oklahoma. We investigated a piece of land near Tulsa
that had a toll bridge crossing it. It used to be part
of an Indian reservation but had been taken over by
the state.

"Just Black was laid out as the decoy, and I was
going to be the fool. After our friend from New York
hired a secretary and had his cards printed, Black
approached the mark with a proposition. He told him
that he had heard that our mark was the only white
man colored people could trust. He named some of
the poor fools that had been taken by that crook. It
just goes to show you how white folks can be de-
ceived by their own deception. The mark believed
Black.

"Black told him about his friend who was half
Indian and half colored and how some Northern
white estate agent had found out that he was the
sole owner of a piece of valuable land and the
Northerner wanted to buy it. At first the man acted
like he smelled a rat, but from the way he gobbled
up the proposition, turns out what he thought he
smelled was some nigger money on his top lip.

"He asked the whereabouts of the land but Black
put him off. He told his cracker that he just wanted
to make sure that he would be interested. The mark
allowed how he was being interested, so Black said
he would tell his friend and they'd get in touch with
him. Black met the mark for about three weeks in
cars and in alleys and kept putting him off until the
white man was almost crazy with anxiety and greed
and then accidentally it seemed Black let drop the
name of the Northern real estate agent who wanted
the property. From that moment on we knew we
had the big fish on the line and all we had to do was
to pull him in.

"We expected him to try to contact our store,
which he did. That cracker went to our setup and
counted on his whiteness to ally him with Spots, our
white boy, but Spots refused to talk about the deal

except to say the land had been thoroughly investigated by the biggest real estate concern in the South and that if our mark did not go around raising dust he would make sure that there would be a nice piece of money in it for him. Any obvious inquiries as to the rightful ownership of the land could alert the state and they would surely push through a law prohibiting the sale. Spots told the mark he would keep in touch with him. The mark went back to the store three or four times but to no avail, then just before we knew he would crack, Black brought me to see him. That fool was as happy as a sissy in a C.C.C. camp. You would have thought my neck was in a noose and he was about to light the fire under my feet. I never enjoyed taking anybody so much.

"Anyhow, I played scary at first but Just Black told me that this was one white man that our people could trust. I said I did not trust no white man because all they wanted was to get a chance to kill a Black man legally and get his wife in the bed. (I'm sorry, Clidell.) The mark assured me that he was the only white man who did not feel like that. Some of his best friends were colored people. In fact, if I didn't know it, the woman who raised him was a colored woman and he still sees her to this day. I let myself be convinced and then the mark began to drag the Northern whites. He told me that they made Negroes sleep in the street in the North and that they had to clean out toilets with their hands in the North and even things worse than that. I was shocked and said, 'Then I don't want to sell my land to that white man who offered seventy-five thousand dollars for it.' Just Black said, 'I wouldn't know what to do with that kind of money,' and I said that all I wanted was to have enough money to buy a home for my old mom, to buy a business and to make one trip to Harlem. The mark asked how much would that cost and I said I reckoned I could do it on fifty thousand dollars.

"The mark told me no Negro was safe with that

kind of money. That white folks would take it from him. I said I knew it but I had to have at least forty thousand dollars. He agreed. We shook hands. I said it would do my heart good to see the mean Yankee go down on some of 'our land.' We met the next morning and I signed the deed in his car and he gave me the cash.

"Black and I had kept most of our things in a hotel over in Hot Springs, Arkansas. When the deal was closed we walked to our car, drove across the state line and on to Hot Springs.

"That's all there was to it."

When he finished, more triumphant stories rainbowed around the room riding the shoulders of laughter. By all accounts those storytellers, born Black and male before the turn of the twentieth century, should have been ground into useless dust. Instead they used their intelligence to pry open the door of rejection and not only became wealthy but got some revenge in the bargain.

It wasn't possible for me to regard them as criminals or be anything but proud of their achievements.

The needs of a society determine its ethics, and in the Black American ghettos the hero is that man who is offered only the crumbs from his country's table but by ingenuity and courage is able to take for himself a Lucullan feast. Hence the janitor who lives in one room but sports a robin's-egg-blue Cadillac is not laughed at but admired, and the domestic who buys forty-dollar shoes is not criticized but is appreciated. We know that they have put to use their full mental and physical powers. Each single gain feeds into the gains of the body collective.

Stories of law violations are weighed on a different set of scales in the Black mind than in the white. Petty crimes embarrass the community and many people wistfully wonder why Negroes don't rob more banks, embezzle more funds and employ graft in the unions. "We are the victims of the world's most comprehensive robbery. Life demands a balance. It's all right if we do a little robbing now." This belief appeals particularly to one who is unable to compete legally with his fellow citizens.

My education and that of my Black associates were quite different from the education of our white schoolmates. In the classroom we all learned past participles, but in the streets and in our homes the Blacks learned to drop *s*'s from plurals and suffixes from past-tense verbs. We were alert to the gap separating the written word from the colloquial. We learned to slide out of one language and into another without being conscious of the effort. At school, in a given situation, we might respond with "That's not unusual." But in the street, meeting the same situation, we easily said, "It be's like that sometimes."

30

JUST LIKE Jane Withers and Donald O'Connor I was going on a vacation. Daddy Bailey invited me to spend the summer with him in southern California and I was jumpy with excitement. Given our father's characteristic air of superiority, I secretly expected him to live in a manor house surrounded by grounds and serviced by a liveried staff.

Mother was all cooperation in helping me to shop for summer clothes. With the haughtiness San Franciscans have for people who live in the warmer climate, she explained that all I needed were lots of shorts, pedal pushers, sandals and blouses because "southern Californians hardly ever wear anything else."

Daddy Bailey had a girl friend, who had begun corresponding with me some months before, and she was to meet me at the train. We had agreed to wear white carnations to identify each other, and the porter kept my flower in the diner's Frigidaire until we reached the small hot town.

On the platform my eyes skimmed over the whites and searched among the Negroes who were walking up and down expectantly. There were no men as tall as Daddy, and no really glamorous ladies (I had decided that given his first choice, all his succeeding women would be startlingly beautiful). I saw a little girl who wore a white flower, but dismissed her as improbable. The platform emptied as we walked by each other time after time. Finally she stopped me with a disbelieving "Marguerite?" Her voice screeched with shock and maturity. So, after all, she wasn't a little girl. I, too, was visited with unbelief.

She said, "I'm Dolores Stockland."

Stunned but trying to be well mannered, I said, "Hello. My name is Marguerite."

Daddy's girl friend? I guessed her to be in her early twenties. Her crisp seersucker suit, spectator pumps and gloves informed me that she was proper and serious. She was of average height but with the unformed body of a girl and I thought that if she was planning to marry our father she must have been horrified to find herself with a nearly six-foot prospective stepdaughter who was not even pretty. (I found later that Daddy Bailey had told her that his children were eight and nine years old and cute as buttons. She had such a need to believe in him that even though we corresponded at a time when I loved the multisyllabic words and convoluted sentences she had been able to ignore the obvious.)

I was another link in a long chain of disappointments. Daddy had promised to marry her but kept delaying until he finally married a woman named Alberta, who was another small tight woman from the South. When I met Dolores she had all the poses of the Black bourgeoisie without the material basis to support the postures. Instead of owning a manor house and servants, Daddy lived in a trailer park on the outskirts of a town that was itself the outskirts of town. Dolores lived there with him and kept the house clean with the orderliness of a coffin. Artificial flowers reposed waxily in glass vases. She was on close terms with her washing machine and ironing board. Her hairdresser could count on absolute fidelity and punctuality. In a word, but for intrusions her life would have been perfect. And then I came along.

She tried hard to make me into something she could reasonably accept. Her first attempt, which failed utterly, concerned my attention to details. I was asked, cajoled, then ordered to care for my room. My willingness to do so was hampered by an abounding ignorance of how it should be done and a fumbling awkwardness with small objects. The dresser in my room was covered with little porcelain white women holding parasols, china dogs, fat-bellied cupids and blown-glass animals of every persuasion. After making the bed, sweeping my room and hanging up the clothes, if and when I remembered to dust the bric-a-brac, I unfailingly held one too tightly and crunched off a leg or two, or too loosely and dropped it, to shatter it into miserable pieces.

Daddy wore his amused impenetrable face constantly. He seemed positively diabolic in his enjoyment of our discomfort. Certainly Dolores adored her outsize lover, and his elocution (Daddy Bailey never spoke, he orated), spiced with the rolling *ers* and *errers*, must have been some consolation to her in their less-than-middle-class home. He worked in the kitchen of a naval hospital and they both said he was a medical dietician for the United States Navy. Their Frigidaire was always stocked with newly acquired pieces of ham, half roasts and quartered chickens. Dad was an excellent cook. He had been in France during World War I and had also worked as doorman at the exclusive Breakers' Hotel; as a result he often made Continental dinners. We sat down frequently to coq au vin, prime ribs au jus, and cotelette Milanese with all the trimmings. His speciality, however, was Mexican food. He traveled across the border weekly to pick up condiments and other supplies that graced our table as pollo en salsa verde and enchilada con carne.

If Dolores had been a little less aloof, a little more earthy, she could have discovered that those ingredients were rife in her town proper, and Dad had no need to travel to Mexico to buy provisions. But she would not be caught so much as looking into one of the crusty Mexican *mercados*, let alone venturing inside its smelliness. And it also sounded ritzy to say, "My husband, Mr. Johnson, the naval dietician, went over to Mexico to buy some things for our dinner." That goes over large with other ritzy people who go to the white area to buy artichokes.

Dad spoke fluent Spanish, and since I had studied for a year we were able to converse slightly. I believe that my talent with a foreign language was the only quality I had that impressed Dolores. Her mouth was too taut and her tongue too still to attempt the strange sounds. Admittedly, though, her English, like everything else about her, was absolutely perfect.

We indulged in a test of strength for weeks as Dad stood figuratively on the sidelines, neither cheering nor booing but enjoying himself greatly. He asked me once if I "er liked errer my mother." I thought he meant my mother, so I answered yes—she was beautiful and gay and very kind. He said he wasn't talking about Vivian, he meant Dolores. Then I explained that I didn't like her because she was mean and petty and full of pretense. He laughed, and when I added she didn't like me because I was so tall and arrogant and wasn't clean enough for her, he laughed harder and said something like "Well, that's life."

One evening he announced that on the next day he was going to Mexico to buy food for the weekend. There was nothing unusual about his pronouncement until he added that he was taking me along. He filled the shocked silence with the information that a trip to Mexico would give me an opportunity to practice Spanish.

Dolores' silence might have been brought on by a jealous reaction, but mine was occasioned by pure surprise. My father had not shown any particular pride in me and very little affection. He had not taken me to his friends or to southern California's few points of interest. It was incredible that I was to be included in something as exotic as a trip to Mexico. Well, I quickly reasoned, I deserved it. After all, I was his daughter and my vacation fell far short of what I had expected a vacation to be. Had I protested that I would like Dolores to go along, we might have been spared a display of violence and near tragedy. But my young mind was filled with self, and my imagination shivered at the prospect of seeing sombreros, rancheros, tortillas and Pancho Villa. We spent a quiet night. Dolores mended her perfect underwear, and I pretended to read a novel. Dad listened to the radio with a drink in his hand and watched what I now know was a pitiful spectacle.

In the morning, we set out on the foreign adventure. The dirt roads of Mexico fulfilled all my longing for the unusual. Only a few miles from California's slick highways and, to me, tall buildings, we were bumping along on gravel streets that could have competed in crudeness with the worst paths in Arkansas, and the landscape boasted adobe huts or cabins walled with corrugated metal. Dogs, lean and dirty, slunk around the houses, and children played innocently in the nude or near nude with discarded rubber tires. Half the population looked like Tyrone Power and Dolores Del Rio, and the other half like Akim Tamiroff and Katina Paxinou, maybe only fatter and older.

Dad gave no explanation as we drove through the border town and headed for the interior. Although surprised, I refused to indulge my curiosity by questioning him. After a few miles we were stopped by a uniformed guard. He and Dad exchanged familiar greetings and Dad got out of the car. He reached back into the pocket of the door and took a bottle of liquor into the guard's kiosk. They laughed and talked for over a half hour as I sat in the car and tried to translate the muffled sounds. Eventually they came out and walked to the car. Dad still had the bottle but it was only half full. He asked the guard if he would like to marry me. Their Spanish was choppier than my school version but I understood. My father added as an inducement the fact that I was only fifteen years old. At once the guard leaned into the car and caressed my cheek. I supposed that he thought before that I was not only ugly but old, too, and that now the knowledge that I was probably unused attracted him. He told Dad that he would marry me and we would have "many babies." My father found that promise the funniest thing he had heard since we left home. (He had laughed uproariously when Dolores didn't answer my goodbye and I explained as we drove away that she hadn't heard.) The guard was not discouraged by my attempts to get away from his probing hands and I would have squirmed to the driver's seat had not Dad opened the door and got in. After many *adiós*'s and *bonita*s and *esposita*s Dad started the car, and we were on our grimy way again.

Signs informed me that we were headed for Ensenada. In those miles, along the twisted roads beside the steep mountain, I feared that I would never get back to America, civilization, English and wide streets again. He sipped from the bottle and sang snatches of Mexican songs as we climbed the tortuous mountain road. Our destination turned out not to be the town of Ensenada, after all, but about five miles out of the city limits. We pulled up in the dirt yard of a *cantina* where half-clothed children chased mean-looking chickens around and around. The noise of the car brought women to the door of the ramshackle building but didn't distract the single-minded activity of either the grubby kids or the scrawny fowls.

A woman's voice sang out, "Baylee, Baylee." And suddenly a claque of women crowded to the door and overflowed into the yard. Dad told me to get out of the car and we went to meet the women. He explained quickly that I was his daughter, which everyone thought to be uncontrollably funny. We were herded into a long room with a bar at one end. Tables sat lopsidedly on a loose-plank floor. The ceiling caught and held my attention. Paper streamers in every possible color waved in the near-still air, and as I watched a few fell to the floor. No one seemed to notice, or if they did, it was obviously unimportant that their sky was falling in. There were a few men on stools at the bar, and they greeted my father with the ease of familiarity. I was taken around and each person was told my name and age. The formal high school "*Cómo está usted?*" was received as the most charming utterance possible. People clapped me on the back, shook Dad's hand and spoke a rat-a-tat Spanish that I was unable to follow. Baylee was the hero of the hour, and as he warmed under the uninhibited show of affection I saw a new side of the man. His quizzical smile disappeared and he stopped his affected way of talking (it would have been difficult to wedge *er*s into that rapid Spanish).

It seemed hard to believe that he was a lonely person, searching relentlessly in bottles, under women's skirts, in church work and lofty job titles for his "personal niche," lost before birth and unrecovered since. It was obvious to me then that he had never belonged in Stamps, and less to the slow-moving, slow-thinking Johnson family. How maddening it was to have been born in a cotton field with aspirations of grandeur.

In the Mexican bar, Dad had an air of relaxation which I had never seen visit him before. There was no need to pretend in front of those Mexican peasants. As he was, just being himself, he was sufficiently impressive to them. He was an American. He was Black. He spoke Spanish fluently. He had money and he could drink tequila with the best of them. The women liked him too. He was tall and handsome and generous.

It was a fiesta party. Someone put money in the jukebox and drinks were served to all the customers. I was given a warm Coca-Cola. The music poured out of the record machine as high-tenored voices wavered and held, wavered and held for the passionate rancheros. Men danced, at first alone, then with each other and occasionally a woman would join the foot-stomping rites. I was asked to dance. I hesitated because I wasn't sure I'd be able to follow the steps, but Dad nodded and encouraged me to try. I had been enjoying myself for at least an hour before I realized it. One young man had taught me how to put a sticker on the ceiling. First, all the sugar must be chewed out of Mexican gum, then the bartender gives a few slips of paper to the aspirant, who writes either a proverb or a sentimental remark on the strip. He takes the soft gum from his mouth and sticks it to the end of the streamer. Choosing a less densely covered area of the ceiling he aims at the spot, and as he throws he lets out a bloodcurdling scream which would not be out of place in a bronco-busting rodeo. After a few squeaky misses, I overcame my reserve and tore my tonsils loose with a yell that would have been worthy of Zapata. I was happy, Dad was proud and my new friends were gracious. A woman brought *chicharrones* (in the South they're called cracklings) in a greasy newspaper. I ate the fried pig skins, danced, screamed and drank the extra-sweet and sticky Coca-Cola with the nearest approach to abandonment I had ever experienced. As new revelers joined the celebration I was introduced as la niña de Baylee, and as quickly accepted. The afternoon sun failed in its attempt to

light the room through the single window, and the
press of bodies and scents and sounds melted to give
us an aromatic and artificial twilight. I realized that
I hadn't seen my father for some time. "*Dónde
está mi padre?*" I asked my dancing partner. My
formal Spanish must have sounded as pretentious to
the ears of the paisano as "Whither goeth my sire?"
would have sounded to a semi-literate Ozark moun-
taineer. In any case it brought on a howl of laughter,
a bear-crushing embrace and no answer. When the
dance was finished, I made my way through the
squeeze of the people as unobtrusively as possible. A
fog of panic nearly suffocated me. He wasn't in the
room. Had he made an arrangement with the guard
back at the pass? I would not put it beyond him. My
drink had been spiked. The certainty made my
knees weak, and dancing couples blurred before my
eyes. Dad was gone. He was probably halfway back
home with the money from my sale in his pocket. I
had to get to the door, which seemed miles and
mountains away. People stopped me with "*Dónde
vas?*" My response was something as stiff and double meaning as "*Yo voy por ventilarme,*" or "I am
going to air out." No wonder I was a big hit.

Seen through the open door Dad's Hudson sat in
lonely splendor. He hadn't left me, after all. That
meant, of course, that I hadn't been drugged. I
immediately felt better. No one followed me into
the yard where the late afternoon sun had tenderized the midday harshness. I decided to sit in his car
and wait for him since he couldn't have gone far. I
knew he was with a woman, and the more I thought
about it, it was easy to figure which one of the gay
señoritas he had taken away. There had been a
small neat woman with very red lips who clung to
him avidly when we first arrived. I hadn't thought of
it at the time but had simply recorded her pleasure.
In the car, in reflection, I played the scene back.
She had been the first to rush to him, and that was
when he quickly said "This is my daughter" and

"She speaks Spanish." If Dolores knew, she would crawl up in her blanket of affectations and die circumspectly. The thought of her mortification kept me company for a long time, but the sounds of music and laughter and Cisco Kid screams broke into my pleasant revengeful reveries. It was, after all, getting dark and Dad must have been beyond my reach in one of the little cabins out back. An awkward fear crept up slowly as I contemplated sitting in the car all night alone. It was a fear distantly related to the earlier panic. Terror did not engulf me wholly, but crawled along my mind like a tedious paralysis. I could roll up the windows and lock the door. I could lie down on the floor of the car and make myself small and invisible. Impossible! I tried to staunch the flood of fear. Why was I afraid of the Mexicans? After all, they had been kind to me and surely my father wouldn't allow his daughter to be ill treated. Wouldn't he? Would he? How could he leave me in that raunchy bar and go off with his woman? Did he care what happened to me? Not a damn, I decided, and opened the flood gates for hysteria. Once the tears began, there was no stopping them. I was to die, after all, in a Mexican dirt yard. The special person that I was, the intelligent mind that God and I had created together, was to depart this life without recognition or contribution. How pitiless were the Fates and how helpless was this poor Black girl.

I made out his shadow in the near gloom and was about to jump out and run to him when I noticed that he was being propelled by the small woman I had seen earlier and a man. He wobbled and lurched but they held him up firmly and guided his staggering toward the door of the *cantina*. Once he got inside we might never leave. I got out of the car and went to them. I asked Dad if he wouldn't like to get into the car and rest a little. He focused enough to recognize me and answered that that was exactly what he wanted; he was a little tired and he'd like to rest before we set out for his place. He told his friends his wishes in Spanish and they steered him to the car. When I opened the front door he said No, he'd lie down on the back seat for a little while. We got him into the car and tried to arrange his long legs comfortably. He began snoring even as we tugged at him. It sounded like the beginning of a deep and long sleep, and a warning that, after all, we were to spend the night in the car, in Mexico.

I thought fast as the couple laughed and jabbered at me in incomprehensible Spanish. I had never driven a car before, but I had watched carefully and my mother was declared to be the best driver in San Francisco. *She* declared it, at least. I was superbly intelligent and had good physical coordination. Of course I could drive. Idiots and lunatics drove cars, why not the brilliant Marguerite Johnson? I asked the Mexican man to turn the car around, again in my exquisite high school Spanish, and it took about fifteen minutes to make myself understood. The man must have asked me if I could drive, but I didn't know the Spanish for the verb "to drive," so I kept repeating "*Si, si*" and "*Gracias*" until he got in and headed the car toward the highway. He showed his understanding of the situation by his next action. He left the motor running. I put my foot on the accelerator and clutch, jiggled the gear-shift and raised both feet. With an ominous roar we leaped out of the yard.

As we shook onto the shelf of the road the car nearly stalled and I stamped both feet again on the pedal and clutch. We made no progress and an awful amount of noise, but the motor didn't stop. I understood then that in order to go forward I would have to lift my feet off the pedals, and if I did so abruptly the car would shake like a person with St. Vitus Dance. With that complete understanding of the principle of motor locomotion, I drove down the mountainside toward Calexico, some fifty miles away. It is hard to understand why my vivid imagination and tendency toward scariness didn't provide me with gory scenes of bloody crashes on a *risco de Mexico*. I can only think that my every sense was concentrated on steering the bucking car.

When it became totally dark, I fumbled over knobs, twisting and pulling until I succeeded in finding the lights. The car slowed down as I centered on that search, and I forgot to step on the pedals, and the motor gurgled, the car pitched and the engine stopped. A bumbling sound from the back told me that Dad had fallen off the seat (I had been expecting this to happen for miles). I pulled the hand brake and carefully considered my next move. It was useless to think of asking Dad. The fall on the floor had failed to stir him, and I would be unable to do so. No car was likely to pass us—I hadn't seen any motor vehicles since we passed the guard's house early in the day. We were headed downhill, so I reasoned that with any luck we might coast right up to Calexico—or at least to the guard. I waited until I formulated an approach to him before releasing the brake. I would stop the car when we reached the kiosk and put on my siddity air. I would speak to him like the peasant he was. I would order him to start the car and then tip him a quarter or even a dollar from Dad's pocket before driving on.

With my plans solidly made, I released the brake and we began coasting down the slope. I also pumped the clutch and the accelerator, hoping that the action would speed our descent, and wonder of wonders the motor started again. The Hudson went crazy on the hill. It was rebelling and would have leaped over the side of the mountain, to all our destruction, in its attempt to unseat me had I relaxed control for a single second. The challenge was exhilarating. It was me, Marguerite, against the elemental opposition. As I twisted the steering wheel and forced the accelerator to the floor I was controlling Mexico, and might and aloneness and inexperienced youth and Bailey Johnson, Sr., and death and insecurity, and even gravity.

After what seemed like one thousand and one nights of challenge the mountain began to level off and we started passing scattered lights on either side of the road. No matter what happened after that I had won. The car began to slow down as if it had been tamed and was going to give up without grace. I pumped even harder and we finally reached the guard's box. I pulled on the hand brake and came to a stop. There would be no need for me to speak to the guard since the motor was running, but I had to wait until he looked into the car and gave me the signal to continue. He was busy talking to people in a car facing the mountain I had just conquered. The light from his hut showed him bent from the waist with his upper torso completely swallowed by the mouth of the open window. I held the car in instant readiness for the next lap of our journey. When the guard unfolded himself and stood erect I was able to see he was not the same man of the morning's embarrassment. I was understandably taken aback at the discovery and when he saluted sharply and barked "*Pasa*" I released the brake, put both feet down and lifted them a bit too sharply. The car outran my intention. It leaped not only forward but left as well, and with a few angry spurts propelled itself onto the side of the car just pulling off. The crash of scraping metal was followed immediately by a volley of Spanish hurled at me from all directions. Again, strangely enough, fear was absent from my sensations. I wondered in this order: was I hurt, was anyone else hurt, would I go to jail, what were the Mexicans saying, and finally, had Dad awakened? I was able to answer the first and last concern promptly. Buoyed by the adrenalin that had flooded my brain as we careened down the mountainside, I had never felt better, and my father's snores cut through the cacophony of protestations outside my window. I got out of the car, intending

to ask for the *policías*, but the guard beat me to the
punch. He said a few words, which were strung
together like beads, but one of them was *policías*.
As the people in the other car fumbled out, I tried
to recover my control and said loudly and too gra-
ciously, "*Gracias, señor.*" The family, some eight or
more people of every age and size, walked around
me, talking heatedly and sizing me up as if I might
have been a statue in a city park and they were a
flock of pigeons. One said "*Joven,*" meaning I was
young. I tried to see which one was so intelligent.
I would direct my conversation to him or her, but
they shifted positions so quickly it was impossible to
make the person out. Then another suggested "*Bor-
racho.*" Well, certainly, I must have smelled like a
tequila farm, since Dad had been breathing out the
liquor in noisy respirations and I had kept the windows closed against the cold night air. It wasn't
likely that I would explain that to these strangers
even if I could. Which I couldn't. Someone got the
idea to look into the car, and a scream brought us all
up short. People—they seemed to be in the hundreds—crowded to the windows and more screams
erupted. I thought for a minute that something awful might have happened. Maybe at the time of the
crash ... I, too, pushed to the window to see, but
then I remembered the rhythmic snores, and coolly
walked away. The guard must have thought he had
a major crime on his hands. He made moves and
sounds like "Watch her" or "Don't let her out of your
sight." The family came back, this time not as close
but more menacing, and when I was able to sort out
one coherent question, "*Quién es?*" I answered dryly and with all the detachment I could summon, "*Mi
padre.*" Being a people of close family ties and
weekly fiestas they suddenly understood the situation. I was a poor little girl thing who was caring for
my drunken father, who had stayed too long at the
fair. *Pobrecita.*

The guard, the father and one or two small chil-

dren began the herculean job of waking Dad. I
watched coolly as the remaining people paraded,
making figure eights around me and their badly
bruised automobile. The two men shook and tugged
and pulled while the children jumped up and down
on my father's chest. I credit the children's action for
the success of the effort. Bailey Johnson, Sr., woke
up in Spanish. "*Qué tiene? Qué pasa? Qué qui-
ere?*" Anyone else would have asked, "Where am I?"
Obviously, this was a common Mexican experience.
When I saw he was fairly lucid I went to the car,
calmly pushed the people away, and said from the
haughty level of one who has successfully brought to
heel a marauding car and negotiated a sneaky
mountain, "Dad, there's been an accident." He recognized me by degrees and became my pre-Mexican-
fiesta father.

"An accident, huh? Er, who was at fault? You,
Marguerite? Errer was it you?"

It would have been futile to tell him of my master-
ing his car and driving it nearly fifty miles. I didn't
expect or even need, now, his approbation.

"Yes, Dad, I ran into a car."

He still hadn't sat up completely, so he couldn't
know where we were. But from the floor where he
rested, as if that was the logical place to be, he said,
"In the glove compartment. The insurance papers.
Get them and er give them to the police, and then
come back."

The guard stuck his head in the other door before
I could form a scathing but polite response. He asked
Dad to get out of the car. Never at a loss, my father
reached in the glove compartment, and took out the
folded papers and the half bottle of liquor he had
left there earlier. He gave the guard one of his
pinch-backed laughs, and descended, by joints, from
the car. Once on the ground he towered over the
angry people. He took a quick reading of his location
and the situation, and then put his arm around the
other driver's shoulder. He kindly, not in the least

condescendingly, bent to speak to the guard, and
the three men walked into the hut. Within easy
minutes, laughter burst from the shack and the crisis
was over, but so was the enjoyment.

Dad shook hands with all the men, patted the
children and smiled winsomely at the women. Then,
and without looking at the damaged cars, he eased
himself behind the steering wheel. He called me to
get in, and as if he had not been helplessly drunk a
half hour earlier, he drove unerringly toward home.
He said he didn't know I could drive, and how did I
like his car? I was angry that he had recovered so
quickly and felt let down that he didn't appreciate
the greatness of my achievement. So I answered yes
to both the statement and the question. Before we
reached the border he rolled down the window, and
the fresh air, which was welcome, was uncom-
fortably cold. He told me to get his jacket from the
back seat and put it on. We drove into the city in a
cold and private silence.

31

DOLORES WAS SITTING, it seemed, in the same place as
the night before. Her pose was so similar it was hard
to believe she had gone to sleep, eaten breakfast or
even patted her firm hairdo. Dad said sportily, "Hello, kid," and walked toward the bathroom. I greeted
her: "Hello, Dolores" (we had long dropped the
pretense of familial relationship). She responded,
briefly but politely, and threaded her attention
through the eye of her needle. She was now
prudently making cute kitchen curtains, which
would soon starchily oppose the wind. Having nothing more to say, I went to my room. Within minutes
an argument ensued in the living area that was as
audible to me as if the separating walls were muslin
sheets.

charge, I would not be able to live, to continue to live with Mother, and I so wanted to.

I walked to Dolores, enraged at the threat. "I'm going to slap you for that, you silly old bitch." I warned her and I slapped her. She was out of the chair like a flea, and before I could jump back she had her arms around me. Her hair was under my chin and she wrapped her arms, it seemed two or three times, around my waist. I had to push her shoulders with all my strength to unlock the octopus hold. Neither of us made a sound until I finally shoved her back onto the sofa. Then she started screaming. Silly old fool. What did she expect if she called my mother a whore? I walked out of the house. On the steps I felt something wet on my arm and looked down to find blood. Her screams still sailed through the evening air like skipping stones, but I was bleeding. I looked carefully on my arm, but there was no cut. I put my arm back to my waist and it brought fresh blood as I pulled it away. I *was* cut. Before I could fully understand, or comprehend enough to respond, Dolores opened the door, screaming still, and upon seeing me, instead of slamming the door she ran like a mad woman down the stairs. I saw a hammer in her hand, and without wondering if I would be able to take it from her, I fled. Dad's car sat in a yard twice in one day offering magnificent refuge. I jumped in, rolled up the windows and locked the door. Dolores flitted around the car, screaming like a banshee, her face bedizened with fury.

Daddy Bailey and the neighbors he was visiting responded to the screams and crowded around her. She shouted that I had jumped on her and tried to kill her and Bailey had better not bring me back in the house. I sat in the car, feeling the blood slip down to my buttocks as the people quieted and cooled her rage. My father motioned to me to open the window, and when I did he said he would take

Dolores inside but I should stay in the car. He would be back to attend to me.

The events of the day swarmed over me and made my breathing difficult. After all the decisive victories of the day my life was to end in sticky death. If Dad stayed a very long time in the house, I was too afraid to go to the door and ask for him, and besides, my feminine training would not allow me to walk two steps with blood on my dress. As I had always feared, no, known, the trials had been for nothing. (The dread of futility has been my life-long plague.) Excitement, apprehension, release and anger had drained me of mobility. I waited for Fate, the string puller, to dictate my movements.

My father came down the steps in a few minutes and angrily slammed into the car. He sat in a corner of blood and I gave no warning. He must have been pondering what to do with me when he felt the damp on his trousers.

"What the hell is this?" He hunched himself up on a hip and brushed the pants. His hand showed red in the porch's cast-off light. "What is this, Marguerite?"

I said with a coldness that would have done him proud, "I've been cut."

"What do you mean, cut?"

It only lasted a precious minute, but I managed once to see my father perplexed.

"Cut." It was so delicious. I didn't mind draining away into the plaid seat cushions.

"When ? By whom?"

Daddy, even in a critical moment, wouldn't say "By who?"

"Dolores cut me." The economy of words showed my contempt for them all.

"How badly?"

I would have reminded him that I was no doctor and therefore was ill equipped to do a thorough examination, but impudence would have diminished my lead.

"I don't know."

He put the car in gear, smoothly, and I enviously realized that although I had driven his car I didn't know how to drive.

I thought we were en route to an emergency hospital, and so with serenity I made plans for my death and will. As I faded into time's dateless night, I would say to the doctor, "The moving finger writes and having writ, moves on . . ." and my soul would escape gracefully. Bailey was to have my books, my Lester Young records and my love from the next world. I had groggily surrendered myself to oblivion when the car stopped.

Dad said, "O.K., kid, errer let's go."

We were in a strange driveway, and even before I got out of the car he was on the steps of a typical southern California ranch-type house. The doorbell chimed, and he beckoned me up the steps. When the door opened he signaled me to stand outside. After all, I was dripping, and I could see the living room was carpeted. Dad went in but didn't quite close the door, and a few minutes later a woman called to me in a whisper from the side of the house. I followed her into a recreation room, and she asked me where I was hurt. She was quiet and her concern seemed sincere. I pulled off my dress and we both looked into the open flesh on my side. She was as pleased as I was disappointed that the edges of the wound had begun to clot. She washed witch hazel over the rupture and taped me tightly with extra-long Band-Aids. Then we went into the living room. Dad shook hands with the man he'd been talking to and thanked my emergency nurse and we left.

In the car he explained that the couple were his friends and he had asked the wife to look at me. He said he told her if the laceration wasn't too deep he would be grateful if she treated it. Otherwise he'd have to take me to a hospital. Could I imagine the scandal if people found out that his, Bailey Johnson's, daughter had been cut by his lady friend? He was after all a Mason, an Elk, a naval dietician and the first Negro deacon in the Lutheran church. No Negro in the city would be able to hold his head up if our misfortune became common knowledge. While the lady (I never knew her name) dressed my wound he had telephoned other friends and made arrangements for me to spend the night with them. At another strange trailer, in yet another mobile park, I was taken in and given night clothes and a bed. Dad said he'd see me around noon the next day.

I went to bed and slept as if my death wish had come true. In the morning neither the empty and unfamiliar surroundings nor the stiffness of my side bothered me. I made and ate a big breakfast and sat down with a slick magazine to wait for Dad.

At fifteen life had taught me undeniably that surrender, in its place, was as honorable as resistance, especially if one had no choice.

When my father came, with a jacket thrown over the striped cotton uniform he wore as a naval dietician, he asked how I felt, gave me a dollar and a half and a kiss, and said he'd drop by late in the evening. He laughed as usual. Nervous?

Alone, I imagined the owners returning to find me in their house, and realized that I didn't even remember what they looked like. How could I bear their contempt or their pity? If I disappeared Dad would be relieved, not to mention Dolores. I hesitated nearly too long. What would I do? Did I have the nerve to commit suicide? If I jumped in the ocean wouldn't I come up all bloated like the man Bailey saw in Stamps? The thought of my brother made me pause. What would he do? I waited a patience and another patience and then he ordered me to leave. But don't kill yourself. You can always do that if things get bad enough.

I made a few tuna sandwiches, lumpy with pickles, put a Band-Aid supply in my pocket, counted my money (I had over three dollars plus some Mexican coins) and walked out. When I heard the door slam I knew the decision had jelled. I had no key and nothing on earth would induce me to stand around until Dad's friends returned to pityingly let me back in.

Now that I was out free, I set to thinking of my future. The obvious solution to my homelessness concerned me only briefly. I could go home to Mother, but I couldn't. I could never succeed in shielding the gash in my side from her. She was too perceptive not to notice the crusty Band-Aids and my favoring the wound. And if I failed to hide the wound we were certain to experience another scene of violence. I thought of poor Mr. Freeman, and the guilt which lined my heart, even after all those years, was a nagging passenger in my mind.

32

I SPENT THE DAY wandering aimlessly through the bright streets. The noisy penny arcades with their gaggle-giggle of sailors and children and the games of chance were tempting, but after walking through one of them it was obvious that I could only win more chances and no money. I went to the library and used a part of my day reading science fiction, and in its marble washroom I changed my bandage.

On one flat street I passed a junkyard, littered with the carcasses of old cars. The dead hulks were somehow so uninviting that I decided to inspect them. As I wound my way through the discards a temporary solution sprang to my mind. I would find a clean or cleanish car and spend the night in it. With the optimism of ignorance I thought that the morning was bound to bring a more pleasant solution. A tall-bodied gray car near the fence caught my eye. Its seats were untorn, and although it had no wheels or rims it sat evenly on its fenders. The

idea of sleeping in the near open bolstered my sense
of freedom. I was a loose kite in a gentle wind
floating with only my will for an anchor. After de-
ciding upon the car, I got inside and ate the tuna
sandwiches and then searched the floorboards for
holes. The fear that rats might scurry in and eat off
my nose as I slept (some cases had been recently
reported in the papers) was more alarming than the
shadowed hulks in the junkyard or the quickly descending night. My gray choice, however, seemed
rat-tight, and I abandoned my idea of taking another walk and decided to sit steady and wait for sleep.

My car was an island and the junkyard a sea, and
I was all alone and full of warm. The mainland was
just a decision away. As evening became definite the
street lamps flashed on and the lights of moving cars
squared my world in a piercing probing. I counted
the headlights and said my prayers and fell asleep.

The morning's brightness drew me awake and I
was surrounded with strangeness. I had slid down
the seat and slept the night through in an ungainly
position. Wrestling with my body to assume an upward arrangement, I saw a collage of Negro, Mexican and white faces outside the windows. They
were laughing and making the mouth gestures of
talkers but their sounds didn't penetrate my refuge.
There was so much curiosity evident in their
features that I knew they wouldn't just go away
before they knew who I was, so I opened the door,
prepared to give them any story (even the truth)
that would buy my peace.

The windows and my grogginess had distorted
their features. I had thought they were adults and
maybe citizens of Brobdingnag, at least. Standing
outside, I found there was only one person taller
than I, and that I was only a few years younger than
any of them. I was asked my name, where I came
from and what led me to the junkyard. They accepted my explanation that I was from San Francisco, that my name was Marguerite but that I was

called Maya and I simply had no place to stay. With a generous gesture the tall boy, who said he was Bootsie, welcomed me, and said I could stay as long as I honored their rule: No two people of opposite sex slept together. In fact, unless it rained, everyone had his own private sleeping accommodations. Since some of the cars leaked, bad weather forced a doubling up. There was no stealing, not for reasons of morality but because a crime would bring the police to the yard; and since everyone was underage, there was the likelihood that they'd be sent off to foster homes or juvenile delinquent courts. Everyone worked at something. Most of the girls collected bottles and worked weekends in greasy spoons. The boys mowed lawns, swept out pool halls and ran errands for small Negro-owned stores. All money was held by Bootsie and used communally.

During the month that I spent in the yard I learned to drive (one boy's older brother owned a car that moved), to curse and to dance. Lee Arthur was the only boy who ran around with the gang but lived at home with his mother. Mrs. Arthur worked nights, so on Friday evening all the girls went to his house for a bath. We did our laundry in the Laundromat, but those things that required ironing were taken to Lee's house and the ironing chore was shared, as was everything else.

On Saturday night we entered the jitterbug contest at the Silver Slipper, whether we could dance or not. The prizes were tempting ($25 to first couple, $10 to second and $5 to third), and Bootsie reasoned that if all of us entered we had a better chance. Juan, the Mexican boy, was my partner, and although he couldn't dance any better than I, we were a sensation on the floor. He was very short with a shock of straight black hair that swished around his head when he pivoted, and I was thin and black and tall as a tree. On my last weekend at the yard, we actually won the second prize. The dance we performed could never be duplicated or described except to say that the passion with which we threw each other around the small dance area was similar to the zeal shown in honest wrestling matches and hand-to-hand combat.

After a month my thinking processes had so changed that I was hardly recognizable to myself. The unquestioning acceptance by my peers had dislodged the familiar insecurity. Odd that the homeless children, the silt of war frenzy, could initiate me into the brotherhood of man. After hunting down unbroken bottles and selling them with a white girl from Missouri, a Mexican girl from Los Angeles and a Black girl from Oklahoma, I was never again to sense myself so solidly outside the pale of the human race. The lack of criticism evidenced by our ad hoc community influenced me, and set a tone of tolerance for my life.

I telephoned Mother (her voice reminded me of another world) and asked her to send for me. When she said she was going to send my air ticket to Daddy, I explained that it would be easier if she simply sent my fare to the airline, then I'd pick it up. With the easy grace characteristic of Mother when she was given a chance to be magnanimous she agreed.

The unrestrained life we had led made me believe that my new friends would be undemonstrative about my leaving. I was right. After I picked up my ticket I announced rather casually that I would be leaving the following day. My revelation was accepted with at least the equal amount of detachment (only it was not a pose) and everyone wished me well. I didn't want to say goodbye to the junkyard or to my car, so I spent my last night at an all-night movie. One girl, whose name and face have melted into the years, gave me "an all-enduring friendship ring," and Juan gave me a black lace handkerchief just in case I wanted to go to church sometime.

I arrived in San Francisco, leaner than usual, fairly unkempt, and with no luggage. Mother took one look and said, "Is the rationing that bad at your father's? You'd better have some food to stick to all those bones." She, as she called it, turned to, and soon I sat at a clothed table with bowls of food, expressly cooked for me.

I was at a home, again. And my mother was a fine lady. Dolores was a fool and, more important, a liar.

33

THE HOUSE SEEMED smaller and quieter after the trip south, and the first bloom of San Francisco's glamour had dulled around the edges. Adults had lost the wisdom from the surface of their faces. I reasoned that I had given up some youth for knowledge, but my gain was more valuable than the loss.

Bailey was much older too. Even years older than I had become. He had made friends during that youth-shattering summer with a group of slick street boys. His language had changed. He was forever dropping slangy terms into his sentences like dumplings in a pot. He may have been glad to see me, but he didn't act much like it. When I tried to tell him of my adventures and misadventures, he responded with a casual indifference which stilled the tale on my lips. His new companions cluttered the living room and halls wearing zoot suits and wide-brimmed hats and dangling long snaky chains hooked at their belts. They drank sloe gin secretly and told dirty jokes. Although I had no regrets, I told myself sadly that growing up was not the painless process one would have thought it to be.

In one area my brother and I found ourselves closer. I had gotten the knack of public dancing. All the lessons with Mother, who danced so effortlessly, had not borne immediate fruit. But with my newly and dearly bought assurance I could give myself up to the rhythms and let them propel me where they willed.

Mother allowed us to go to the big band dances in the crowded city auditorium. We danced the jitterbug to Count Basie, the Lindy and the Big Apple to Cab Calloway, and the Half Time Texas Hop to Duke Ellington. In a matter of months cute Bailey and his tall sister were famous as those dancing fools (which was an apt description).

Although I had risked my life (not intentionally) in her defense, Mother's reputation, good name and community image ceased, or nearly ceased, being of interest to me. It was not that I cared for her less but that I concerned myself less about everything and everyone. I often thought of the tedium of life once one had seen all its surprises. In two months, I had become blasé.

Mother and Bailey were entangled in the Oedipal skein. Neither could do without or do with the other; yet the constrictions of conscience and society, morality and ethos dictated a separation. On some flimsy excuse, Mother ordered Bailey out of the house. On an equally flimsy excuse he complied. Bailey was sixteen, small for his age, bright for any and hopelessly in love with Mother Dear. Her heroes were her friends and her friends were big men in the rackets. They wore two-hundred-dollar Chesterfield coats, Busch shoes at fifty dollars a pair, and Knox hats. Their shirts were monogrammed and their fingernails manicured. How could a sixteen-year-old boy hope to compete with such overshadowing rivals? He did what he had to do. He acquired a withered white prostitute, a diamond ring on his little finger and a Harris tweed coat with raglan sleeves. He didn't consciously consider the new possessions the open sesame to Mother Dear's vault of acceptance. And she had no idea that her preferences prodded him to such excesses.

From the wings I heard and watched the pavane

of tragedy move steadily toward its climax. Interception and even the thought of it was impossible. Easier to plan an obstruction to a sunrise or a hurricane. If Mother was a beautiful woman who exacted the tribute of obeisance from all men, she was also a mother, and "a damn good one." No son of hers was going to be exploited by a used-up white whore, who wanted to milk him of his youth and spoil him for adulthood. Hell, no.

Bailey, for his part, was her son and she was his mother. He had no intention of taking low even from the most beautiful woman in the world. The fact that she happened to be his mother did nothing to weaken his resolve.

Get out? Oh, hell, yes. Tomorrow? What's wrong with today? Today? What about right now? But neither could move until all the measured steps had been negotiated.

During the weeks of bitter wrangling I sat in hopeless wonder. We were not allowed profanity or even obvious sarcasm, but Bailey looped his language around his tongue and issued it out to Mother in alum drops. She threw her "ing bings" (passionate explosions guaranteed to depilate the chest of the strongest man) and was sweetly sorry (only to me) after.

I had been left out of their power/love struggles. It would be more correct to say that since neither needed a claque I was forgotten on the sidelines.

It was a little like Switzerland in World War II. Shells were bursting all around me, souls were tortured and I was powerless in the confines of imposed neutrality—hopes were dying. The confrontation, which brought relief, had come on an ordinary unheralded evening. It was after eleven o'clock, so I left my door ajar, hoping to hear Mother go out, or the creak of Bailey easing up the stairs.

The record player on the first floor volumed up Lonnie Johnson singing, "Tomorrow night, will you remember what you said tonight?" Glasses clinked and voices rubbed each other. A party was shimmering below and Bailey had defied Mother's eleven o'clock curfew. If he made it in before midnight, she might be satisfied with slapping him across the face a few times with her lashing words.

Twelve o'clock came and went at once, and I sat up in bed and laid my cards out for the first of many games of solitaire.

"Bailey!"

My watch hands made the uneven V of one o'clock.

"Yes, Mother Dear?" En garde. His voice thrust sweet and sour, and he accented the "dear."

"I guess you're a man ... Turn down that record player." She shouted the last to the revelers.

"I'm your son, Mother Dear." A swift parry.

"Is it eleven o'clock, Bailey?" That was a feint, designed to catch the opponent offguard.

"It's after one o'clock, Mother Dear." He had opened up the game, and the strokes from then on would have to be direct.

"Clidell is the only man in this house, and if you think you're so much of a man ..." Her voice popped like a razor on a strap.

"I'm leaving now, Mother Dear." The deferential tone heightened the content of his announcement. In a bloodless coup he had thrust beneath her visor.

Now, laid open, she had no recourse but to hurry along the tunnel of her anger, headlong.

"Then Goddammit, get your heels to clicking." And her heels were clicking down the linoleum hall as Bailey tap-danced up the stairs to his room.

When rain comes finally, washing away a low sky of muddy ocher, we who could not control the phenomenon are pressed into relief. The near-occult feeling: The fact of being witness to the end of the world gives way to tangible things. Even if the succeeding sensations are not common, they are at least not mysterious.

Bailey was leaving home. At one o'clock in the morning, my little brother, who in my lonely days of inferno dwelling had protected me from goblins, gnomes, gremlins and the devils, was leaving home.

I had known all along the inevitable outcome and that I dared not poke into his knapsack of misery, even with the offer to help him carry it.

I went to his room, against my judgment, and found him throwing his carefully tended clothes into a pillowcase. His maturity embarrassed me. In his little face, balled up like a fist, I found no vestige of my brother, and when, not knowing what to say, I asked if I could help, he answered, "Leave me the shit alone."

I leaned on the doorjamb, lending him my physical presence but said no more.

"She wants me out, does she? Well, I'll get out of here so fast I'll leave the air on fire. She calls herself a mother? Huh! I'll be damned. She's seen the last of me. I can make it. I'll always make it."

At some point he noticed me still in the doorway, and his consciousness stretched to remember our relationship.

"Maya, if you want to leave now, come on. I'll take care of you."

He didn't wait for an answer, but as quickly went back to speaking to his soul. "She won't miss me, and I sure as hell won't miss her. To hell with her and everybody else."

He had finished jamming his shoes on top of his shirts and ties, and socks were wadded into the pillowcase. He remembered me again.

"Maya, you can have my books."

My tears were not for Bailey or Mother or even myself but for the helplessness of mortals who live on the sufferance of Life. In order to avoid this bitter end, we would all have to be born again, and born with the knowledge of alternatives. Even then?

Bailey grabbed up the lumpy pillowcase and pushed by me for the stairs. As the front door slammed, the record player downstairs mastered the house and Nat King Cole warned the world to "straighten up and fly right." As if they could, as if human beings could make a choice.

Mother's eyes were red, and her face puffy, the next morning, but she smiled her "everything is everything" smile and turned in tight little moons, making breakfast, talking business and brightening the corner where she was. No one mentioned Bailey's absence as if things were as they should be and always were.

The house was smudged with unspoken thoughts and it was necessary to go to my room to breathe. I believed I knew where he headed the night before, and made up my mind to find him and offer him my support. In the afternoon I went to a bay-windowed house which boasted ROOMS, in green and orange letters, through the glass. A woman of any age past thirty answered my ring and said Bailey Johnson was at the top of the stairs.

His eyes were as red as Mother's had been, but his face had loosened a little from the tightness of the night before. In an almost formal manner I was invited into a room with a clean chenille-covered bed, an easy chair, a gas fireplace and a table.

He began to talk, covering up the unusual situation that we found ourselves in.

"Nice room, isn't it? You know it's very hard to find rooms now. The war and all ... Betty lives here [she was the white prostitute] and she got this place for me ... Maya, you know, it's better this way ... I mean, I'm a man, and I have to be on my own ..."

I was furious that he didn't curse and abuse the Fates or Mother or at least act put upon.

"Well"—I thought to start it—"If Mother was really a mother, she wouldn't have——"

He stopped me, his little black hand held up as if I were to read his palm. "Wait, Maya, she was right. There is a tide and time in every man's life——"

"Bailey, you're sixteen."

"Chronologically, yes, but I haven't been sixteen for years. Anyway, there comes a time when a man must cut the apron strings and face life on his own ... As I was saying to Mother Dear, I've come to—"

"When were you talking to Mother ... ?"

"This morning, I said to Mother Dear—"

"Did you phone her?"

"Yes. And she came by here. We had a very fruitful discussion"—he chose his words with the precision of a Sunday school teacher—"She understands completely. There is a time in every man's life when he must push off from the wharf of safety into the sea of chance ... Anyway, she is arranging with a friend of hers in Oakland to get me on the Southern Pacific. Maya, it's just a start. I'll begin as a dining-car waiter and then a steward, and when I know all there is to know about that, I'll branch out ... The future looks good. The Black man hasn't even begun to storm the battlefronts. I'm going for broke myself."

His room smelled of cooked grease, Lysol and age, but his face believed the freshness of his words, and I had no heart nor art to drag him back to the reeking reality of our life and times.

Whores were lying down first and getting up last in the room next door. Chicken suppers and gambling games were rioting on a twenty-four-hour basis downstairs. Sailors and soldiers on their doom-lined road to war cracked windows and broke locks for blocks around, hoping to leave their imprint on a building or in the memory of a victim. A chance to be perpetrated. Bailey sat wrapped in his decision and anesthetized by youth. If I'd had any suggestion to make I couldn't have penetrated his unlucky armor. And, most regrettable, I had no suggestion to make.

"I'm your sister, and whatever I can do, I'll do it."

"Maya, don't worry about me. That's all I want you to do. Don't worry. I'll be okey-dokey."

I left his room because, and only because, we had said all we could say. The unsaid words pushed roughly against the thoughts that we had no craft to verbalize, and crowded the room to uneasiness.

34

LATER, MY ROOM had all the cheeriness of a dungeon and the appeal of a tomb. It was going to be impossible to stay there, but leaving held no attraction for me, either. Running away from home would be anticlimactic after Mexico, and a dull story after my month in the car lot. But the need for change bulldozed a road down the center of my mind.

I had it. The answer came to me with the suddenness of a collision. I would go to work. Mother wouldn't be difficult to convince; after all, in school I was a year ahead of my grade and Mother was a firm believer in self-sufficiency. In fact, she'd be pleased to think that I had that much gumption, that much of her in my character. (She liked to speak of herself as the original "do-it-yourself girl.")

Once I had settled on getting a job, all that remained was to decide which kind of job I was most fitted for. My intellectual pride had kept me from selecting typing, shorthand or filing as subjects in school, so office work was ruled out. War plants and shipyards demanded birth certificates, and mine would reveal me to be fifteen, and ineligible for work. So the well-paying defense jobs were also out. Women had replaced men on the streetcars as conductors and motormen, and the thought of sailing up and down the hills of San Francisco in a dark-blue uniform, with a money changer at my belt, caught my fancy.

Mother was as easy as I had anticipated. The world was moving so fast, so much money was being made, so many people were dying in Guam, and

Germany, that hordes of strangers became good friends overnight. Life was cheap and death entirely free. How could she have the time to think about my academic career?

To her question of what I planned to do, I replied that I would get a job on the streetcars. She rejected the proposal with: "They don't accept colored people on the streetcars."

I would like to claim an immediate fury which was followed by the noble determination to break the restricting tradition. But the truth is, my first reaction was one of disappointment. I'd pictured myself, dressed in a neat blue serge suit, my money changer swinging jauntily at my waist, and a cheery smile for the passengers which would make their own work day brighter.

From disappointment, I gradually ascended the emotional ladder to haughty indignation, and finally to that state of stubbornness where the mind is locked like the jaws of an enraged bulldog.

I would go to work on the streetcars and wear a blue serge suit. Mother gave me her support with one of her usual terse asides, "That's what you want to do? Then nothing beats a trial but a failure. Give it everything you've got. I've told you many times, 'Can't do is like Don't Care.' Neither of them have a home."

Translated, that meant there was nothing a person can't do, and there should be nothing a human being didn't care about. It was the most positive encouragement I could have hoped for.

In the offices of the Market Street Railway Company, the receptionist seemed as surprised to see me there as I was surprised to find the interior dingy and the décor drab. Somehow I had expected waxed surfaces and carpeted floors. If I had met no resistance, I might have decided against working for such a poor-mouth-looking concern. As it was, I explained that I had come to see about a job. She asked, was I sent by an agency, and when I replied that I was not, she told me they were only accepting applicants from agencies.

The classified pages of the morning papers had listed advertisements for motorettes and conductorettes and I reminded her of that. She gave me a face full of astonishment that my suspicious nature would not accept.

"I am applying for the job listed in this morning's *Chronicle* and I'd like to be presented to your personnel manager." While I spoke in supercilious accents, and looked at the room as if I had an oil well in my own backyard, my armpits were being pricked by millions of hot pointed needles. She saw her escape and dived into it.

"He's out. He's out for the day. You might call tomorrow and if he's in, I'm sure you can see him." Then she swiveled her chair around on its rusty screws and with that I was supposed to be dismissed.

"May I ask his name?"

She half turned, acting surprised to find me still there.

"His name? Whose name?"

"Your personnel manager."

We were firmly joined in the hypocrisy to play out the scene.

"The personnel manager? Oh, he's Mr. Cooper, but I'm not sure you'll find him here tomorrow. He's . . . Oh, but you can try."

"Thank you."

"You're welcome."

And I was out of the musty room and into the even mustier lobby. In the street I saw the receptionist and myself going faithfully through paces that were stale with familiarity, although I had never encountered that kind of situation before and, probably, neither had she. We were like actors who, knowing the play by heart, were still able to cry afresh over the old tragedies and laugh spontaneously at the comic situations.

The miserable little encounter had nothing to do with me, the me of me, any more than it had to do with that silly clerk. The incident was a recurring dream, concocted years before by stupid whites and it eternally came back to haunt us all. The secretary and I were like Hamlet and Laertes in the final scene, where, because of harm done by one ancestor to another, we were bound to duel to the death. Also because the play must end somewhere.

I went further than forgiving the clerk, I accepted her as a fellow victim of the same puppeteer.

On the streetcar, I put my fare into the box and the conductorette looked at me with the usual hard eyes of white contempt. "Move into the car, please move on in the car." She patted her money changer.

Her Southern nasal accent sliced my meditation and I looked deep into my thoughts. All lies, all comfortable lies. The receptionist was not innocent and neither was I. The whole charade we had played out in that crummy waiting room had directly to do with me, Black, and her, white.

I wouldn't move into the streetcar but stood on the ledge over the conductor, glaring. My mind shouted so energetically that the announcement made my veins stand out, and my mouth tighten into a prune.

I WOULD HAVE THE JOB. I WOULD BE A CONDUCTORETTE AND SLING A FULL MONEY CHANGER FROM MY BELT. I WOULD.

The next three weeks were a honeycomb of determination with apertures for the days to go in and out. The Negro organizations to whom I appealed for support bounced me back and forth like a shuttlecock on a badminton court. Why did I insist on that particular job? Openings were going begging that paid nearly twice the money. The minor officials with whom I was able to win an audience thought me mad. Possibly I was.

Downtown San Francisco became alien and cold, and the streets I had loved in a personal familiarity were unknown lanes that twisted with malicious intent. Old buildings, whose gray rococo façades housed my memories of the Forty-Niners, and Diamond Lil, Robert Service, Sutter and Jack London, were then imposing structures viciously joined to keep me out. My trips to the streetcar office were of the frequency of a person on salary. The struggle expanded. I was no longer in conflict only with the Market Street Railway but with the marble lobby of the building which housed its offices, and elevators and their operators.

During this period of strain Mother and I began our first steps on the long path toward mutual adult admiration. She never asked for reports and I didn't offer any details. But every morning she made breakfast, gave me carfare and lunch money, as if I were going to work. She comprehended the perversity of life, that in the struggle lies the joy. That I was no glory seeker was obvious to her, and that I had to exhaust every possibility before giving in was also clear.

On my way out of the house one morning she said, "Life is going to give you just what you put in it. Put your whole heart in everything you do, and pray, then you can wait." Another time she reminded me that "God helps those who help themselves." She had a store of aphorisms which she dished out as the occasion demanded. Strangely, as bored as I was with clichés, her inflection gave them something new, and set me thinking for a little while at least. Later when asked how I got my job, I was never able to say exactly. I only knew that one day, which was tiresomely like all the others before it, I sat in the Railway office, ostensibly waiting to be interviewed. The receptionist called me to her desk and shuffled a bundle of papers to me. They were job application forms. She said they had to be filled in triplicate. I had little time to wonder if I had won or not, for the standard questions reminded me of the necessity for dexterous lying. How old was I? List my previous jobs, starting from the last held and go backward to the first. How much money did I earn, and why did I leave the position? Give two references (not relatives).

Sitting at a side table my mind and I wove a cat's ladder of near truths and total lies. I kept my face blank (an old art) and wrote quickly the fable of Marguerite Johnson, aged nineteen, former companion and driver for Mrs. Annie Henderson (a White Lady) in Stamps, Arkansas.

I was given blood tests, aptitude tests, physical coordination tests, and Rorschachs, then on a blissful day I was hired as the first Negro on the San Francisco streetcars.

Mother gave me the money to have my blue serge suit tailored, and I learned to fill out work cards, operate the money changer and punch transfers. The time crowded together and at an End of Days I was swinging on the back of the rackety trolley, smiling sweetly and persuading my charges to "step forward in the car, please."

For one whole semester the streetcars and I shimmied up and scooted down the sheer hills of San Francisco. I lost some of my need for the Black ghetto's shielding-sponge quality, as I clanged and cleared my way down Market Street, with its honky-tonk homes for homeless sailors, past the quiet retreat of Golden Gate Park and along closed undwelled-in-looking dwellings of the Sunset District.

My work shifts were split so haphazardly that it was easy to believe that my superiors had chosen them maliciously. Upon mentioning my suspicions to Mother, she said, "Don't worry about it. You ask for what you want, and you pay for what you get. And I'm going to show you that it ain't no trouble when you pack double."

She stayed awake to drive me out to the car barn

at four thirty in the mornings, or to pick me up when I was relieved just before dawn. Her awareness of life's perils convinced her that while I would be safe on the public conveyances, she "wasn't about to trust a taxi driver with her baby."

When the spring classes began, I resumed my commitment with formal education. I was so much wiser and older, so much more independent, with a bank account and clothes that I had bought for myself, that I was sure that I had learned and earned the magic formula which would make me a part of the gay life my contemporaries led.

Not a bit of it. Within weeks, I realized that my schoolmates and I were on paths moving diametrically away from each other. They were concerned and excited over the approaching football games, but I had in my immediate past raced a car down a dark and foreign Mexican mountain. They concentrated great interest on who was worthy of being student body president, and when the metal bands would be removed from their teeth, while I remembered sleeping for a month in a wrecked automobile and conducting a streetcar in the uneven hours of the morning.

Without willing it, I had gone from being ignorant of being ignorant to being aware of being aware. And the worst part of my awareness was that I didn't know what I was aware of. I knew I knew very little, but I was certain that the things I had yet to learn wouldn't be taught to me at George Washington High School.

I began to cut classes, to walk in Golden Gate Park or wander along the shiny counter of the Emporium Department Store. When Mother discovered that I was playing truant, she told me that if I didn't want to go to school one day, if there were no tests being held, and if my school work was up to standard, all I had to do was tell her and I could stay home. She said that she didn't want some white woman calling her up to tell her something about her child that she didn't know. And she didn't want to be put in the position of lying to a white woman because I wasn't woman enough to speak up. That put an end to my truancy, but nothing appeared to lighten the long gloomy day that going to school became.

To be left alone on the tightrope of youthful unknowing is to experience the excruciating beauty of full freedom and the threat of eternal indecision. Few, if any, survive their teens. Most surrender to the vague but murderous pressure of adult conformity. It becomes easier to die and avoid conflicts than to maintain a constant battle with the superior forces of maturity.

Until recently each generation found it more expedient to plead guilty to the charge of being young and ignorant, easier to take the punishment meted out by the older generation (which had itself confessed to the same crime short years before). The command to grow up at once was more bearable than the faceless horror of wavering purpose, which was youth.

The bright hours when the young rebelled against the descending sun had to give way to twenty-four-hour periods called "days" that were named as well as numbered.

The Black female is assaulted in her tender years by all those common forces of nature at the same time that she is caught in the tripartite crossfire of masculine prejudice, white illogical hate and Black lack of power.

The fact that the adult American Negro female emerges a formidable character is often met with amazement, distaste and even belligerence. It is seldom accepted as an inevitable outcome of the struggle won by survivors and deserves respect if not enthusiastic acceptance.

35

The Well of Loneliness was my introduction to lesbianism and what I thought of as pornography. For months the book was both a treat and a threat. It allowed me to see a little of the mysterious world of the pervert. It stimulated my libido and I told myself that it was educational because it informed me of the difficulties in the secret world of the pervert. I was certain that I didn't know any perverts. Of course I ruled out the jolly sissies who sometimes stayed at our house and cooked whopping eight-course dinners while the perspiration made paths down their made-up faces. Since everyone accepted them, and more particularly since they accepted themselves, I knew that their laughter was real and that their lives were cheerful comedies, interrupted only by costume changes and freshening of make-up.

But true freaks, the "women lovers," captured yet strained my imagination. They were, according to the book, disowned by their families, snubbed by their friends and ostracized from every society. This bitter punishment was inflicted upon them because of a physical condition over which they had no control.

After my third reading of *The Well of Loneliness* I became a bleeding heart for the downtrodden misunderstood lesbians. I thought "lesbian" was synonymous with hermaphrodite, and when I wasn't actively aching over their pitiful state, I was wondering how they managed simpler body functions. Did they have a choice of organs to use, and if so, did they alternate or play favorite? Or I tried to imagine how two hermaphrodites made love, and the more I pondered the more confused I became. It seemed that having two of everything other people had, and four where ordinary people just had two, would complicate matters to the point of giving up the idea of making love at all.

It was during this reflective time that I noticed how heavy my own voice had become. It droned and drummed two or three whole tones lower than my schoolmates' voices. My hands and feet were also far from being feminine and dainty. In front of the mirror I detachedly examined my body. For a sixteen-year-old my breasts were sadly undeveloped. They could only be called skin swellings, even by the kindest critic. The line from my rib cage to my knees fell straight without even a ridge to disturb its direction. Younger girls than I boasted of having to shave under their arms, but my armpits were as smooth as my face. There was also a mysterious growth developing on my body that defied explanation. It looked totally useless.

Then the question began to live under my blankets: How did lesbianism begin? What were the symptoms? The public library gave information on the finished lesbian—and that woefully sketchy—but on the growth of a lesbian, there was nothing. I did discover that the difference between hermaphrodites and lesbians was that hermaphrodites were "born that way." It was impossible to determine whether lesbians budded gradually, or burst into being with a suddenness that dismayed them as much as it repelled society.

I had gnawed into the unsatisfying books and into my own unstocked mind without finding a morsel of peace or understanding. And meantime, my voice refused to stay up in the higher registers where I consciously pitched it, and I had to buy my shoes in the "old lady's comfort" section of the shoe stores.

I asked Mother.

Daddy Clidell was at the club one evening, so I sat down on the side of Mother's bed. As usual she woke completely and at once. (There is never any yawning or stretching with Vivian Baxter. She's either awake or asleep.)

"Mother, I've got to talk to you ..." It was going to kill me to have to ask her, for in the asking wouldn't it be possible that suspicion would fall on my own normality? I knew her well enough to know that if I committed almost any crime and told her the truth about it she not only wouldn't disown me but would give me her protection. But just suppose I was developing into a lesbian, how would she react? And then there was Bailey to worry about too.

"Ask me, and pass me a cigarette." Her calmness didn't fool me for a minute. She used to say that her secret to life was that she "hoped for the best, was prepared for the worst, so anything in between didn't come as a surprise." That was all well and good for most things but if her only daughter was developing into a ...

She moved over and patted the bed, "Come on, baby, get in the bed. You'll freeze before you get your question out."

It was better to remain where I was for the time being.

"Mother ... my pocketbook ..."

"Ritie, do you mean your vagina? Don't use those Southern terms. There's nothing wrong with the word 'vagina.' It's a clinical description. Now, what's wrong with it?"

The smoke collected under the bed lamp, then floated out to be free in the room. I was deathly sorry that I had begun to ask her anything.

"Well? ... Well? Have you got crabs?"

Since I didn't know what they were, that puzzled me. I thought I might have them and it wouldn't go well for my side if I said I didn't. On the other hand, I just might not have them, and suppose I lied and said I did?

"I don't know, Mother."

"Do you itch? Does your vagina itch?" She leaned on one elbow and jabbed out her cigarette.

"No, Mother."

"Then you don't have crabs. If you had them, you'd tell the world."

I wasn't sorry or glad not to have them, but made a mental note to look up "crabs" in the library on my next trip.

She looked at me closely, and only a person who knew her face well could have perceived the muscles relaxing and interpreted this as an indication of concern.

"You don't have a venereal disease, do you?"

The question wasn't asked seriously, but knowing Mother I was shocked at the idea. "Why, Mother, of course not. That's a terrible question." I was ready to go back to my room and wrestle alone with my worries.

"Sit down, Ritie. Pass me another cigarette." For a second it looked as if she was thinking about laughing. That would really do it. If she laughed, I'd never tell her anything else. Her laughter would make it easier to accept my social isolation and human freakishness. But she wasn't even smiling. Just slowly pulling in the smoke and holding it in puffed cheeks before blowing it out.

"Mother, something is growing on my vagina."

There, it was out. I'd soon know whether I was to be her ex-daughter or if she'd put me in a hospital for an operation.

"Where on your vagina, Marguerite?"

Uh-huh. It was bad all right. Not "Ritie" or "Maya" or "Baby." "Marguerite."

"On both sides. Inside." I couldn't add that they were fleshy skin flaps that had been growing for months down there. She'd have to pull that out of me.

"Ritie, go get me that big *Webster's* and then bring me a bottle of beer."

Suddenly, it wasn't all that serious. I was "Ritie" again, and she just asked for beer. If it had been as awful as I anticipated, she'd have ordered Scotch and water. I took her the huge dictionary that she had bought as a birthday gift for Daddy Clidell and laid it on the bed. The weight forced a side of the mattress down and Mother twisted her bed lamp to beam down on the book.

When I returned from the kitchen and poured her beer, as she had taught Bailey and me beer should be poured, she patted the bed.

"Sit down, baby. Read this." Her fingers guided my eyes to VULVA. I began to read. She said, "Read it out loud."

It was all very clear and normal-sounding. She drank the beer as I read, and when I had finished she explained it in every-day terms. My relief melted the fears and they liquidly stole down my face.

Mother shot up and put her arms around me.

"There's nothing to worry about, baby. It happens to every woman. It's just human nature."

It was all right then to unburden my heavy, heavy heart. I cried into the crook of my arm. "I thought maybe I was turning into a lesbian."

Her patting of my shoulder slowed to a still and she leaned away from me.

"A lesbian? Where the hell did you get that idea?"

"Those things growing on my . . . vagina, and my voice is too deep and my feet are big, and I have no hips or breasts or anything. And my legs are so skinny."

Then she did laugh. I knew immediately that she wasn't laughing at me. Or rather that she was laughing at me, but it was something about me that pleased her. The laugh choked a little on the smoke in its way, but finally broke through cleanly. I had to give a small laugh too, although I wasn't tickled at all. But it's mean to watch someone enjoy something and not show your understanding of their enjoyment.

When she finished with the laughter, she laid it

down a peal at a time and turned to me, wiping her eyes.

"I made arrangements, a long time ago, to have a boy and a girl. Bailey is my boy and you are my girl. The Man upstairs, He don't make mistakes. He gave you to me to be my girl and that's just what you are. Now, go wash your face, have a glass of milk and go back to bed."

I did as she said but I soon discovered my new assurance wasn't large enough to fill the gap left by my old uneasiness. It rattled around in my mind like a dime in a tin cup. I hoarded it preciously, but less than two weeks later it became totally worthless.

A classmate of mine, whose mother had rooms for herself and her daughter in a ladies' residence, had stayed out beyond closing time. She telephoned me to ask if she could sleep at my house. Mother gave her permission, providing my friend telephoned her mother from our house.

When she arrived, I got out of bed and we went to the upstairs kitchen to make hot chocolate. In my room we shared mean gossip about our friends, giggled over boys and whined about school and the tedium of life. The unusualness of having someone sleep in my bed (I'd never slept with anyone except my grandmothers) and the frivolous laughter in the middle of the night made me forget simple courtesies. My friend had to remind me that she had nothing to sleep in. I gave her one of my gowns, and without curiosity or interest I watched her pull off her clothes. At none of the early stages of undressing was I in the least conscious of her body. And then suddenly, for the briefest eye span, I saw her breasts. I was stunned.

They were shaped like light-brown falsies in the five-and-ten-cent store, but they were real. They made all the nude paintings I had seen in museums come to life. In a word they were beautiful. A universe divided what she had from what I had. She was a woman.

My gown was too snug for her and much too long, and when she wanted to laugh at her ridiculous image I found that humor had left me without a promise to return.

Had I been older I might have thought that I was moved by both an esthetic sense of beauty and the pure emotion of envy. But those possibilities did not occur to me when I needed them. All I knew was that I had been moved by looking at a woman's breasts. So all the calm and casual words of Mother's explanation a few weeks earlier and the clinical terms of Noah Webster did not alter the fact that in a fundamental way there was something queer about me.

I somersaulted deeper into my snuggery of misery. After a thorough self-examination, in the light of all I had read and heard about dykes and bulldaggers, I reasoned that I had none of the obvious traits—I didn't wear trousers, or have big shoulders or go in for sports, or walk like a man or even want to touch a woman. I wanted to be a woman, but that seemed to me to be a world to which I was to be eternally refused entrance.

What I needed was a boyfriend. A boyfriend would clarify my position to the world and, even more important, to myself. A boyfriend's acceptance of me would guide me into that strange and exotic land of frills and femininity.

Among my associates, there were no takers. Understandably the boys of my age and social group were captivated by the yellow- or light-brown-skinned girls, with hairy legs and smooth little lips, and whose hair "hung down like horses' manes." And even those sought-after girls were asked to "give it up or tell where it is." They were reminded in a popular song of the times, "If you can't smile and say yes, please don't cry and say no." If the pretties were expected to make the supreme sacrifice in order to "belong," what could the unattractive female do? She who had been skimming along on life's turning but never-changing periphery had to be

W9-BEW-566

C I T Y P A C K
Amsterdam

By Teresa Fisher

2ND EDITION

Fodor's Travel Publications, Inc.
New York • Toronto • London • Sydney • Auckland

WWW.FODORS.COM

About this book

KEY TO SYMBOLS

✚	map reference on the fold-out map accompanying this book (see below)	🚌	nearest bus route
✉	address	⛴	nearest riverboat or ferry stop
☎	telephone number	♿	facilities for visitors with disabilities
🕐	opening hours	✋	admission charge
🍴	restaurant or café on premises or nearby	↔	other nearby places of interest
🚇	nearest subway or Metro train station	❓	tours, lectures, or special events
		➤	indicates the page where you will find a fuller description
🚉	nearest railroad station	ℹ	tourist information

Citypack Amsterdam is divided into six sections to cover the six most important aspects of your visit to Amsterdam. It includes:

- The author's view of the city and its people
- Itineraries, walks, and excursions
- The top 25 sights to visit—as selected by the author
- Features about different aspects of the city that make it special
- Detailed listings of restaurants, hotels, stores, and nightlife
- Practical information

In addition, easy-to-read side panels provide fascinating extra facts and snippets, highlights of places to visit, and invaluable practical advice.

CROSS-REFERENCES

To help you make the most of your visit, cross-references, indicated by ➤, show you where to find additional information about a place or subject.

MAPS

The fold-out map in the wallet at the back of the book is a comprehensive street plan of Amsterdam. All the map references given in the book refer to this map. For example, the Westerkerk in the Westermarkt on Prinsengracht has the following information: ✚ **65** indicating the grid square of the map in which the Westerkerk will be found.

The downtown maps found on the inside front and back covers of the book itself are for quick reference. They show the Top 25 Sights, described on pages 24–48, plotted by number (**1** – **25** , not page number) from west to east across the city.

AREA CODE

The telephone code for Amsterdam is 020. If you call Amsterdam from outside the Netherlands, dial the country code (0031) followed by 20; to call a number in the city from elsewhere in the Netherlands, dial 020 then the subscriber number; to call a number in Amsterdam from inside the city, dial only the subscriber number.

AMSTERDAM
life

INTRODUCING AMSTERDAM

In their view

"Where else in the world are all life's commodities and all conceivable curiosities to be found as easily as here? In what other country can one find such absolute freedom?"

—René Descartes (1596–1650)

"This city seems to be double: one can also see it in the water: and the reflection of these distinguished houses in these canals makes this spot a fairyland."

—Jean-François Regnard (1655–1709)

The Keizersgracht seen from the tower of the Westerkerk

Few cities arouse such contradictory feelings in visitors as Amsterdam: old yet modern, beautiful yet sordid, sleepy yet energetic, international in outlook yet provincial in character. One thing on which all agree, though, is that it is the most exciting, sophisticated, and alluring of Dutch cities, and a place that is sure to leave a lasting impression on anyone who goes there.

Strolling along the grand horseshoe-shaped canals of the inner city, with their magnificent patrician mansions, imagine Amsterdam in its 17th-century heyday, when it became the richest city in Europe, headquarters of an empire and world capital of culture and commerce. Gentlemen's, Emperor's, and Prince's Canals: their names reflect the grandeur of the Golden Age. Over five thousand of the buildings along these canals are classified monuments. At night, tiny white lights define the humpback bridges, and, as the Dutch seldom draw their curtains, you can catch glimpses of their homes at dusk— trendy warehouse conversions, perhaps, or the gilded ceilings of grand salons, all with potted plants the size of half-grown trees and bunches of fresh flowers.

Romantic, picture-book images such as these are easy to find in Amsterdam. Some people

wear clogs, cheese is sold in bright yellow rounds, the parks are ablaze with tulips in May, and windmills are on the horizon. Modern Amsterdam is not in the least quaint and time-less, though. It has many other aspects, less pic-turesque perhaps, but more interesting.

Historically, Amsterdam has been tolerant of minority groups, and over the centuries has pro-vided sanctuary for victims of persecution. As a result, over a hundred different cultures, includ-ing many from the former Dutch colonies, now try to live harmoniously in this cosmopolitan city. Its tolerance has also provided the city with problems. Ever since the 1960s, when Amsterdam became the hippie capital of Europe, it has been trying to cope with "drugs tourism." Today its "smoking" coffee shops, where the sale and use of soft drugs is tolerated, are the city's main attraction for many young people. The Rosse Buurt, or Red Light District, with its sleazy sex shops and barely clad prostitutes touting for business at their windows, has become a focus for criminal activity.

There is no denying, however, that the atmosphere in Holland's capital has changed over the past 25 years. The hippies, squatters, and *provos* (anti-establishment rebels) of the '60s are now the conform-ing citizens of the '90s. The authorities are trying to play down the old capital of counter-culture image and present a more conventional view of a city where culture and fine arts—and business—flourish.

The Netherlands claims the highest concentra-tion of museums in the world, and Amsterdam boasts some of the most famous. The Rijksmuseum, with its unrivalled collection of Dutch art and the Van Gogh Museum, are, for many, reason enough to visit the city. The top museums and galleries are clustered near the

Herring city

If there had been no herring, Amsterdam might never have come into existence. In the Middle Ages, the Dutch discovered a method of curing these fish, and they became a staple food. Herring fishermen built a dam across the river Amstel and a small fishing village developed, called Amstelledamme. Its site is now Dam, Amsterdam's main square.

Colorful cheeses are a traditional part of Dutch food

Amsterdam in winter has a special charm

Double Dutch

Double Dutch (gibberish), *going Dutch* (sharing expenses equally), *a Dutch treat* (a party or outing for which the participants pay), and *Dutch courage* (false bravery fueled by alcohol)—the numerous, mostly derogatory "Dutch" expressions that litter the English language emerged during the 17th century and reflect the British view of their major rivals in maritime trade at the time.

Concertgebouw, Holland's world-renowned concert hall, favored by the finest performers of classical music. There is much more to Amsterdam than classic temples of culture: many of the city's museums are quirky and off-beat; and there's enough experimental art, music, theater, and dance to satisfy the most rigorously avant-garde.

Most of the city's cultural and historic sights are packed into a small area. The best way to see them all is to walk, or to hurtle around, in true Amsterdam style, on a bicycle. The city is crammed with tiny, quirky shops, offering everything from diamonds to Delftware and from trendy hemp clothing to haute couture. There are bars to suit all moods—dark, cozy brown cafés (traditional old bars stained with centuries of tobacco smoke); designer bars; and gin-tasting houses, called *proeflokalen*, bars attached to old gin (*jenever*) distilleries, where customers could sample before buying. Once businesses close for the day, the outgoing Amsterdammers take to the streets, walking, shopping, or drinking in the sidewalk cafés before eating out at restaurants serving cuisine from around the world, and then moving on to nightspots that tempt even the most jaded visitor. However you choose to describe it—laid-back, paradoxical, impulsive, addictive—Amsterdam embodies modern life.

AMSTERDAM IN FIGURES

People
- Population (1998): 724,908, including 140 nationalities, 30,000 university students, around 9,000 heroin addicts, 7,000 prostitutes, and 3,600 police officers
- Historical growth: 1500—9,000 inhabitants; 1550—30,000; 1650—220,000; 1900—510,000; 1963—868,000
- 8.5 million tourists visit annually

City
- Total area of city: 80 square miles
- Area of water: 7.7 square miles
- Number of districts: 30
- Height: 10 feet below sea level
- Average temperatures: January 36°F, July 62°F
- Landmarked buildings: 6,850
- 28 public parks; 220,000 trees; 600,000 flowering bulbs
- Bicycles: 400,000

Leisure
- 141 art galleries; 65 theaters and concert halls; 42 museums; 40 cinemas; 36 discos
- 1,400 cafés and bars; 750 restaurants; 550 coffee shops
- 10,334 stores

Canals
- 160 (total length of 45 miles), with 2,500 registered houseboats, 1,281 bridges, 120 waterbikes, 90 islands, and 70 glass-topped *rondvaartboten* (tour boats)
- Flushed with fresh water: four times a week
- Rubbish: 27 million gallons dredged each year, including up to 10,000 bicycles

On Rembrandtplein, one of Amsterdam's 1,400 cafés

A CHRONOLOGY

13th century	Herring fishermen settle on the Amstel. A dam is built across the Amstel. In 1300 the settlement is given city status.
1345	City becomes a pilgrimage center (➤ 40).
1421	The first of several great fires; wooden houses banned in 1669 to reduce fire risk.
1425	First horseshoe canal, the Singel, is dug.
1517	Protestant Reformation in Germany; Lutheran and Calvinist ideas take root in Amsterdam.
1519	Amsterdam becomes part of the Spanish empire and nominally Catholic.
1566	Iconoclast movement against the church.
1567–68	The Duke of Alba executes thousands of Protestants; start of the Eighty Years' War against Spanish rule.
1578	Amsterdam capitulates to William of Orange; Calvinists take power.
1595–97	First voyage by Dutch traders to Indonesia.
17th century	Dutch Golden Age; the city becomes the most important port in the world.
1602	Dutch East India Company founded (➤ 12).
1613	Work starts on the Grachtengordel (Canal Ring).
1620–37	Tulip mania (➤ 38).
1632	Rembrandt moves to Amsterdam from Leiden; dies in poverty 1669 (➤ 12).
1648	End of war with Spain, which recognizes Dutch independence. Work begins on a new town hall, now the Koninklijk Paleis (➤ 36).
1652–54	First of a series of wars with Britain for maritime supremacy.

1784	British navy destroys Dutch fleet.
1806	Napoleon Bonaparte takes over republic, and establishes his brother Louis Napoleon as king.
1813	After defeat of Napoleon, Prince William VI of Orange returns from exile; crowned King William I in 1814.
1876	North Sea Canal opens: brings new prosperity.
1914–18	World War I. Netherlands neutral.
1928	Amsterdam Olympics: women athletes enter.
1940–45	German Occupation in World War II.
1942	Anne Frank's family go into hiding in a house on the Prinsengracht; betrayed by an unknown informant in August 1944 (► 12, 31).
1948	Karel Appel helps found the CoBrA (Copenhagen, Brussels, Amsterdam) modern art movement, laying the foundations of abstract expressionism.
1940s–50s	Holland withdraws from overseas empire.
1952	Amsterdam–Rhine Canal opens.
1960s–70s	Hippies from all over Europe flock to the city.
1964–67	Anti-Establishment riots in Amsterdam.
1973	Van Gogh Museum opens (► 26).
1980	Queen Beatrix crowned; city named Holland's capital.
1989	City government falls because of weak anti-vehicle laws. New laws are passed to make Amsterdam eventually free of motor traffic.
1990	Van Gogh centenary exhibition attracts 890,000 visitors.
1998–99	Redevelopment of Museumplein, with a park and lake in the square; new wing added to Van Gogh Museum, another planned for Stedelijk Museum of Modern Art (► 25, 26).

11

PEOPLE & EVENTS FROM HISTORY

A popular monarch

Beatrix, Queen of the Netherlands, came to the throne when her mother, Queen Juliana, abdicated on April 30, 1980. Beatrix, born in 1938, was crowned at the Nieuwe Kerk. Her great popularity is reflected in the celebrations on her official birthday (*Koninginnedag*, April 30)—a national holiday, when the entire city becomes one massive street party with market stalls, music, dancing, and drinking in the jam-packed streets.

FOUNDING OF THE NETHERLANDS

In the mid-16th century the Low Countries rebelled against the religious and political oppression of Spanish rule. The resistance was led by Prince William of Orange, better known as William the Silent. In 1578 he took control of Amsterdam in a bloodless coup. The city's Catholic magistrates and clergy were deported, and Amsterdam was declared a Calvinist city within the new Dutch Republic of 1579.

DUTCH EAST INDIA COMPANY (VOC)

In 1602 a number of Amsterdam companies joined together to create the *Verenigde Oost-Indische Compagnie* (VOC) to control Dutch trading. It soon became the world's largest trading company, enjoying tremendous prosperity in the 17th century. But a series of wars in the late 17th and early 18th centuries exhausted the country. Faced also with commercial competition from Britain and France, the VOC went into decline and in 1799 was declared bankrupt.

REMBRANDT

Rembrandt Harmenszoon van Rijn (1606–69) was the most influential Dutch artist of the 17th century. Marrying a wealthy heiress in 1634, he spent his most successful years as a painter in Amsterdam; commissions poured in from wealthy patrons, beneficiaries of Amsterdam's Golden Age. Yet changing tastes in art, plus the untimely death of his wife, Saskia, in 1642, left Rembrandt impoverished (➤ 28, 30, 44).

ANNE FRANK

Anne Frank (1929–45) dreamed of becoming a famous writer. In 1942, with Holland under Nazi occupation, Anne's father hid his family in a house beside the Prinsengracht. Her journal during their 25 months of confinement was to posthumously realize her youthful ambition; she died at Belsen just before the war's end. *The Diary of a Young Girl*, published 1947, is read and loved worldwide; yet it not only brings her to life as an individual, but has become a voice of the many silenced in the Holocaust (➤ 31).

AMSTERDAM
how to organize your time

13

ITINERARIES

These itineraries take you to some of Amsterdam's main sights. Almost all places of interest are within walking distance of each other, and the city's layout of concentric canals and crisscrossing streets forms a grid that is easy to orient. Itinerary One is based around Dam square, with Four nearby to the west on the Canal Ring. The second itinerary lies to the southwest of the center, while Itinerary Three takes in the east side.

ITINERARY ONE	HISTORIC CITY
Morning	Visit the Amsterdams Historisch Museum (➤ 35) to get an idea of the city's colorful history. Then stop at the Begijnhof (➤ 34), Holland's finest almshouses.
Lunch	Try Caffé Esprit (➤ 69) or a Dutch restaurant, such as Haesje Claes (➤ 62).
Afternoon	Enjoy the street entertainment between visits to the sumptuous Koninklijk Paleis (Royal Palace ➤ 36) and Nieuwe Kerk (➤ 37), both on the dam (now Dam square) that gave Amsterdam its name.
Evening	Having reserved in advance, if possible, go to a classical music concert at the Concertgebouw (➤ 54 and 78) or Beurs van Berlage, or opera or dance at the Muziektheater (➤ 55, 77 and 78).

ITINERARY TWO	ART TREASURES
Morning	See part of the Rijksmuseum's immense collection (➤ 28)—start with the paintings of the Golden Age. Then stroll through the Vondelpark (➤ 24).
Lunch	Picnic in the park or head for Leidseplein (➤ 27) for its cafés and restaurants.
Afternoon	Return to the Museumsplein for the Van Gogh Museum (➤ 26), or the Stedelijk Museum (➤ 25) that specializes in modern art. Neither should be missed.

Malevich painting in the Stedelijk Museum

14

ITINERARY THREE	**MARITIME HISTORY**
Morning	It's easy to imagine 17th-century Amsterdam at the peak of its maritime success during an early morning stroll around the Western Islands (➤ 51). A bus ride from here (🚌 **22, 28**) takes you to the Eastern Islands and the Scheepvaart Museum (➤ 47).
Lunch	Enjoy a snack at the Scheepvaart Museum restaurant.
Afternoon	Head for the Tropenmuseum (➤ 48), which re-creates tropical scenes, or walk to the Hortus Botanicus (➤ 58), the botanical gardens beside Artis Zoo (➤ 59). Continue to the Museum Willet-Holthuysen (➤ 42), built for a wealthy Golden Age merchant.
Evening	Take a candlelit canal cruise (➤ 19) and see the Golden Age buildings and canal bridges lit up.

Clogs—popular souvenirs though no longer everyday wear

ITINERARY FOUR	**SIGHTSEEING AND SHOPPING**
Morning	Avoid lines by arriving early at Anne Frankhuis (➤ 31). Then climb the tower of the nearby Westerkerk (➤ 30) for its breathtaking views.
Lunch	By now, you will have earned one of the Pancake Bakery's delicious *pannekoeken* (➤ 68).
Afternoon	Explore the Grachtengordel (Canal Ring) (➤ 29, 32, 50–51), and go souvenir shopping (➤ 70–76). Don't forget the Bloemenmarkt (➤ 38) for bulbs and Stoeltie Diamonds (➤ 43).
Evening	Explore the Rosse Buurt (➤ 39).

WALKS

Characteristic gables along the Singel

THE CANAL RING AND JORDAAN

After breakfast at La Ruche (➤69) in De Bijenkorf department store, leave Dam square via Paleisstraat; continue straight on over the scenic Singel, Herengracht, and Keizersgracht canals; and then turn right alongside Prinsengracht to pass the impressively high tower of the Westerkerk and the nearby Anne Frankhuis (Anne Frank's House). Cross over Prinsengracht and double back on yourself for a few yards along the west bank of the canal until you reach the peaceful, leafy Bloemgracht canal. Turn right here, take the second right up Tweede Leliedwarsstraat, cross over Egelantiersgracht, and turn right along its shady bank and then immediately left up Tweede Egelantiersdwarsstraat into the heart of the bohemian Jordaan district. Take time to soak up the atmosphere in one of its numerous cafés and browse in its tiny designer boutiques.

Walk on to Lijnbaansgracht, and then turn right on to Lindengracht, once a canal and now site of a splendid Saturday food market, to Brouwersgracht (➤ 50), one of Amsterdam's most attractive canals, lined with traditional Dutch barges and houseboats. Pause for a prelunch drink at the Papeneiland brown café (reputedly Amsterdam's oldest café, ➤ 80) on the corner of Prinsengracht. Cross Brouwersgracht at Herengracht and continue along Brouwersgracht to the Singel. Cross by the sluice gates and turn right along the eastern side of the Singel, past Amsterdam's narrowest house facade (No. 7) and the Poezenboot—a houseboat refuge for stray cats. To conclude the walk, turn left at Torenstraat, cross Spui and go along Molensteeg. Continue across Nieuwezijds Voorburgwal, past Nieuwe Kerk on the left and return to Dam square, for a tasty lunch of Dutch specialties at De Roode Leeuw (➤ 62).

THE SIGHTS

- Nieuwe Kerk (➤ 37)
- Koninklijk Paleis (➤ 36)
- Singel (➤ 33)
- Canal Ring (➤ 29, 32, 50)
- Westerkerk (➤ 30)
- Anne Frankhuis (➤ 31)
- Jordaan district (➤ 52)

INFORMATION

Distance 2.5 miles
Time 1–2 hours
Start/End point Dam
➕ H5
▭ Tram 4, 9, 14, 16, 20, 24, 25

MARKETS AND MUSEUMS

Leaving Dam square via Paleisstraat, turn left onto Nieuwezijds Voorburgwal, where a stamp and coin market is held (the Postzegelmarkt ► 53). About 100 yards farther on the left, narrow Sint Luciensteeg leads to the Amsterdams Historisch Museum. Pass through the Schuttersgalerij (Civic Guard Gallery) into a narrow lane of whitewashed houses called Gedempte Begijnensloot. At the southern end, a stone archway on your right brings you into the calm of the leafy, cobbled, Begijnhof courtyard. A further archway leads to Spui that, with its cluster of sidewalk cafés, makes a good coffee stop on a sunny day. On Fridays, you will find a bustling market of antiquarian books here, and on Sundays the stalls sell paintings and prints.

Head southwest from Spui and turn left along the edge of the Singel. Cross the bridge onto Koningsplein and Amsterdam's ravishing flower market, the Bloemenmarkt. Your next landmark, the Munttoren (Mint Tower) at Muntplein, is easy to spot. Turn right along the Amstel and follow it just past the Blauwbrug (Blue Bridge). Turn right along Herengracht to make a short detour to the Willet-Holthuysen Museum, which gives a rare glimpse inside one of the canal's elegant patrician mansions. On your return, cross the bridge to reach the Waterlooplein flea market, a hodgepodge of stalls, some with trendy clothes and others cluttered with junk. Tucked away at the far end of the market is the Museum het Rembrandthuis (Rembrandt's House), which is not to be missed. End your walk with a drink on the terrace of Café Dantzig (► 68) opposite the Muziektheater (► 55, 77 and 78) where you can watch the barges chugging up the Amstel River.

THE SIGHTS

- Amsterdams Historisch Museum (► 35)
- Begijnhof (► 34)
- Markets (► 53)
- Singel (► 33)
- Bloemenmarkt (► 38)
- Munttoren (► 55)
- Blauwbrug (► 54)
- Museum Willet-Holthuysen (► 42)
- Museum het Rembrandthuis (► 44)

INFORMATION

Distance 1.5 miles
Time 1–2 hours
Start point Dam
➕ H5
🚊 Tram 4, 9, 14, 16, 20, 24, 25
End point: Café Dantzig
➕ H5
🚇 Waterlooplein

Waterlooplein flea market

EVENING STROLLS

Red Light District signs pull no punches

ROSSE BUURT (RED LIGHT DISTRICT)

From Dam square, turn up Warmoesstraat (by Hotel Krasnapolsky), the city's oldest street. After the police station, turn right down Lange Niezel and then right again at Oudezijds Voorburgwal, past the venerable Oude Kerk (➤ 40), incongruous in this seedy place. Cross the canal at Stoofstraat, then turn right on to Oudezijds Achterburgwal, pass the Hash Marihuana Hemp Museum, where you can learn everything you maybe never wanted to know about hash, marijuana, and hemp. Cross the bridge and follow Oude Hoogstraat to the Pillenbrug (pill-bridge), often crowded with junkies by the drug-paraphernalia store, the Head Shop. Cross the bridge and go left (north) up Klovenierburgswal to the Waag (the old weigh-house) at Nieuwmarkt. Turn left, back to Oudezijds Achterburgwal, then right along the canal past the Tattoo Museum, devoted to the art of body illustration, and the gloomy displays of the Erotic Museum. At the canal's end, go right along Vredenburgerstraat to Zeedijk (➤ 52). Follow the road to the left back to Warmoesstraat for dinner. (➤ 93, Precautions.)

SQUARES AND CANALS

From Dam square, take Paleisstraat to Singel (➤ 33) and turn south along the canalside, passing Spui and the Flower Market (➤ 38) to Rembrandtplein. Head south across Thorbeckeplein from the neon lights and pulsating music in the cafés on Rembrandtplein, and turn left on to the silent, stately Herengracht (➤ 32). Turn right on to the Amstel for a view of the illuminated Skinny Bridge (➤ 45). The next right takes you back along Keizersgracht to the enchanting Reguliersgracht. Turn right and then left to reach Herengracht's magically lit "Golden Bend." Cross over Vijzelstraat, then turn left and follow Nieuwe Spiegelstraat, passing a long line of antique shops as far as Lijnbaansgracht. Turn right here and at the canal's end cut across Max Euweplein, past the glitzy Casino and along the Lido, where you will finally reach the lively Leidseplein (➤ 27).

INFORMATION

Red Light District
Distance 1.5 miles
Time 1 hour
Start/End point Dam
✚ H5
🚋 Tram 4, 9, 14, 16, 20, 24, 25

Squares and canals
Distance 1.5 miles
Time 1 hour
Start point Rembrandtplein
✚ H5
🚋 Tram 4, 9, 14, 20
End point Leidseplein
✚ G6
🚋 Tram 1, 2, 5, 6, 7, 10, 20

SIGHTSEEING TOURS

ON THE WATER

Holland International ✉ Prins Hendrikkade 33a ☎ 6227788 🕐 Year-round Cruises every 15 minutes (30 minutes in winter) in glass-topped boats, called *rondvaartboten*.

Canal Bus Tours ✉ Weteingschans 24 ☎ 6239886 There is a water-bus service around the city, and two theme tours: *Rembrandt* and *City on the Water*.

Rederij Lovers Amsterdam ✉ Prins Hendrikkade 25–27 ☎ 6222181 🕐 Daily in summer, fewer in winter Candlelit canal cruises for romantics, with music and refreshments, as well as a commentary.

Museumboat ✉ Stationsplein 8 ☎ 6222181 Links seven jetties near the 20 major museums, so that you can combine canal cruising with museum visits. A day ticket costs f25; service runs every 30–45 minutes.

A boat tour gives a different view

ON DRY LAND

Yellow Bike Tours ✉ Nieuwezijds Kolk 29 ☎ 6206940 🕐 Daily Apr–Oct View the city at a sedate pace or head out to the waterlands north of Amsterdam to visit windmills and a clog factory.

Tourist Tram ✉ Centraal Station ☎ 0900/9292 🕐 Sun, in summer & holidays An hourly tram linking city sights.

Amsterdam Travel and Tours ✉ Dam 10 ☎ 6276236 🕐 Fri 9pm Organized walking tour of the Red Light District.

Audio Tourist ✉ Oude Spiegelstraat 9 ☎ 4215580 🕐 Apr–Sep: daily 9–6. Oct–Mar: Tue–Sun 10–5 Guide yourself around town with the help of a map and audio cassette.

FROM THE AIR

KLM Helicopter Tours ✉ Schiphol Airport ☎ 4747747 🕐 Depends on weather Breathtaking views of the city.

Watery ways

The view of Amsterdam from the water is unforgettable. Alternatives to the glass-topped tour boats are water taxi (✉ Stationsplein 8 ☎ 6222181), or pedal boat, rented from Canal Bike (✉ Weteringschans 24 ☎ 6265574) for f12.50 per person per hour for 1–2 people; f10 for 3–4 people (with a f50 deposit).

EXCURSIONS

HAARLEM

As you wander through the historic heart of Haarlem it is hard to believe that this is the eighth largest city in Holland and the center of Dutch printing, pharmaceutical, and bulb-growing industries. The brick-paved, traffic-free streets are lined with elegant Renaissance buildings, and have hardly changed since the town's 17th-century heyday. For centuries, the town's main meeting place has been the lively main square—Grote Markt—today bordered with busy sidewalk cafés. The nearby Grote Kerk boasts one of the world's largest and finest organs, an ornate instrument that has drawn many renowned composers to the city, including Handel and Mozart. Haarlem's greatest attraction, however, is the Frans Hals Museum, home of the world's best collection of works by this painter. A short cruise can be taken along the river from the Gravenstenenbrug lift bridge.

KEUKENHOF GARDENS

These gardens at the heart of the *Bloembollenstreek* bulb-growing region rank among the most famous in the world. The site— 69 acres of wooded park close to Lisse—was acquired in 1949 as a showcase. Visit between March and late May, when more than seven million bulbs are in bloom, laid out in brilliant swathes of red, yellow, pink, and blue. Few people leave without a bag of bulbs for their own garden.

Keukenhof Gardens blaze with color

DELFT

The name of this charming old town is known the world over for its blue-and-white pottery, but it was also the birthplace of the artist Johannes Vermeer (1632–75). His simple grave can be seen in the Oude Kerk along with those of other eminent Delft citizens, including Antonie van Leeuwenhoek, inventor of the microscope.

William of Orange (▶ 12) led his revolt against Spanish rule from the Prinsenhof in Delft. The building now houses the city museum, which includes a collection of rare antique Delftware. Halfway up the stairs can still be seen the holes made by the bullets that killed William in 1584. His elaborate marble tomb, designed by Hendrick de Keyser in 1614, lies in the Nieuwe Kerk.

EDAM

Famous for its ball-shaped cheeses wrapped in wax (red for export, yellow for local consumption), Edam is everyone's idea of a typical Dutch town—full of narrow, tree-shaded canals lined by gabled, red-roofed houses and crossed by wooden lift bridges. Edam enjoyed its heyday during the Golden Age, when shipbuilding, fishing, and cheese brought prosperity. A traditional cheese market still takes place on Wednesday mornings in July and August. The colorful cheeses arrive by boat and are weighed at the Kaasmarkt's 16th-century weighhouse. The method for producing longlasting pressed cheeses was perfected in the Middle Ages, though the process is now automated. You can see it in action at three farms near Edam; leaflets are available from the tourist office (VVV) in the Town Hall.

Delftware

Delftware was developed from majolica in the 16th century by immigrant Italian potters who produced wall tiles with motifs of Dutch landscapes, animals, and flowers. Over the next hundred years, trade with the East brought other influences; delicate Chinese porcelain inspired finer work. By 1652 De Porceleyne Fles was one of 32 thriving potteries here. Today it is the only original Delftware factory in production, and offers daily guided tours.

WHAT'S ON

Amsterdam's year is punctuated with fairs, festivals, and street parties celebrating everything from cycling to Santa Claus, including the party to end all parties, the Queen's birthday. For details of events pick up a copy of the main English language listings magazine *What's On*, available from newsagents and tourist offices, or the free monthly *Amsterdam Times*, obtainable from larger hotels.

February	*Carnival*, celebrated as a preamble to Lent.
	Dockers' Strike Commemoration (Feb 25 ➤ 46).
March	*Stille Omgang* (second Sun): silent procession celebrating Amsterdam's miracle (➤ 40).
April	*National Museum Weekend* (mid-month): free or reduced entrance to all museums.
	Koninginnedag (Apr 30): the Queen's birthday.
	World Press Photo Exhibition (end-Apr).
May	*Remembrance Day* (May 4): two minutes' silence at 8PM following a ceremony at Dam square in remembrance of World War II victims.
	Liberation Day (May 5): celebrations marking the end of the German Occupation in 1945.
	National Windmill Day (second Sat ➤ 60).
	National Cycling Day (second Sun).
June	*Holland Festival:* international arts festival.
	Open-air Theater Season in Vondelpark (until mid-August ➤ 24).
	Grachtenloop canal race (second Sun): along the banks of Prinsengracht and Vijzelgracht.
July	*Summer Festival:* alternative arts festival.
August	*Dammen Op De Dam* (mid-Aug): open-air checkers tournament in Dam square.
	Prinsengracht concert (last Fri): classical music recitals on barges outside the Hotel Pulitzer.
September	*Bloemencorso* (first Sat): parade of flower-laden floats from Aalsmeer to Amsterdam.
	National Monument Day (second Sat): monuments and buildings, usually closed, are open.
	Jordaan Folk Festival (first week): music, street parties, games, and eating and drinking.
October	*Antiques Fair* (last weekend): open house at the antiques shops of the Spiegelkwartier.
November	*Sinterklaas* (Santa Claus) *Parade* (➤ 57).
December	*Pakjesavond* (Dec 5): parcel evening, Holland's traditional day for present giving (➤ 57).
	Oudejaarsavond (Dec 31): New Year's Eve—wild street parties, fireworks, and champagne.

AMSTERDAM's
top 25 sights

The sights are shown on the maps on the inside front cover and inside back cover, numbered **1–25** *from west to east across the city*

VONDELPARK

A favorite place for people-watching, full of joggers, sunbathers, frisbee-throwers, and bookworms. Let yourself be entertained by musicians, mime artists, and acrobats in this welcome splash of green near the city center.

INFORMATION

- ➕ E7–G6
- ✉ Stadhouderskade
- 🕐 Dawn–dusk daily
- 🍴 Café Vertigo (SS), Het Ronde Blauwe Theehouse (SS)
- 🚊 Tram 1, 2, 3, 5, 6, 12, 20
- 🚢 Museumboat stop 3
- ♿ Good
- ↔ Stedelijk Museum (➤ 25), Van Gogh Museum (➤ 26), Leidseplein (➤ 27)
- ❓ Open-air summer festival of theater and concerts

Open-air auditorium in Vondelpark

Pleasure gardens Amsterdam's largest and oldest municipal park—a 118-acre rectangle of former marshland—was first opened in 1865. The designers, J.D. and L.P. Zocher, intentionally moved away from the symmetrical Dutch garden, creating in the romantic English-style with lengthy pathways, open lawns, ornamental lakes, meadows, and woodland containing 120 varieties of tree, including catalpa, chestnut, cypress, oak, and poplar. Financed by wealthy local residents, the Nieuwe Park (as it was then called) became the heart of a luxurious new residential district, overlooked by elegant town houses and villas. Two years later, a statue of Holland's best-known playwright, Joost van den Vondel (1587–1679)—a Dutch contemporary of Shakespeare—was erected in the park and its present name was adopted. Today, with its wide open spaces, fragrant rose garden, playgrounds, bandstand, and teahouses, it remains a popular destination for family outings. It also has the Dutch Film Museum, an absolute must for cinephiles.

Like a summer-long pop festival The heyday of the always-colorful Vondelpark was in the 1970s, when hippies flocked to Amsterdam, attracted by the city's tolerance for soft drugs. Vondelpark soon became their main gathering place; the bubble burst at the end of the decade and the hippies dispersed. All that now remains are street musicians, flea markets, and the occasional aging hippy.

STEDELIJK MUSEUM

One of the world's leading modern art museums. From Henri Matisse to Kazimir Malevich and Piet Mondrian, from Paul Klee to Vasily Kandinsky and Edward Keinholz, this gallery is an essential stop for art enthusiasts.

Controversial The Stedelijk or Municipal Museum, Amsterdam's foremost venue for contemporary art, was founded in 1895. Its collection of over 25,000 paintings, sculptures, drawings, graphics, and photographs contains works by some of the great names of modern art (van Gogh, Cézanne, Picasso, Monet, Chagall), but the main emphasis is on progressive postwar movements and the exhibitions highlight the very latest, often highly controversial, trends in contemporary art. There is not enough space to keep the entire collection on view, but an extension is planned to open around 2002.

House of Museums In 1938 the Stedelijk became Holland's National Museum of Modern Art, but it achieved its worldwide avant-garde reputation in 1945–63, when it was under the dynamic direction of Willem Sandberg. He put much of its existing collection in storage and created a House of Museums in which art, photography, dance, theater, music, and cinema were all represented in innovative shows.

Cutting edge Museum highlights include suprematist paintings by Malevich; works by Mondrian, Gerrit Rietveld and other exponents of the Dutch *De Stijl* school; and a remarkable collection of almost childlike paintings by the *CoBrA* movement, founded in defiance of the artistic complacency of postwar Europe, and named after the native cities of its members—Copenhagen, Brussels, and Amsterdam.

HIGHLIGHTS

- *The Parakeet and the Mermaid*, Matisse (1952–3)
- *The Women of the Revolution*, Kiefer (1986)
- *My Name as Though it were Written on the Surface of the Moon*, Nauman (1986)
- *Sitting Woman with Fish Hat*, Picasso (1942)
- *The Appelbar*, Appel (1951)
- *Beanery*, Kienholz (1965)
- Rietveld furniture collection

INFORMATION

- G6
- Paulus Potterstraat 13
- 5732911
- Daily 11–5; public hols 11–4. Closed Jan 1
- Restaurant (SS)
- Tram 2, 3, 5, 12, 16, 20
- Very good
- Moderate
- Vondelpark (➤ 24), Van Gogh Museum (➤ 26), Rijksmuseum (➤ 28)
- Lectures, films, and concerts. Book guided tours

Top: Special exhibitions are a feature of the Stedelijk Museum

3

VAN GOGH MUSEUM

- *The Potato Eaters* (1885)
- *Self-portrait as a Painter* (1888)
- *Bedroom at Arles* (1888)
- *Vase with Sunflowers* (1888)
- *Wheatfield with Crows* (1890)

DID YOU KNOW?

- Van Gogh sold only one painting in his life time
- Record price for a van Gogh painting is f93million (1990 *Portrait of Dr. Gachet*)

INFORMATION

- G6
- Paulus Potterstraat 7
- 5705200
- Daily 10–5. Closed Jan 1
- Self-service restaurant (SS)
- Tram 2, 3, 5, 12, 16, 20
- Museumboat stop 4
- Excellent
- Expensive
- Stedelijk Museum (➤ 25)
  Rijksmuseum (➤ 28)

Top: Bedroom at Arles.
Below: a self-portrait

It is a moving experience to trace this great artist's tragic life and extraordinary achievement, through such a comprehensive display of his art, his Japanese prints, and contemporary works.

World's largest van Gogh collection Of his 900 paintings and 1,200 drawings, the Van Gogh Museum has 200 and 500 respectively, together with 850 letters, Vincent's Japanese print collection, and works by friends and influential contemporaries, including Gauguin, Monet, Bernard, and Pissarro. Van Gogh's paintings are arranged chronologically, starting with works from 1880 to 1887, a period characterized by realistic landscape paintings and peasant scenes in heavy tones. This period is typified by *The Potato Eaters* (1885).

Colorful palette The broad brush strokes and bold colors that characterize van Gogh's works of 1887–90 show the influence of his 1886 move to Paris and the effect of Impressionism, most striking in street and café scenes. Tired of city life, he moved in 1888 to Arles where, intoxicated by the intense sunlight and the brilliant colors of Provence, he painted many of his finest works, including *Harvest at La Crau* and the *Sunflowers* series. After snipping off a bit of his ear and offering it to a local prostitute, van Gogh voluntarily entered an asylum in St. Remy, where his art took an expressionistic form. His mental anguish may be seen in the way he painted gnarled trees and menacing skies, as in the desolate *Wheatfield with Crows*. Shortly after completing this picture, at the age of 37, he shot himself.

New space In May 1999 the museum reopened after eight months of renovation, and construction of a new, ellipse-shaped wing designed by Japanese architect Kisho Kurokawa.

LEIDSEPLEIN

This square represents Amsterdam's nightlife at its vibrant best. It is filled with sidewalk cafés, ablaze with neon and a-buzz with jugglers, musicians, and fire eaters. Be sure to spend at least one evening here.

Party center for centuries During the Middle Ages, farmers on their way to market unloaded their carts here, at the outskirts of the city. At the turn of the century, artists and writers gathered here; in the 1930s Leidseplein was the site of many clashes between political factions, and it became the main site of anti-Nazi rallies during the war. In the 1960s it was the stomping ground of the *Pleiners* (Dutch Mods), and in 1992 it witnessed wild celebrations following local soccer team Ajax's UEFA Cup victory. Today, despite the constant flow of trams through the square, you will always find fire eaters, sword-swallowers, and other street entertainment. By night, dazzling neon lights and crowded café terraces seating over 1,000 people transform the square into an Amsterdam hot spot, busy until the early hours. Look for two notable buildings, both protected monuments: the distinctive red-brick Stadsschouwburg (Municipal Theater), with its wide verandah and little turrets, and the art nouveau American Hotel, with its striking art deco Café Américain.

Winter wonderland Whatever the season, Leidseplein remains one of the city's main meeting places. In winter, when most tourists have returned home, it becomes quintessentially Dutch. Most of the outdoor café terraces disappear and locals huddle together for a drink and a chat in heated covered terraces, or inside the cafés. It is also *the* place to be on New Year's Eve.

HIGHLIGHTS

- American Hotel (1904)
- Stadsschouwburg (1894)
- Street entertainment

INFORMATION

- G6
- Leidseplein
- Restaurants and cafés (S–SSS)
- Tram 1, 2, 5, 6, 7, 10, 20
- Museumboat stop 3
- Vondelpark (➤ 24), Rijksmuseum (➤ 28), Prinsengracht (➤ 29)

Top: cafés in Leidseplein at night. Below: a stilt walker entertains

5

RIJKSMUSEUM

HIGHLIGHTS

- *The Night Watch*, Rembrandt (1642)
- *The Jewish Bride*, Rembrandt (1665)
- *The Milk Maid*, Vermeer
- *Flower Piece*, Jan Brueghel
- *Winter Landscape with Iceskaters*, Avercamp
- *The Merry Family*, Steen

INFORMATION

- G6
- Stadhouderskade 42
- 6747000
- Daily 10–5. Closed Jan 1
- Café/restaurant (SS)
- Tram 2, 5, 6, 7, 10, 20
- Museumboat stop 4
- Very good
- Expensive
- Stedelijk Museum (➤ 25), Van Gogh Museum (➤ 26)
- Audio-tour

Top: The Merry Family, *Jan Steen. Below:* Self-portrait as the Apostle Paul, *Rembrandt*

28

Holland's biggest museum has a mind-numbing seven million items in its catalog (not all on view), ranging from the world's most important collection of Dutch Golden Age masterpieces, through detailed model sailing ships, to dollhouses.

Masterpieces Housed in a palatial red-brick building designed by P.J.H. Cuypers and opened in 1885, the Rijksmuseum boasts an unrivaled collection of Old Master paintings in more than 250 rooms, a library with 250,000 volumes, a million prints and drawings, and thousands of sculptures and other artifacts. The museum's first floor traces the course of Dutch painting from religious pieces of the medieval era to the rich paintings of the Renaissance and the Golden Age, including works by Rembrandt, Vermeer, Hals, and Steen. Pride of place goes to Rembrandt's *The Night Watch* (1642). This vast, dramatic canvas—one of his largest and most famous compositions, portraying a militia company—is a showpiece of 17th-century Dutch art. It was originally even bigger, but Rembrandt cut it down considerably, reputedly to get it through a doorway. Displayed in the adjacent room is a copy of *The Night Watch* attributed to Lundens, in the original form.

Treasures Along with the remarkable Dutch paintings, the museum's riches include a collection of Delftware and Meissen porcelain, countless sculptures and Asian treasures, a fascinating section on Dutch history, and two ingeniously made dollhouses—scaled-down copies of old canal houses with sumptuous 17th-century period furnishings. The refurbished south wing of the museum contains a magnificent collection of Dutch Romantic works and Impressionist paintings by local artists.

PRINSENGRACHT

Of the three canals that form the Grachtengordel (Canal Ring), Prinsengracht is in many ways the most atmospheric, with its magnificent merchants' homes, converted warehouses, and flower-laden houseboats.

Prince William's canal Prinsengracht ("Prince's Canal"), named after William of Orange (▶ 12), was dug at the same time as Herengracht and Keizersgracht as part of a massive 17th-century expansion scheme. Together these three form the city's distinctive horseshoe-shaped canal network. Less exclusive than the other two waterways, with smaller houses, Prinsengracht became an important thoroughfare lined with warehouses and merchants' homes. Cargo would be unloaded from ships into fifth-floor storehouses by means of the massive hoist-beams seen today in the gables of many buildings (and still used for lifting furniture). Some houses were built with a deliberate tilt, to protect their facades from the goods as they were hoisted.

Floating homes Today, you'll also see some of Amsterdam's most beautiful houseboats moored along Prinsengracht, near Brouwersgracht and alongside the ivy-covered quays close to the Amstel. Amsterdammers have long lived in houseboats, but the housing crisis after World War II skyrocketed the population of boat-people, so that there are more than 2,500 legal houseboats in Amsterdam, all with a postal address and power hook-ups. The unofficial figure is a lot higher. You will see a variety of craft on Prinsengracht, some more seaworthy than others, ranging from solid old Rhine barges to chalet-like rafts, boats with greenhouses and gardens, and trendy studio homes.

HIGHLIGHTS

- Amstelkerk (▶ 57)
- Anne Frankhuis (▶ 31)
- Noorderkerk (▶ 57)
- Noordermarkt (▶ 53)
- Westerkerk (▶ 30)

DID YOU KNOW?

- Prinsengracht is 2.8 miles long, 6 feet deep and 80 feet wide to accommodate 4 lanes of shipping
- A law (dating from 1565) restricts the lean of canal houses to 1:25

INFORMATION

- ✚ G4–G6, H6
- 🍴 Bars, cafés, restaurants (S–SSS)
- 🚊 Tram 1, 2, 4, 5, 13, 14, 16, 17, 20, 24, 25
- 🚢 Museumboat stop 2
- ↔ Herengracht (▶ 32), Anne Frankhuis (▶ 31), Westerkerk (▶ 30)

WESTERKERK

This is the most beautiful of the four churches built in the 17th century to the north, south, east, and west of the city center. The views from the tall tower are unsurpassable.

HIGHLIGHTS

- Climbing the tower
- Organ, Johannes Duyschot (1686)
- Anne Frank statue, Mari Andriessen
- Rembrandt memorial column
- Grave of Rembrandt's son, Titus

DID YOU KNOW?

- The church was consecrated in 1631
- The tower contains 48 bells
- The largest bell weighs 16,500lb. and its hammer weight is 440lb.

INFORMATION

- ✚ G5
- ✉ Prinsengracht 281, Westermarkt
- ☎ 6247766
- 🕐 Church mid-Apr to mid-Sep Mon–Sat 10–4; Sun 1–5. Tower Jun to mid-Sep, Wed–Sat 10–4
- 🚊 Tram 13, 14, 17, 20
- ⛴ Museumboat stop 2
- ♿ Few
- 🎟 Inexpensive (tower)
- ↔ Prinsengracht (▶ 29), Anne Frankhuis (▶ 31)
- ❓ Carillon concerts most Tue at noon

Masterwork The West Church, the church most visited by tourists in the city, has the largest nave of any Dutch Protestant church, and the tallest tower and largest congregation in Amsterdam. It is the masterwork of Dutch architect Hendrick de Keyser, who died in 1621, one year after construction began. Designed to serve the wealthy bourgeoisie living in the stylish new mansions of the Canal Ring, it was eventually completed by his son Pieter with Cornelis Dancker in 1631. To its tower they added the gaudy golden crown—a symbol of the city granted by Habsburg Emperor Maximilian 150 years earlier. The sweeping views over the Prinsengracht gables from the top of the tower, popularly called "Lange Jan" (Tall John), make the 280-foot climb worthwhile. Outside the church, people often lay wreaths at the foot of the statue of Anne Frank (▶ 31), who used to listen to the church bells while she was in hiding, before the bells were melted down by the Nazis.

Interior The simple, whitewashed interior is laid out in the shape of a double Greek cross. The massive organ is decorated with musical instruments and frescoes of the Evangelists by Gerard de Lairesse, who was one of Rembrandt's pupils. Rembrandt himself was buried here on October 8, 1669; although no trace of his pauper's grave remains, there is a memorial to him in the north aisle, near the grave of his son, Titus. The church's opening hours for visitors are not guaranteed; it may be closed at the times stated.

ANNE FRANKHUIS

"My greatest wish is to be a journalist, and later on, a famous writer...after the war, I'd like to publish a book called 'The Secret Annex.' It remains to be seen whether I'll succeed, but my diary can serve as a basis."

Unfulfilled wish On Thursday May 11, 1944, just under three months before she was captured by the Nazis, Anne Frank wrote these poignant words in her diary. She never saw it published, but died in the concentration camp at Belsen near the end of World War II, at the age of 15.

"The Secret Annex" After Nazi Germany invaded the Netherlands in 1940, increasingly severe anti-Semitic measures were introduced. In 1942, the Frank and van Daan families went into hiding. For the next two years, Anne Frank kept a diary describing daily life and the families' isolation and fear of discovery—until they were betrayed to the Nazis in 1944. Her father was the only member of the group to survive. In 1947, following her wishes, he published her diary, calling it *Het Achterhuis* (The Secret Annex). Today, over half a million visitors annually make their way through the revolving bookcase that conceals the entrance into the small, gloomy rooms so vividly described in the diary. Mementos on the walls include a map showing the Allied armies' advance from Normandy. Penciled lines mark the children's growth. The building is preserved by the Anne Frank Foundation, an organization founded to combat racism and anti-Semitism and to promote "the ideals set down in the Diary of Anne Frank." In one entry Anne wrote: "I want to go on living even after my death!" Thanks to her diary, this wish, at least, came true.

DID YOU KNOW?

- The Nazis occupied Amsterdam for five years
- Of Holland's 140,000 prewar Jewish population only 16,000 survived

INFORMATION

- ✚ G4
- ✉ Prinsengracht 263
- ☎ 5567100
- 🕐 Sep–Mar: daily 9–5. Apr–Aug: daily 9–9. Closed Dec 25, Jan 1, Yom Kippur
- 🚋 Tram 13, 14, 17, 20
- 🚤 Museumboat stop 2
- ♿ None
- 💷 Expensive
- ↔ Prinsengracht (➤ 29), Westerkerk (➤ 30)
- ❓ 5-minute introductory film

Top: the revolving bookcase. Below: sculpture of Anne Frank

9

HERENGRACHT

INFORMATION

- ✚ H4, H6, G4–G6
- 🍴 Bars, cafés, and restaurants (S–SSS)
- 🚃 Tram 1, 2, 4, 5, 13, 14, 16, 17, 20, 24, 25
- 📷 Museumboat stop 5
- ↔ Singel (➤ 33), Museum Willet-Holthuysen (➤ 42)

Exploring the city's grandest canal is like going back through time to Amsterdam's Golden Age. These gilded houses are a case study of four centuries of Dutch architectural styles.

The Gentlemen's Canal Herengracht takes its name from the rich merchants and traders of Amsterdam's heyday, and was the first of three concentric canals dug early in the 17th century to house the city's fast-growing population. Attracting the wealthiest merchant aristocrats, it has the largest, most ostentatious houses, 400 of which are now protected monuments. The houses had to conform to many building standards. Even the color of the front doors— "Amsterdam green"—was regulated. Taxes were levied according to the width of the canal frontage, hence the rows of tall, narrow residences.

Gable-spotting Canal house owners expressed themselves in the elaborate decoration of their houses' gables and facades, and you can find every imaginable design along Herengracht. The earliest and most common are the *step* gable and the *spout* gable. Amsterdam's first *neck* gable (No. 168) was built in 1638 by Philip Vingboons, and the *bell* gable became popular early in the 18th century. Around this time, Louis XIV-style facades were fashionable. Number 475 is a fine example—nicknamed "the jewel of canal houses."

The Golden Bend Amsterdam's most extravagant mansions, with double fronts, were built between Leidsestraat and Vijzelstraat, along the stretch of the canal since dubbed the "Golden Bend." To this day, it remains the most prestigious address in town.

Top: a bell gable beside the Herengracht

SINGEL

On first glance, this canal looks like any other major waterway in the city. Look a little closer, though, and you will discover some of Amsterdam's most unusual and enchanting sights.

Former city "belt" From its construction in the early 15th century until the late 16th century, the city limits were marked by the Singel (originally *Cingle*, meaning "belt"), the city's defensive moat. Then, in 1586, the city council decided to build quays along the Singel's west bank and to convert the moat into a canal for large freight ships. Thus the Singel became the first of Amsterdam's concentric canals, and its curved shape established the horseshoe layout of the city. With the coming of the railroads, canal transportation became less important and the Singel began to acquire a more residential character. Many warehouses are now converted into homes. The Nieuwe Haarlemmersluis, at the junction of Singel and Brouwersgracht, is opened nightly to top up the city's canals.

Flowers and floating felines Perhaps the most unusual house is No. 7. The narrowest house in Amsterdam, it was made no wider than a front door in order to minimize property taxes (►32). Opposite is the *Poezenboot*, a houseboat that is a refuge for stray cats. Look out, too, for the Torensluis (Tower Lock, on the Singel's widest bridge); in the 17th century it was used as a prison. The bridge has a monument to Multatuli (1820–87), one of the Netherlands' greatest writers. Europe's only floating flower market, the Bloemenmarkt, is also on the Singel.

HIGHLIGHTS

- Poezenboot
- Bloemenmarkt (► 38)
- Torensluis prison cell
- Munttoren (► 55)
- No. 7: narrowest house facade
- No. 2, 36, 74, 83: unusual facades

INFORMATION

- ✚ H4, G5–H5
- ✉ Singel
- 🕐 Poezenboot: 1–4PM daily
- 🍴 Cafés and restaurants (S–SSS)
- 🚊 Tram 13, 14, 17, 20
- ♿ Poezenboot: none
- 💰 Poezenboot: free
- ↔ Bloemenmarkt (► 38), Herengracht (► 32), Koninklijk Paleis (► 36), Begijnhof (► 34)

The Bloemenmarkt brings a riot of color to the Singel

BEGIJNHOF

Tranquillity characterizes Amsterdam's many hofjes (almshouses), none more so than this leafy oasis. The cobbled courtyard, edged with delightful buildings resembling dollhouses, looks almost like a film set.

INFORMATION

- ✚ H5
- ✉ Gedempte Begijnsloot (entrance in Spui)
- 🕐 Dawn till dusk
- 🚌 Tram 1, 2, 5
- ♿ Good
- 🎟 Free
- ↔ Amsterdams Historisch Museum (➤ 35), Singel (➤ 33)

Below: one of Amsterdam's oldest buildings, the Wooden House

Pious women A tiny, unlikely looking gateway leads to the Begijnhof, the oldest and finest *hofje* in the country (almshouses were charitable lodgings for the poor). This secluded community of magnificently restored old houses and gardens clustered around a small church lies a stone's throw from the main shopping thoroughfare. It was built in 1346 as a sanctuary for the *Begijnen* or Beguines, unmarried women who wanted to live in a religious community without becoming nuns. In return for modest lodging, they devoted themselves to the care of the poor and sick. Today, the Begijnhof is a residence for single women earning less than f35,000 ($18,500) a year, and has a five-year waiting list.

Two churches The Begijnkerk (1419), which dominates the courtyard, was confiscated from the Beguines during the Alteration in 1578 (➤ 12). The women continued to worship secretly until religious tolerance was restored over 200 years later, in 1795. Meanwhile, their precious church became a warehouse until 1607, when it was given to the Presbyterian community and renamed the Engelse Kerk (English Church). The simple interior contains pulpit panels designed by Piet Mondrian. Nearby, het Houten Huys (the Wooden House, 1477) is one of only two remaining wood-fronted houses in Amsterdam. It was built before 1521, when the use of wood as a building material was banned, following a series of fires. Look out for a nearby courtyard, with walls dotted with gable stones salvaged from demolished Begijnhof houses.

AMSTERDAMS HISTORISCH MUSEUM

Do make this excellent museum your first port of call. Once you have a grasp of Amsterdam's colorful history, walks around town are all the more rewarding.

The building This lively, informative museum traces the growth of Amsterdam from a 13th-century fishing village to bustling metropolis, through an impressive collection of paintings, maps, models, and historical artifacts. They are displayed chronologically in one of the city's oldest buildings. Originally a monastery, it was occupied by the city orphanage (Burger-weeshuis) for nearly 400 years, until 1975, when it was converted into a museum. Most of the present structure dates from the 16th and 17th centuries. Throughout, you can still see evidence of its former use—notably the ceiling paintings in the Regent's Chamber and the numerous portraits of children, including Jan Carel van Speyck, who later in life became a Dutch naval hero.

The collections The first rooms of the museum chronicle the city's early history and its rise to prominence in trade and commerce. The displays include furniture, memorabilia, and a map that illuminates each 25-year period of growth through the centuries. The museum's main focus is on the Golden Age and colonial expansion. Paintings and photographs illustrate the growing welfare problems of the 19th and early 20th centuries, and a small collection of relics from World War II shows how the Nazi occupation affected the city's population, 10 percent of which was Jewish. Finally, in the adjoining Schuttersgalerij, don't miss the portraits of the dapper Civic Guard, an armed civilian force formed in the late 14th century to police the city.

HIGHLIGHTS

- *View of Amsterdam*, Cornelis Anthonisz (1538), the oldest city map
- *The Meal of the 17 Guardsmen of Company H*, Cornelis Anthonisz (1533), in the Schuttersgalerij
- *The First Steamship on the IJ*, Nicolaas Bavo (1816)
- *Governesses at the Burgher Orphanage*, Adriaen Backer (1683)
- *Girls from the Civic Orphanage*, Nicolaas van der Waay (1880)
- Bell room

INFORMATION

- ✚ H5
- ✉ Kalverstraat 92, Nieuwezijds Voorburgwal 357, St Luciensteeg 27
- ☎ 5231822
- 🕐 Mon–Fri 10–5; Sat, Sun 11–5. Closed Jan 1, Apr 30, Dec 25
- 🍴 David and Goliath Café (SS)
- 🚋 Tram 1, 2, 4, 5, 9, 16, 20, 24, 25
- ♿ Very good
- 🚤 Museumboat stop 5
- 💷 Moderate
- ↔ Begijnhof (► 34), Koninklijk Paleis (► 36)
- ❓ Guided tours on request: telephone in advance

Top: Armor on display in the Amsterdams Historisch Museum

KONINKLIJK PALEIS

HIGHLIGHTS

- Views of Dam square
- Tribunal
- Citizen's Hall
- Facade

DID YOU KNOW?

- The state bought the palace in 1936 for f10 million
- The palace rests on 13,659 piles driven 60 feet into the ground
- It is 265 feet long and 125 feet wide
- The bell tower is 119 feet high

INFORMATION

- H5
- Dam
- 6204060
- Jun–Aug: Tue–Thu 1–4, other days 12:30–5. Sep–May: phone for details. Closed public hols and when the Queen is in residence
- Tram 4, 9, 14, 16, 20, 24, 25
- Good
- Moderate
- Nieuwe Kerk (➤ 37), Amsterdams Historisch Museum (➤ 35), Begijnhof (➤ 34)

Don't be put off by the Royal Palace's sober exterior. Stern and heavy, it belies the lavish decoration inside—a reminder of the power of Amsterdam in its heyday.

Civic pride At the height of the Golden Age, architect Jacob van Campen was commissioned to design Europe's largest and grandest town hall, and its classical design was a startling and progressive departure from the Dutch Renaissance style. The poet Constantyn Huygens called the Stadhuis "the world's Eighth Wonder" and to this day it remains the city's only secular building on such a grand scale. Note the facade's astonishing wealth of decoration, numerous statues, an elaborate pediment, and a huge cupola crowned by a galleon weather vane. During the seven years of construction, a heated argument developed as to whether a tower for the Nieuwe Kerk should have priority over a town hall. This was resolved when the old town hall burned down, and in 1655 the mayor moved into his new building.

Palatial splendor The town hall was transformed into a royal palace in 1808 after Napoleon made his brother Louis King of Holland. Today it serves as an occasional residence for Queen Beatrix, whose principal palace is in The Hague. Inside, be sure to see the Tribunal and the sumptuous Burgerzaal (Citizen's Hall), running the length of the palace, with the entire eastern and western hemispheres mapped out on the floor. The Tribunal was once the city's main courtroom, and condemned prisoners were taken from here to be hanged publicly in Dam square. The graceful Schepenzaal (Council Chamber), where the city aldermen met, has Rembrandt pupil Ferdinand Bol's painting of *Moses the Lawgiver*.

NIEUWE KERK

Considering its turbulent history, it is something of a miracle that Holland's magnificent national church has survived. Hearing its organ is a real treat.

Not so new The "New" Church actually dates from the 15th century, when Amsterdam was growing at such a rate that the "Old" Church (Oude Kerk, ►40) was no longer sufficient. Construction started in 1408 but the church was several times destroyed by fire. After the Alteration in 1578, (when Amsterdam officially became Protestant), and a further fire in 1645, the church was rebuilt and reconsecrated in 1648. It has no spire: following years of fierce debate, the money designated for its construction was spent to complete the Royal Palace (► 36). It does have one of the finest of Amsterdam's 42 historic church organs—a Schonat-Hagerbeer organ, dating from 1650–73, with 5,005 pipes and a full-voiced sound that easily fills the church's vast interior.

Famous names At the time of the Alteration (► 12), Amsterdam's churches were largely stripped of their treasures, and the Nieuwe Kerk was no exception. The altar space has since been occupied by the tomb of Holland's most valiant naval hero, Admiral de Ruyter, one of many names from Dutch history, including poets P. C. Hooft and Joost van den Vondel, buried in the church. A window dated 1650 shows the granting of the city's coat of arms by William IV. Another, by Otto Mengelberg to mark her 40th year as queen, shows Wilhelmina at her inauguration in 1898. Dutch monarchs have been inaugurated here, from William I in 1815 to Beatrix in 1980. Although it is no longer a place of worship, it holds regular exhibitions and organ recitals.

Top: tomb of Michiel de Ruyter. Above: the Nieuwe Kerk from Dam Square

HIGHLIGHTS

- Organ, Hans Schonat and Jacob Hagerbeer (1650–73)
- Organ case, Jacob van Campen (1645)
- Pulpit, Albert Vinckenbrinck (1649)
- Tomb of Admiral de Ruyter, Rombout Verhulst (1681)

INFORMATION

✚	H5
✉	Dam
☎	6268168
◷	Variable
🍴	Nieuwe Café (SS)
🚊	Tram 1, 2, 4, 5, 9, 13, 14, 16, 17, 20, 24, 25
♿	Good
🎟	Varies with exhibitions
↔	Koninklijk Paleis (► 36)

37

BLOEMENMARKT

HIGHLIGHTS

- De Tuin bulb stand (opposite Singel 502) (▶ 71)
- Van Zoomeren cactus display (opposite Singel 526)
- Vazoplant pots and stands (opposite Singel 514)

INFORMATION

Tulipa Whittalli *from Curtis's Botanical Magazine* c1795

Golden sunflowers, deep blue irises, delicately scented roses, and row upon row of tulips and brightly packaged tulip bulbs—the barges that serve as stalls for Amsterdam's fragrant flower market are ablaze with color, whatever the season.

Floating market During the 17th and 18th centuries there were approximately 20 floating markets in Amsterdam, at least two of which gratified the Dutch passion for tulips. Nurserymen would sail up the Amstel from their smallholdings and moor here to sell their wares directly from their boats. Today, the stalls at this, the city's only remaining floating market, are permanently moored. Offering a vast variety of seasonal flowers, plants, pots, shrubs, and herbs, they are supplied by the florists of Aalsmeer and the region around Haarlem (▶ 20), at the horticultural heart of Holland. With over 40,000 acres of the country devoted to bulb growing, it is easy to see why the Dutch are nicknamed "the florists of Europe."

Tulip mania Tulips were first spotted in Turkey by Dutch diplomats, who brought them back to Holland around 1600. Shortly afterwards, a Leiden botanist discovered ways of changing their shape and color, and tulip cultivation rapidly became a national obsession. Prices soared, with single bulbs fetching up to f3,000 (an average worker's annual salary was f150). Some were even exchanged for houses, and an abundance of still life paintings was produced to capture prize blooms on canvas. In 1637, the bubble burst, and many people lost entire fortunes. Prices are more realistic today and tulip bulbs are popular souvenirs for tourists; the Bloemenmarkt remains the best place to buy the many varieties.

ROSSE BUURT

Amsterdam's Red Light District, bathed in a lurid red neon glow, and full of gaping tourists, junkies, and pickpockets, is one of the city's greatest attractions.

Sex for sale Because of the port and its sailor population, sex is, and long has been, big business in Amsterdam. As early as the 15th century, Amsterdam was infamous as a center of prostitution, and the lure of the Red Light District proves irresistible to most visitors to the city today. Crowds clog the narrow alleyways, sex shops, peep shows, and suggestively named bars, while bored prostitutes beckon from their pink-lit windows. But there is more to the Red Light District than sex. Among the sleaziness, there are scattered some welcoming, ordinary cafés, bars, and restaurants. "Normal" people live here, too, and go about their everyday business in what, behind the tawdry facade, is an interesting part of the old city.

Drug central The Red Light District is also frequented by drug dealers, and here you will find the great majority of Amsterdam's psychedelic, marijuana-selling "smoking" coffee shops (➤ 69). The Hash Marihuana Hemp Museum on Oudezijds Achterburgwal is the only museum in Europe tracing the history of hashish and the cannabis plant, and is next to the world's only Cannabis Connoisseurs' Club.

Precautions Watch your wallet, avoid eye contact with any undesirable characters, do not take photographs of prostitutes, and avoid poorly lit alleyways. Even though the evening is the liveliest time to visit, it is best not to wander around alone. Stay alert in the Red Light District and exercise caution in quiet areas at night, or avoid them completely.

DID YOU KNOW?

- Possession of drugs is technically illegal but the authorities tolerate possession of up to one ounce of soft drugs (cannabis, hashish and marijuana) for personal use
- Drug-dealing is not allowed. "Smoking" coffee shops are tolerated (➤ 69)
- 30 percent of the city's hard-drug users carry the AIDS virus
- Brothels were legalized in 1990
- Half of Amsterdam's prostitutes are foreign

INFORMATION

➕ H4–H5
✉ Borders roughly denoted by Zeedijk (north), Kloveniersburgwal (east), Damstraat (south), and Warmoesstraat (west)
🍴 Restaurants, bars, cafés (S–SSS)
🚇 Centraal Station, Nieuwmarkt
🚋 Tram 4, 9, 14, 16, 20, 24, 25
🔄 Oude Kerk (➤ 40), Museum Amstelkring (➤ 41)

OUDE KERK

Surrounded by the cafés, bars, and sex shops, the Old Church represents an island of spirituality in the Red Light District. The contrast is typical of Amsterdam.

HIGHLIGHTS

- Great Organ, Vatermüller
- Stained-glass windows, Lambert van Noort (1555)
- Carillon, F. Hemony (1658)

INFORMATION

- ✚ H5
- ✉ Oudekerksplein 1
- ☎ 6258284
- 🕐 Mon–Sat 11–5; Sun 1–5. Closed Jan 1, Apr 30
- 🚌 Tram 4, 9, 16, 20, 24, 25
- ♿ Good
- 💰 Moderate
- ↔ Rosse Buurt (➤ 39), Museum Amstelkring (➤ 41)
- ❓ Frequent organ recitals and carillon concerts

The 18th-century Great Organ

History Amsterdam's oldest church, dedicated to St. Nicholas, the patron saint of seafarers, was built in 1306 to replace a wooden chapel that probably dated from the late 1200s. Over the centuries the church escaped the great fires that devastated so much of the city, and the imposing basilica you see today dates largely from the 14th century. Its graceful tower, added in 1565–67, contains one of the finest carillons in Holland. In the 16th century Jan Pieters Sweelinck, Holland's best-known composer, was organist here.

Miracle In the 14th century, the Oude Kerk became one of Europe's pilgrimage centers following a miracle: Communion bread regurgitated by a dying man and thrown on the fire, would not burn, and the sick man did not die. Today, thousands of Catholics still take part in the annual *Stille Omgang*, a silent nocturnal procession, but as the Oude Kerk is now Protestant, it no longer follows the ancient pilgrim route to the church, going instead to the Begijnhof.

Sober interior The stark, impressive interior has a triple nave and elaborate vaulting. Three magnificent windows in the Lady Chapel survived the Alteration, as did the finely carved choir stools. In the 1960s some delicate 14th-century paintings were found behind layers of blue paint in the vaults. The tombstone of Rembrandt's first wife, Saskia van Uylenburg, is still in the church even though poverty drove him to sell her grave plot.

MUSEUM AMSTELKRING

Not only is this tiny museum one of the city's most surprising, it is also off the beaten tourist track, tucked away in a small, inconspicuous canal house on the edge of the Red Light District.

Best-kept secret In 1578, when the Roman Catholic city council was replaced by a Protestant one (▶ 12), Roman Catholic churches were closed throughout the city. In 1661, while Catholic church services were still forbidden, a wealthy merchant named Jan Hartman built a residence on the Oudezijds Voorburgwal, and two adjoining houses in the Heintje Hoeckssteeg. He ran a sock shop on the first floor, lived upstairs, rented out the spare rooms in the buildings behind and cleverly converted the top two stories of the canal house, and the attics of all three buildings, into a secret Catholic church. Religious freedom only returned with the French occupation of the Netherlands in 1795.

Hidden church This "schuilkerk" was just one of many clandestine churches that sprang up throughout the city, but it is the only one that has been completely preserved. It was saved from demolition in 1888 by a group of historians called the Amstelkring (Amstel "circle"), who nicknamed the church "Our Dear Lord in the Attic." To find a three-story, galleried church at the top of a series of increasingly steep staircases is an awesome experience. With seating for 200 people, magnificent ecclesiastical statuary, silver, paintings, a collapsible altar, and a huge organ, it is hard to believe that the services held here were really secret. Look for the resident priest's tiny hidden bedroom under the stairs, and the confessional on the landing. The rest of the complex has been restored, and provides a taste of domestic life in the 17th century.

HIGHLIGHTS

- Church of "Our Dear Lord in the Attic"
- Altar painting *The Baptism of Christ*, Jacob de Wit (1716)
- Priest's bedroom
- Confessional
- Drawing room
- Kitchen

DID YOU KNOW?

- The altarpiece is one of three paintings by Jacob de Wit, designed to be interchangeable
- The church is still a consecrated place of worship

INFORMATION

- ✚ H4
- ✉ Oudezijds Voorburgwal 40
- ☎ 6246604
- 🕐 Mon–Sat 10–5; Sun, public hols 1–5. Closed Jan 1, Apr 30
- 🚉 Centraal Station
- 🚊 Tram 4, 9, 16, 20, 24, 25
- 🚉 Centraal Station
- 🚢 Museumboat stop 1
- ♿ None
- 💶 Moderate
- ↔ Rosse Buurt (▶ 39), Oude Kerk (▶ 40)
- ❓ Classical concerts during winter

Top: "Our Dear Lord in the Attic"

MUSEUM WILLET-HOLTHUYSEN

HIGHLIGHTS

- Blue Room
- Dining Room
- Porcelain and silver collections
- Kitchen
- Garden Room
- Garden

INFORMATION

- H5–H6
- Herengracht 605
- 5231870
- Mon–Fri 10–5; Sat, Sun 11–5
- Waterlooplein
- Tram 4, 9, 14, 20
- Museumboat stop 6
- None
- Moderate
- Herengracht (▶ 32), Magere Brug (▶ 45), Joods Historisch Museum (▶ 46)

Behind the impressive facade of this gracious mansion lies a sumptuously furnished home with a delightful garden, a rare luxury in Amsterdam.

Insight This beautifully preserved house on Herengracht, Amsterdam's most elegant canal (▶ 32), was built in 1687 for Jacob Hop, a wealthy member of the city council. It changed hands many times and eventually, in 1855, came into the possession of a glass merchant named Pieter Gerard Holthuysen. On his death, it became the home of his daughter Sandra and her husband, the art-collector Abraham Willet, who together built up a valuable collection of glass, silver, ceramics, and paintings. The couple bequeathed the house and its contents to the city in 1895, to be used as a museum. For many years it was visited so rarely that people joked that it was the best place for a gentleman to meet his mistress unobserved. However, following extensive restoration in 1996, the museum is attracting an increasing number of visitors, and providing a rare insight into life in the grand canal-houses in the 17th to 19th centuries.

Luxury and grandeur The rooms are lavishly decorated with inlaid wood and lacquered paneling with painted ceilings. Be sure to see the Blue Room, formerly the preserve of the gentlemen of the house, and the 17th-century kitchen, with its original plumbing. Guests would be served tea in the tiny, round Garden Room that, painted in the customary pale green, looks out over an immaculate French-style formal garden, lined with topiary and studded with statues. This is one of the city's few surviving 18th-century gardens—and is a jewel not to be missed.

STOELTIE DIAMONDS

When you tour this diamond-polishing factory, be assured there is no pressure to buy, but the allure of all those dazzling jewels may well leave you mesmerized.

Diamonds are forever Amsterdam's association with diamonds dates from the 16th century, when Antwerp was taken by the Spanish and thousands of refugees fled north, including Jewish diamond cutters and the city's most prosperous Jewish merchants. Amsterdam's guild controls prevented them from entering most other trades so they soon established new businesses processing diamonds and dealing in the stones, and were thriving. By the 19th century, they were employing thousands of workers, and when vast fields of diamonds were discovered in South Africa in 1867, most of the stones were brought to Amsterdam to be cut. Amsterdam reigned as the diamond capital of the world until World War II, when most of the city's Jewish workers were deported to concentration camps. Because few returned, Antwerp regained its leadership of the world diamond market after the war, but diamonds from Amsterdam are known for their quality and outstanding workmanship.

Tour Many of Amsterdam's 24 diamond-polishing factories offer tours. Stoeltie's, which lasts about 30 minutes, includes a brief history of diamonds, their many industrial applications, how they are mined and the fine art of diamond production, a surprisingly grimy process considering the brilliant product. It is fascinating to watch the craft workers at their benches, deftly cutting, polishing, sorting, and setting the glittering gems. Stoeltie Diamonds is one of five members of the Amsterdam Diamond Foundation, a symbol of quality and fair dealing, though not necessarily of modest prices.

DID YOU KNOW?

- The first records of Amsterdam's diamond industry date from 1586
- At its peak, it employed over 10,000 workers
- Only 20 percent of diamonds are used in jewelry
- The world's largest-ever cut diamond, the Cullinan I ("Star of Africa") weighs 530 carats. The world's smallest-ever cut diamond has 57 facets and weighs 0.0012 carats. Both were processed in Amsterdam
- The General Dutch Diamond Workers Union, founded in 1894, was the first union in the world to win an eight-hour working day

INFORMATION

- ➕ H5
- ✉ Wagenstraat 13–17
- ☎ 6237601
- 🕐 Daily 9–5
- Ⓠ Waterlooplein
- 🚊 Tram 4, 9, 14, 20
- ♿ Very good
- 🎟 Free
- ↔ Museum Willet-Holthuysen (➤ 42)

Top: working on diamonds

21

Museum het Rembrandthuis

HIGHLIGHTS

- *Self-portrait with a Surprised Expression*
- *Jan Six*
- *Five Studies of the Head of Saskia and One of an Older Woman*
- *View of Amsterdam*
- *Christ Shown to the People*

INFORMATION

- ✚ H5
- ✉ Jodenbreestraat 4–6
- ☎ 5200400
- 🕐 Mon–Sat 10–5; Sun, public hols 1–5. Closed Jan 1
- Ⓜ Nieuwmarkt, Waterlooplein
- 🚃 Tram 9, 14, 20
- ⛴ Museumboot stop 6
- ♿ Few
- 🅿 Moderate
- ↔ Joods Historisch Museum (➤ 46), Museum Willet-Holthuysen (➤ 42)
- ❓ Brief film of Rembrandt's life

Below: Self-portrait with Saskia Rembrandt, 1636

The absence of Rembrandt's own belongings from this intimate house is more than compensated for by its collection of his etchings, which is virtually complete. They are fascinating.

From riches to rags In this red-shuttered canal house, Rembrandt spent the happiest and most successful years of his life, producing many of his most famous paintings and prints here. Because of his wife, the wealthy heiress Saskia van Uylenburg, the up-and-coming young artist had been introduced to Amsterdam's patrician class and commissions for portraits had poured in. He had rapidly become an esteemed painter, and bought this large, three-story house in 1639 as a symbol of his newfound respectability. After Saskia's tragic death, age 30, in 1642 shortly after the birth of their son Titus, Rembrandt's work became unfashionable, and in 1656 he was declared bankrupt. The house and most of his possessions were sold in 1658, although Rembrandt continued to live here until 1660. He died a pauper in 1669 (➤ 30).

Funny faces It is a strange experience to see 260 of the 280 etchings ascribed to Rembrandt in the very surroundings in which they were created. His achievements in etching were as important as those in his painting, since his mastery in this medium inspired its recognition as an art form for the first time. Four of his copper etching plates are on display on the first floor, together with an exhibition on traditional etching techniques, and a series of biblical illustrations. Visit the first floor, too, where Rembrandt's studies of street figures are hung alongside some highly entertaining self-portraits in various guises, and some mirror-images of himself making faces.

MAGERE BRUG

This traditional double-leaf Dutch draw-bridge is a much-loved city landmark, and one of the most photographed sights in Amsterdam at night, illuminated by strings of enchanting lights.

Skinny sisters Of Amsterdam's 1,200 or so bridges, the wooden "Skinny Bridge" is, without doubt, the best known. Situated on the Amstel river, it is a 20th-century replica of a 17th-century drawbridge. Tradition has it that, in 1670, a simple footbridge was built by two elderly sisters named *Mager* (meaning 'skinny'), who lived on one side of the Amstel and wanted easy access to their carriage and horses, stabled on the other bank. It seems more likely, however, that the bridge took its name from its narrow girth. In 1772 it was widened and became a double drawbridge, enabling ships of heavy tonnage to sail up the Amstel from the IJ, an inlet of what was then a sea called the Zuider Zee and is today the IJsselmeer, a freshwater lake.

City uproar In 1929 the city council started discussing whether to demolish the old frame, which had rotted. It was to be replaced with an electrically operated bridge. After a huge outcry, the people of Amsterdam voted overwhelmingly to save the original wooden bridge.

The present bridge, made of African azobe wood, was erected in 1969 and its mechanical drive installed in 1994. Every now and then, you can watch the bridge master raising the bridge to let boats through. He then jumps on his bicycle and rides hastily upstream to open the Amstel and Hoge sluice gates, only to mount his bike again and repeat the whole procedure.

DID YOU KNOW?

- 63,000 boats pass under the bridge each year
- Rebuilding in 1969 cost f140,000 ($74,000)
- There are 60 drawbridges in Amsterdam

INFORMATION

- ⊞ H6
- ✉ Amstel
- Ⓠ Waterlooplein
- 🚊 Tram 4, 9, 14, 20
- 🚋 Museumboat stop 6
- ↔ Museum Willet-Holthuysen (➤ 42), Joods Historisch Museum (➤ 46)

Top: the Magere Brug, all lit up at night

JOODS HISTORISCH MUSEUM

HIGHLIGHTS

- Grote Schul (Great Synagogue, 1671)
- Holy Ark (1791)
- Haggadah Manuscript (1734)

DID YOU KNOW?

- 1597 First Jew gained Dutch citizenship
- 1602 Judaism first practiced openly here
- 1671 The Grote Schul became the first synagogue in Western Europe
- 102,000 of the 140,000-strong Dutch Jewish community were exterminated in World War II
- Restoration of the synagogues cost over f13 million (S7 million)

INFORMATION

- ✚ H5
- ✉ Jonas Daniël Meijerplein 2–4
- ☎ 6269945
- 🕐 Daily 11–5. Closed Yom Kippur
- 🍴 Café (SS)
- Ⓜ Waterlooplein
- 🚊 Tram 9, 14, 20
- 🚢 Museumboat stop 6
- ♿ Very good
- 👥 Moderate
- ↔ Museum het Rembrandthuis (➤ 44), Museum Willet-Holthuysen (➤ 42), Magere Brug (➤ 45)

Top: the Great Synagogue

A remarkable exhibition devoted to Judaism and the story of Jewish settlement in Amsterdam, this is of interest whether or not you're Jewish. The most memorable and poignant part portrays the horrors of the Holocaust.

Reconstruction Located in the heart of what used to be a Jewish neighborhood, this massive complex of four synagogues forms the largest and most important Jewish museum outside Israel. The buildings lay in ruins for many years after World War II, and have only recently been painstakingly reconstructed as a monument to the strength of the Jewish faith and to the suffering of the Jewish people under the Nazis.

Historical exhibits The New Synagogue (1752) gives a lengthy, detailed history of Zionism, with displays of religious artifacts. The Great Synagogue (1671), of more general interest, defines the role of the Jewish community in Amsterdam's trade and industry. Downstairs is a chilling exhibition from the war years and a moving collection by Jewish painters, including a series entitled *Life? or Theater?* by Charlotte Salomon, who died in Auschwitz aged 26.

The Dockworker The Nazis occupied Amsterdam in May 1940 and immediately began to persecute the Jewish population. In February 1941, 400 Jews were gathered outside the Great Synagogue by the SS, herded into trucks and taken away. This triggered the February Strike, a general strike led by dockers. Though suppressed after only two days, it was Amsterdam's first open revolt against Nazism and gave impetus to the resistance movement. Every February 25, a ceremony at Andriessen's statue *The Dockworker* commemorates the strike.

24

NEDERLANDS SCHEEPVAART MUSEUM

Holland's glorious seafaring history gets due recognition at this museum, which displays with contemporary flair a superb collection of ships, full-size replicas, and hundreds of models and nautical artifacts.

Admiralty storehouse The vast neoclassical building (1656) that now houses the Maritime Museum was formerly the Dutch Admiralty's central store. Here the East India Company would load their ships prior to the eight-month journey to Jakarta, headquarters of the VOC in Indonesia (► 12). In 1973, the arsenal was converted into this museum, which has the largest collection of ships in the world.

Voyages of discovery An ancient dugout, a re-created section of a destroyer, schooners, and luxury liners depict Holland's remarkable maritime history. Children can peer through periscopes and operate a radar set, while parents marvel at some 500 magnificent model ships and study the charts, instruments, weapons, maps, and globes from the great age of exploration. Don't miss the first-ever sea atlas, the mid-16th century three-masted ship model, or the beautiful royal sloop—the "golden coach on water"—last used in 1962 for Queen Juliana's silver wedding anniversary.

The *Amsterdam* The highlight of the museum is moored alongside—the *Amsterdam*, a replica of the 18th-century Dutch East Indiaman that sank off the English coast in 1749 during her maiden voyage. A vivid film "Voyage to the East Indies" is shown, and in summer, actors become bawdy "sailors," firing cannons, swabbing the decks, loading cargo, and enacting burials at sea. The *Stad Amsterdam*, a replica of a clipper from 1854, began construction at the wharf in 1999.

HIGHLIGHTS

- The *Amsterdam*
- Royal sloop
- Blaeu's World Atlas (Room 1)
- First printed map of Amsterdam (Room 1)
- Three-masted ship (Room 2)
- Wartime exhibits (Rooms 21–24)

INFORMATION

- ✚ J5
- ✉ Kattenburgerplein 1
- ☎ 5232222
- 🕐 Tue–Sat 10–5; Sun & hols 12–5. (Also Mon 10–5 in summer). Closed Jan 1. Crew on board *Amsterdam* in summer Mon–Sat 10:30–4:15; Sun 12:30–4:15. Winter Tue–Sun 11–3
- 🍴 Café (S)
- 🚌 Bus 22, 32
- 🚢 Museumboat stop 7
- ♿ Very good
- 💰 Expensive
- ↔ Artis Zoo (► 59), Hortus Botanicus (► 58)
- ❓ Souvenir and book shop, model-boat kit shop Thu and Fri only, multimedia theater

Top: the ornate stern of the replica of the Amsterdam

47

25

TROPENMUSEUM

HIGHLIGHTS

- Bombay slums
- Arabian souk
- Bangladeshi village
- Indonesian farmhouse
- Indonesian gamelan orchestra
- Pacific carved wooden boats
- Papua New Guinean Bisj Poles
- Puppet and musical instrument collections

INFORMATION

- ✚ K6
- ✉ Linnaeusstraat 2
- ☎ 5688215. Children's Museum ☎ 5688233
- 🕐 Mon–Fri 10–5; Sat, Sun, hols 12–5. Closed Jan 1, Apr 30, May 5, Dec 25. Children's Museum 🕐 Wed afternoons, Sat, Sun; and Mon–Fri during school hols
- 🍴 Café and restaurant Ekeko
- 🚊 Tram 9, 14, 20
- ♿ Very good
- 💲 Expensive
- ⬌ Artis Zoo (➤ 59), Hortus Botanicus (➤ 58)
- ❓ Soeterijn Theater. Shop ☎ 5688233 for further information

Top: statue of a Hindu goddess in the Tropenmuseum

In the extraordinary Tropical Museum, once a hymn to colonialism, colorful reconstructions of street scenes with sounds, photographs, and slide presentations evoke contemporary life in tropical regions.

Foundations In 1859, Frederik Willem van Eeden, a member of the Dutch Society for the Promotion of Industry, was asked to establish a collection of objects from the Dutch colonies "for the instruction and amusement of the Dutch people." The collection started with a simple bow, arrows, and quiver from Borneo and a lacquer water scoop from Palembang, then expanded at a staggering rate, as did the number of visitors. In the 1920s, to house the collection, the palatial Colonial Institute was constructed and adorned with stone friezes to reflect Holland's imperial achievements. In the 1970s, the emphasis shifted away from the glories of colonialism towards an explanation of Third World problems. Beside the museum is the Oosterpark, a pleasant green space.

Another world The precious collections are not displayed in glass cases, but instead are set out in lifelike settings, amid evocative sounds, photographs, and slide presentations, so that you feel as if you've stepped into other continents. Explore a Bombay slum, feel the fabrics in an Arabian souk, have a rest in a Nigerian bar, contemplate in a Hindu temple, or listen to the sounds of Latin America in a café. There is also a theater, the Soeterijn, where visiting performers mount performances of non-Western music, theater, and dance in the evenings. During the day, activities in the children's section, Kindermuseum TMJunior, give youngsters an insight into other cultures.

AMSTERDAM's
best

CANALS & WATERWAYS

See Top 25 sights for:
HERENGRACHT (► 32)
PRINSENGRACHT (► 29)
SINGEL (► 33)

Sunken booty

The canals receive many of the city's unwanted items. More than 25 million gallons of sludge and rubbish are removed annually by a fleet of ten municipal boats: six for recovering floating refuse, one for retrieving bikes (about 10,000 a year), using hooks, and three dredgers. Among the "treasures" they find are stolen wallets, parking meters, cars with failed hand brakes, and even an occasional corpse.

AMSTEL

The river is a busy commercial thoroughfare, with barges carrying goods to and from the port. Its sturdy 18th-century wooden sluice gates are closed four times a week. This enables fresh water from the IJmeer to flow into the canal network.
🚻 H5–H6, H9–H10, J6–J9   🚊 Tram 4, 9, 14, 16, 20, 24, 25

AMSTERDAM–RHINE CANAL

Amsterdam's longest waterway stretches from the IJ to Switzerland.
🚻 M5–M6, N6–N7   🚌 Bus 37, 220, 245

BLAUWBURGWAL

Amsterdam's shortest canal extends between Singel and Herengracht.
🚻 H4   🚊 Tram 1, 2, 5, 13, 17, 20

BLOEMGRACHT AND EGELANTIERSGRACHT

These intimate, narrow thoroughfares in the Jordaan, a retreat from the hustle and bustle of downtown, are lined with colorful small boats.
🚻 G4–G5   🚊 Tram 13, 14, 17, 20

BROUWERSGRACHT

Also in the Jordaan, the Brouwersgracht owes its name to the many breweries established here in the 16th and 17th centuries. Houseboats and the old warehouses that line it (once used to store barley but today converted into luxury apartments) make this leafy canal particularly photogenic.
🚻 G4–H4   🚇 Centraal Station

The junction of the Keizersgracht and the Reguliersgracht

GROENBURGWAL
This idyllic, picturesque canal near the Muziektheater was Monet's favorite.
⊞ H5 🚇 Nieuwmarkt

THE IJ
Amsterdam is situated on precariously low-lying ground at the confluence of the IJ (an inlet of the IJsselmeer lake) and the Amstel river. During Amsterdam's heyday in the 17th century, most maritime activity was centered on the IJ inlet and along Prins Hendrikkade, where the old warehouses were crammed with spices and other exotic produce from the East. Since 1876, access to the sea has been via the North Sea Canal, and the working docks are now to the west. The IJ is busy with barges sailing to and from the port, with pleasure boats, an occasional warship and cruise liner, and the free shuttle ferries to Amsterdam Noord.
⊞ F1–N6 🚇 Centraal Station

A bridge over the Keizersgracht

KEIZERSGRACHT
Together with Prinsengracht and Heren-gracht, this broad, elegant canal, built in 1612 and named Emperor's Canal after Emperor Maximilian I, completes the Grachtengordel (Canal Ring)—the trio of concentric central canals, that, intersected by a series of narrower, radial waterways, make a cobweb of water across the city.
⊞ G4–G6, H6 🚊 Tram 1, 2, 5, 13, 14, 16, 17, 20, 24, 25

LEIDSEGRACHT
One of the most exclusive addresses in town.
⊞ G5–G6 🚊 Tram 1, 2, 5

LOOIERSGRACHT
In the 17th century, the main industry in the Jordaan was tanning, hence the name Tanner's Canal. Many streets are named after the animals whose pelts were used such as Hazenstraat (Hare Street), Reestraat (Deer Street), and Wolvenstraat (Wolf Street).
⊞ G5 🚊 Tram 7, 10, 20

OUDEZIJDS ACHTERBURGWAL AND OUDEZIJDS VOORBURGWAL
In contrast to most of Amsterdam's canals, which are peaceful and romantic, parts of the Oudezijds Achterburgwal and Oudezijds Voorburgwal are lined with glaring, neon-lit bars and sex shops.
⊞ H4–H5 🚊 Tram 4, 9, 16, 20, 24, 25

REGULIERSGRACHT
Seven bridges cross the water here in quick succession. They are best viewed from the water at night, when they are lit by strings of lights.
⊞ H6 🚊 Tram 4, 16, 20, 24, 25

Old docklands
Amsterdam ranks among the world's 15 busiest ports, handling 45 million metric tons per year. It is Nissan's European distribution center and the world's largest cocoa port. The city's old harbor has been taken by developers, but for a taste of its former glory, head for the Scheepvaart Museum (➤ 47) in the Eastern Islands, or to the Western Islands, where the carefully restored 17th-century warehouses, cluttered wharfs, and nautical street names like Zeilmakerstraat (Sailmaker Street) and Touwslagerstraat (Rope Factory Street) offer a glimpse of old Amsterdam. (⊞ G3–H3 ✉ north of the railroad between Wester-Kanal and Westerdoksdijk).

DISTRICTS

See Top 25 sights for
ROSSE BUURT (▶ 39)

A typically ornate gable

CHINATOWN
Amsterdam's 7,000-strong Chinese community earns part of its living from the numerous Chinese restaurants around Nieuwmarkt.
➕ H5 🚊 Nieuwmarkt

JODENHOEK
Jewish refugees first came here in the 16th century and settled on the cheap, marshy land southeast of Nieuwmarkt and bordered by the Amstel. Almost the entire district was razed to the ground at the end of World War II, leaving only a few synagogues (▶ 46) and diamond factories as legacy of a once-thriving community.
➕ H5, J5 🚊 Waterlooplein

DE JORDAAN
This popular bohemian quarter with its labyrinth of picturesque canals, narrow streets, trendy shops, cafés, and restaurants was once a boggy meadow alongside Prinsengracht. A slum in the 17th century, it later became a more respectable working-class district. The name is believed to have come from the French *jardin*, meaning garden.
➕ G4 🚋 Tram 3, 10, 13, 14, 17, 20

Grachtengordel (Canal Ring)

The buildings along the web of canals around the medieval city center are supported on thousands of wooden piles to stop them from sinking. Constructed as part of a massive 17th-century expansion project, the immaculate patrician mansions along Prinsengracht, Keizersgracht, and Herengracht look almost like a toy town in a child's picture book, with their trim brickwork and characterful gables. The best way to enjoy their architectural details is from the water (▶ 19).

DE PIJP
This lively, multicultural area was once one of Amsterdam's most attractive working-class districts outside the Grachtengordel. The bustling Albert Cuypmarkt takes place daily (▶ 53), and there are several diamond-cutting workshops.
➕ H7 🚋 Tram 4, 16, 20, 24, 25

PLANTAGE
The "Plantation" became one of Amsterdam's first suburbs in 1848. Before that, this popular and leafy residential area was parkland.
➕ J5–J6 🚋 Tram 9, 14, 20

ZEEDIJK
Once the sea wall of the early maritime settlement and until recently the haunt of sailors and shady characters, this area on the fringe of the Red Light District is home to several good bars and restaurants.
➕ H4–H5 🚊 Centraal Station 🚋 Tram 1, 2, 4, 5, 9, 13, 16, 17, 20, 24, 25

MARKETS

**See Top 25 sights for
BLOEMENMARKT (▶ 38)**

ALBERT CUYPMARKT

Amsterdam's best-known, least expensive general market, named after a Dutch landscape artist, attracts some 20,000 bargain hunters on busy days.
➕ H7 ✉ Albert Cuypstraat 🕐 Mon–Sat 10–5 🚊 Tram 4, 16, 20, 24, 25

NOORDERMARKT

For a taste of the Jordaan district, head for the lively square surrounding the Noorderkerk. On Monday morning visit the *Lapjesmarkt* textile and secondhand clothing market, and on Saturday try the *Boerenmarkt* for organically grown fresh produce, crafts, and birds.
➕ G4 ✉ Noordermarkt 🕐 Mon, Sat 9–1 🚌 Bus 18, 22, 44

OUDEMANHUISPOORT

Antiquarian bookshops in an 18th-century arcade.
➕ H5 ✉ Oudemanhuispoort 🕐 Mon–Sat 10–4 🚊 Tram 4, 9, 16, 20, 24, 25

POSTZEGELMARKT

A specialist market for stamps, coins, and medals.
➕ H4–H5 ✉ 280 Nieuwezijds Voorburgwal 🕐 Wed, Sat 1–4 🚊 Tram 1, 2, 5, 20

ROMMELMARKT

Rommel means rummaging. Bric-a-brac is your cue to the style of the place.
➕ G5 ✉ Looiersgracht 38 🕐 Sat–Thu 10–5 🚊 Tram 7, 10, 20

WATERLOOPLEIN FLEA MARKET

Amsterdam's liveliest market, full of funky clothes, curiosities, and *junque.*
➕ H5 ✉ Waterlooplein 🕐 Mon–Fri 9–5; Sat 8:30–5:30 🚇 Waterlooplein

ZWARTE MARKT

This huge indoor flea market outside Amsterdam (reputedly Europe's largest) has an Eastern Market overflowing with oriental merchandise.
➕ Off map to northwest ✉ Industriegebied aan de Buitenlandenden, Beverwijk-Oost 🕐 Sat 7–5; Sun (Eastern Market only) 8–6 🚉 Beverwijk-Oost

Markets

Amsterdam resembles a collection of villages, each having its own local market. The daily markets at Ten Katestraat (Kinkerstraat) (➕ F5–F6) and Dapperstraat (➕ K6) are good for fruit and vegetables, and there is a flower market at Amstelveld (➕ H6) every Monday morning. Sunday art markets are held at Spui from March until Christmas (➕ G5–H5) and at Thorbeckeplein from mid-March until November (➕ H6), while you may find a bargain at the Nieuwmarkt antiques market (➕ H5) on Sundays in summer.

Albert Cuypmarkt

BRIDGES, BUILDINGS & MONUMENTS

Bridges

No other city in the world has so many bridges: 1,281. The majority are single or triple-arched hump-backed bridges made of brick and stone with simple cast-iron railings. The oldest bridge is the Torensluis (1648) and the best example of a traditional Dutch drawbridge is the Magere Brug (Skinny Bridge ➤ 45). The cast-iron Blauwbrug (Blue Bridge, 1874) is one of the most traditional, while the 20th-century Waals Eilandsgracht bridge, with its geometric arches, is the most modern.

99 Rokin, a modern interpretation of a canalside house

> **See Top 25 sights for**
> **ANNE FRANK STATUE, WESTERKERK** (➤ 30)
> **HET HOUTEN HUYS, BEGIJNHOF** (➤ 34)
> **JOODS HISTORISCH MUSEUM** (➤ 46)
> **KONINKLIJK PALEIS** (➤ 36)
> **LEIDSEPLEIN (AMERICAN HOTEL)** (➤ 27)
> **MAGERE BRUG** (➤ 45)

BEURS VAN BERLAGE

Designed by Hendrik Berlage and now hailed as an early modernist masterpiece, the former stock exchange provoked outrage when it opened in 1903. It is now a concert hall (➤ 78).

➕ H4–H5 ✉ Damrak 213–279 ☎ 6268936 🕐 Daily 9–5 for exhibitions 🍴 Café Ranieri (SS) 🚊 Tram 4, 9, 16, 20, 24, 25

CENTRAAL STATION

Many travelers get their first glimpse of Amsterdam's architectural wonders at P.J.H. Cuyper's vast neoclassical station (1889), standing defiantly with its back to the River IJ.

➕ H4 ✉ Stationsplein ☎ 0900/9292 🚉 Centraal Station

CONCERTGEBOUW

The orchestra and main concert hall of this elaborate neoclassical building have been renowned worldwide ever since the inaugural concert in 1888.

➕ G7 ✉ Concertgebouwplein 2–6 ☎ 6718345 🕐 Box office Mon–Sat 10–7 🚊 Tram 3, 5, 12, 16, 20

ENTREPOTDOK

The old warehouses at Entrepotdok have been converted into offices and expensive apartments.

➕ J5–L5 ✉ Entrepotdok 🚌 Bus 22

GREENPEACE HEADQUARTERS

This pragmatic city seems an appropriate home for the Greenpeace world headquarters, in a remarkable *Jugendstil* (art nouveau) building dating from 1905.

➕ G4 ✉ Keizersgracht 174 ☎ 4223344
🚊 Tram 13, 14, 17, 20

KERWIN DUINMEYER MONUMENT

Kerwin, a 15-year-old black youth, was stabbed to death in Amsterdam in 1983. It was the first time since World War II that someone had been killed in the city because of race. His statue stands in the Vondelpark as a symbol of the Dutch fight against racism.

➕ F6 ✉ Vondelpark (Jacob Obrechtstraat exit)
🚊 Tram 2, 3, 5, 12, 20

'T LIEVERDJE

In the '60s this little bronze statue of a boy, which

stands so innocently in the middle of the square, became a symbol of the *Provo* movement, and rallying point of frequent anti-establishment demonstrations. The name means "Little Darling."

➕ G5 ✉ Spui
🚋 Tram 1, 2, 5, 20

MUNTTOREN
The tower of the former Mint was part of the southern gateway to the medieval city.

➕ H5 ✉ Muntplein
🚋 Tram 4, 9, 14, 16, 20, 24, 25

MUZIEKTHEATER
Amsterdam's theater for opera and dance is known locally as the "false teeth" because of its white marble paneling and red brick roof. The complex includes the uninspiring buildings of the new town hall (Stadhuis), and the design caused great controversy when it was built in 1986, sparking riots during its construction.

➕ H5 ✉ Waterlooplein 22 🚇 Waterlooplein

National Monument in Dam square, in memory of World War II victims

NATIONAL MONUMENT
The 75-foot obelisk in Dam square contains soil from all the Dutch provinces and former colonies. Every year on May 4, the Queen lays a wreath here.

➕ H5 ✉ Dam 🚋 Tram 4, 9, 14, 16, 20, 24, 25

SCHEEPVAARTHUIS
The peculiarly tapered Maritime House, encrusted with marine decoration, suggests the bow of an approaching ship. Commissioned by seven shipping companies in 1912, it represents one of the most impressive examples of the architecture of the Amsterdam School.

➕ H5–J5 ✉ Prins Hendrikkade 108–111 🚌 Bus 22

SCHREIERSTOREN
The "Weeping Tower" was where tearful wives and girlfriends waved farewell to their seafaring menfolk. They had good reason to weep: in the 18th century, voyages took up to four years and many sailors died.

➕ H4 ✉ Prins Hendrikkade 94–95 🚇 Centraal Station

Homomonument
One of the city's more arresting sculptures is the *Homomonument* (1987) by Dutch artist Karin Daan, on the corner of Westermarkt and Keizersgracht. Consisting of three pink triangles, the sign homosexuals were forced to wear during the German Occupation, it commemorates all those who have been persecuted because of their homosexuality.

MUSEUMS & GALLERIES

Canal-house museums

The grand 17th-century canal house Museum van Loon (Keizersgracht 672) has an impressive family portrait gallery. The Theatermuseum (Herengracht 168) and the Bijbels Museum (Bible Museum) (Herengracht 366), with its religious artifacts, are also in beautiful houses whose interiors alone warrant a visit.

A mug of Heineken

Museum passes

If you intend to visit several museums and galleries, buy a *Museumjaarkaart* from the VVV (tourist office) for f17.50–f47.50 depending on age; it will give you free entry into over 400 museums throughout Holland for one year. The *Amsterdam Culture & Leisure Pass* also offers various discounts, and only costs f36.75.

See Top 25 sights for:
AMSTERDAMS HISTORISCH MUSEUM (▶ 35)
ANNE FRANKHUIS (▶ 31)
FILM MUSEUM (VONDELPARK) (▶ 24)
HASH MARIHUANA HEMP MUSEUM (▶ 40)
JOODS HISTORISCH MUSEUM (▶ 46)
MUSEUM AMSTELKRING (▶ 41)
MUSEUM HET REMBRANDTHUIS (▶ 44)
MUSEUM WILLET-HOLTHUYSEN (▶ 42)
NEDERLANDS SCHEEPVAART MUSEUM (▶ 47)
RIJKSMUSEUM (▶ 28)
VAN GOGH MUSEUM (▶ 26)
STEDELIJK MUSEUM (▶ 25)
TROPENMUSEUM (▶ 48)

HEINEKEN BROUWERIJ
Free tastings of the world's best-known brand of Dutch beer are offered at the end of a comprehensive tour of Heineken's first brewery (no longer in use).
✚ H6 ✉ Stadhouderskade 78 ☎ 5239666 🕐 Guided tours (18 years and over only) Mon–Fri 9:30 and 11. Also Jun to mid-Sep: 1 and 2:30. Jul and Aug: Sat 11, 1, 2:30 🚊 Tram 6, 7, 10, 16, 24, 25 ♿ Few (phone in advance) 💵 Inexpensive

MUSEUM AVIODOME
The National Aerospace Museum has aircraft from 1903 to the '90s, in addition to models of early balloons and heavier-than-air aircraft.
✚ X12 ✉ Westelijke Randweg 201, Schiphol-Centrum ☎ 4068000 🕐 Apr–Sep: 10–5. Oct–Mar: Tue–Fri 10–5; Sat, Sun 12–5. Closed Jan 1, Dec 25 and 31 🚉 Schiphol ♿ Good 💵 Moderate

VERZETSMUSEUM (RESISTANCE MUSEUM)
Rare wartime memorabilia and a fascinating summary of the Dutch resistance during World War II.
✚ J5 ✉ Plantagekerklaan 61a ☎ 6202535 🕐 Tue–Fri 10–5; Sat, Sun 1–5. Closed Jan 1, Apr 30, Dec 25 🚊 Tram 6, 9, 14, 20 ♿ Good 💵 Inexpensive

WERF 'T KROMHOUT MUSEUM
One of the city's few remaining working shipyards, this 18th-century wharf is used for restoring antique vessels, and is open to visitors during working hours.
✚ K5 ✉ Hoogte Kadijk 147 ☎ 6276777 🕐 Mon–Fri 10–4. Closed Sat, Sun, hols 🚌 Bus 22, 28 ♿ Few 💵 Inexpensive

WOONBOOTMUSEUM (HOUSEBOAT MUSEUM)
If you've ever wondered what life is like aboard one of Amsterdam's 2,500 houseboats, here's your chance to find out. The *Hendrika Maria*, built in 1914, was a working canal barge before being converted.
✚ G5 ✉ By Prinsengracht 296 ☎ 4270750 🕐 Tue–Sun 10–5. Closed Mon, public hols 🚊 Tram 1, 2, 5 ♿ None 💵 Inexpensive

PLACES OF WORSHIP

See Top 25 sights for
MUSEUM AMSTELKRING (➤ 41)
NIEUWE KERK (➤ 37)
OUDE KERK (➤ 40)
WESTERKERK (➤ 30)

AMSTELKERK
Squat and wooden, this Calvinist church (1670) was originally meant to be a temporary structure while funds were raised for a larger building elsewhere.
⊞ H6 ✉ Amstelveld ☎ 6238138 ⏲ Closed to public
🚊 Tram 4

FRANCISCUS XAVERIUSKERK
This splendid neo-Gothic church is often dubbed "De Krijtberg" ("Chalk Hill"), because it is built on the site of a former chalk merchant's house.
⊞ G5 ✉ Singel 442–448 ☎ 6231923 ⏲ Services only
🚊 Tram 1, 2, 5, 20

NOORDERKERK
An austere church, the first in Amsterdam to be constructed in the shape of a Greek cross. It was built in 1620–23 for the Protestant workers in the Jordaan district, and is still well attended.
⊞ G4 ✉ Noordermarkt 44–48 ☎ 6266436 ⏲ Mon–Sat 9–6, and services 🚊 Tram 3, 10, 13, 14, 17, 20

PORTUGUESE SYNAGOGUE
Holland's finest synagogue, one of the first of any size in Western Europe. It is remarkable that this imposing building escaped destruction in World War II.
⊞ J5 ✉ Mr Visserplein 3 ☎ 6245351 ⏲ Sun–Fri 10–12:30, 1–4 (closes two hours before sunset on Fri). Closed Jewish holidays, Sun 10–noon Ⓜ Waterlooplein ⛴ Museumboat stop 6

SINT NICOLAASKERK
Amsterdam's main Roman Catholic church (1888) and one of many Dutch churches named after St. Nicholas, the patron saint of sailors. St. Nicholas is also *Sinterklaas* (see panel).
⊞ H4 ✉ Prins Hendrikkade 73 ☎ 6248749 ⏲ Mon–Sat 11–4, and services 🚊 Tram 1, 2, 4, 5, 9, 13, 16, 17, 20, 24, 25

ZUIDERKERK
Holland's first Protestant church (1614) and indisputably one of the city's most beautiful. Its designer, Hendrick de Keyser, lies buried within. The distinctive 265-foot-high tower affords spectacular views of the Nieuwmarkt district.
⊞ H5 ✉ Zuiderkerkhof 72 ☎ 6222962 ⏲ Mon–Wed, Fri 12–5; Thu 12–8 Ⓜ Nieuwmarkt

Zuiderkerk

Sinterklaas

St. Nicholas, or *Sinterklaas*, pays an early visit to the city each year on the third Saturday of November. Accompanied by *Zwarte Piet* (Black Peter), he arrives by boat near Sint Nicolaaskerk and distributes gingerbread to children, then receives the keys to the city from the mayor on Dam square. On December 5 (*Sinterklaasavond* or *Pakjesavond*) he comes during the night with sacks of presents for the sleeping children.

57

PARKS & GARDENS

See Top 25 sights for
OOSTERPARK, TROPENMUSEUM (➤ 48)
VONDELPARK (➤ 24)

Hortus Botanicus

Laid out in 1682, the botanical gardens were originally sponsored by the VOC (➤ 12), whose members brought back plants and seeds from all corners of the earth, to be grown and studied by doctors and apothecaries here. One such plant—a coffee tree—given to Louis XIV of France and cultivated in his American colonies, was the ancestor of the Brazilian coffee plantations. Likewise, the production of palm oil in Indonesia is due to plants initially cultivated here.

Vondelpark

AMSTELPARK

A formal rose garden and a rhododendron valley are two of the seasonal spectacles at this magnificent park, created in 1972 for an international horticultural exhibition. It also offers pony rides, miniature golf, a children's farm, the Rieker windmill (➤ 60), and other attractions. There is a special walk for blind people, and in summer you can tour the park in a miniature train.

➕ H9–H10 ⏰ Dawn–dusk 🍽 Restaurant and café (SS) 🚌 Bus 69, 148, 169

AMSTERDAMSE BOS

Amsterdam's largest park was built on the polders in the 1930s as part of a job creation scheme. It is a favorite family destination on weekends whatever the season—in winter, there is tobogganing and skating; in summer swimming, sailing, and biking. A leisurely tram ride can be taken through the park in colorful antique cars acquired from various European cities.

➕ C10–E10 ⏰ Always open 🍽 Open-air pancake restaurant and café (SS) 🚌 Bus 170, 171, 172

HORTUS BOTANICUS

With more than 8,000 plant species, Amsterdam's oldest botanical garden boasts one of the largest collections in the world. It has spectacular tropical greenhouses, a medicinal herb garden, and a monumental cycad that, at 400 years old, is reputed to be the world's oldest potted plant.

➕ J5 ✉ Plantage Middenlaan 2a ☎ 6258411 ⏰ Apr–Sep: Mon–Fri 9–5; Sat, Sun 11–5. Oct–Mar: Mon–Fri 9–4; Sat, Sun 11–4 🍽 Café (S) 🚊 Tram 7, 9, 14, 20 ♿ Good 💰 Moderate

SARPHATIPARK

Enjoy a picnic bought at nearby Albert Cuypmarkt (➤ 53) in this tiny green oasis dedicated to the 19th-century Jewish doctor and city benefactor, Samuel Sarphati.

➕ H7 ⏰ 9–dusk 🚊 Tram 3, 4, 16, 20, 24, 25

AMSTERDAM FOR CHILDREN

See Top 25 sights for:
ANNE FRANKHUIS (➤ 31)
NEDERLANDS SCHEEPVAART MUSEUM (➤ 47)
TROPENMUSEUM (➤ 48)
VONDELPARK (➤ 24)

ARTIS ZOO (NATURA ARTIS MAGISTRA)

As well as animals, the complex includes museums, an aquarium, and the Planetarium (hourly shows). ➕ J5–J6 ✉ Plantage Kerklaan 38–40 ☎ 5233400 🕐 Daily 9–5 🍴 Restaurant and café 🚋 Tram 7, 9, 14, 20. Artis Express boat from Centraal Station ♿ Good 👎 Very expensive

CIRCUS ELLEBOOG

Learn tightrope walking, juggling, and other circus skills at the Elleboog Circus. Reservations needed. ➕ G5 ✉ Passeerdersgracht 32 ☎ 6269370 🕐 Mon–Fri 10–5; Sat 1:30–5; Sun 10:30–4 🚋 Tram 7, 10, 20 ♿ Good 👎 Moderate

DE KRAKELING THEATER

Mime and puppet shows, for under-12s, and over-12s. ➕ G5 ✉ Nieuwe Passeerderstraat 1 ☎ 6253284 🕐 Shows Mon–Fri 11–4; Sat, Sun 2–4 🚋 Tram 7, 10, 20 ♿ Good 👎 Moderate

KINDERKOOKKAFÉ

A children's restaurant where children between five and twelve can cook, then serve or eat at mini-tables. ➕ H5 ✉ Oudeijds Achterburgwal 193 ☎ 6253257 🕐 Sat cooking 3:30–6, dinner 6–8 (age 8 plus). Sun cooking 2:30–5, high tea 5–6 (age 5 plus). Mon–Fri 1–3 🚋 Nieuwmarkt 👎 Very inexpensive

KINDERBOERDERIJ DE PIJP

A 'children's farm' at the heart of the city. ➕ H7 ✉ Lizzy Ansinghstraat 82 ☎ 6648303 🕐 Wed–Mon 1–5 🚋 Tram 24, 25 ♿ Few 👎 Inexpensive

MADAME TUSSAUD SCENERAMA

Wax models of Rembrandt, Pavarotti, Schwarzenegger, and other characters from the 17th century to the present day, and an amazing 16-foot giant clothed in windmills and tulips. ➕ H5 ✉ Dam 20 ☎ 6229949 🕐 Sep–Jun: 10–5:30. Jul–Aug: 9:30–5:30 🚋 Tram 4, 9, 14, 16, 20, 24, 25 ♿ Good 👎 Very expensive

NEWMETROPOLIS

Children will enjoy learning at this impressive new hands-on, interactive museum of modern technology. ➕ J5 ✉ Oosterdok 2 ☎ 0900/9191100 🕐 Sep–Jun: Mon–Thu 10–6; Fri–Sun 10–9. Jul–Aug: 10–9 🍴 Café 🚌 Bus 22, 32 ♿ Very good 👎 Very expensive

Out of town

Ask the VVV for details on making excursions to Volendam, where villagers still wear traditional costume; the windmill village of Zaanse Schans; to Zuiderzee, for the reconstructed fishing village of Enkhuizen; or to one of Holland's many theme parks, such as the enchanted forest of De Efteling at Kaatsheuvel or the Duinrell water park at Wassenaar, near The Hague.

Punch & Judy

From mid-April until the end of September there are free Punch and Judy performances on Wed 1–5 in Dam square.

Owl statue at the zoo

WINDMILLS

Amsterdam's most central windmill has been converted into a bar

D'ADMIRAAL
Built in 1792 to grind chalk but now unused.
➕ K1 ✉ Noordhollandsch Kanaaldijk, near Jan Thoméepad
🚌 Bus 34, 37, 39, 242

DE BLOEM
This old grain mill, built in 1768, resembles a giant pepper shaker.
➕ F3 ✉ Haarlemmerweg, near Nieuwpoortkade 🚌 Bus 18

DE GOOIER (FUNENMOLEN)
Amsterdam's most central mill (1725) was the first grain mill in Holland to use the streamlined sails that became ubiquitous. Built on a brick base, with an octagonal body and a thatched wooden frame, it has been converted into a small brewery and bar (➤ 81), but its massive sails still occasionally creak into action.
➕ K5 ✉ Funenkade 🚋 Tram 6, 10; Bus 22, 28

DE RIEKER
The finest windmill in Amsterdam was built in 1636 to drain the Rieker polder, and is situated at the southern tip of the Amstelpark. This was one of Rembrandt's favorite painting locations—there is a small statue nearby in his memory. The windmill has been beautifully preserved and is now a private home.
➕ Off map to south ✉ Amsteldijk, near De Borcht 🚌 Bus 148

National Windmill Day

Windmills have been a feature of the Dutch landscape since the 13th century. Much of the Netherlands lies below sea level, and windmills were used to drain the land and extend the shoreline, creating the fertile farmland called *polder*. Some 950 survive, and on National Windmill Day (the second Saturday in May), many turn their sails and are open to the public.

1100 ROE
This old smock mill, shaped like a peasant's smock, was one of a *"gang"* of water mills that once drained the polders. It stands 1,100 roes from the city's outer canal—the word *roe* means both the flat part of a sail that had to be set or reefed according to wind strength, and a unit of measurement (about a foot) used to calculate the distance from the city center.
➕ A5 ✉ Herman Bonpad, Sportpark Ookmeer 🚌 Bus 19, 23

1200 ROE
This early 17th-century post mill, with its impressive platform and revolving cap, was built to help drain the polders.
➕ B3 ✉ Haarlemmerweg, near Willem Molengraaffstraat
🚌 Bus 85

AMSTERDAM
where to...

DUTCH RESTAURANTS

Dutch treats

Numerous restaurants in the city provide a taste of authentic Dutch cuisine. The most delicious dishes include thick split-pea soup (*erwtensoep*), meaty stews (*stamppot*), smoked eel (*gerookt paling*), raw herring (*haring*), sweet and savory pancakes (*pannekoeken*), waffles (*stroopwafels*), and cheeses. Look out for the special "Neerlands Dis" sign (a red, white, and blue soup tureen), which indicates restaurants commended by this organization for their top-quality traditional Dutch cuisine.

A recent trend is towards "New Dutch" cuisine. Traditional dishes are prepared with a lighter touch and presented with greater sophistication, using fresh seasonal products and an adventurous mix of herbs and spices.

DE BLAUWE HOLLANDER ($)
Generous portions of wholesome and modestly priced, if not exactly inspired, fare in a lively bistro setting.
✚ G6 ✉ Leidsekruisstraat 28 ☎ 6233014 ◷ Dinner only 🚊 Tram 1, 2, 5, 6, 7, 10, 20

DORRIUS ($$$)
A sophisticated take on rustic Dutch style. Try the pike and salted cod traditional delicacies, or the cheese soufflé.
✚ H4 ✉ Crowne Plaza Hotel, Nieuwezijds Voorburgwal 5 ☎ 4202224 🚊 Tram 1, 2, 5, 13, 17, 20

DE GEUS ($)
Dutch pea soup, herring in *jenever* (gin), and warm cheesecake in a wood-paneled 1885 interior.
✚ G6 ✉ Korte Leidsedwarsstraat 71 ☎ 6271808 🚊 Tram 1, 2, 5, 6, 7, 10, 20

HAESJE CLAES ($$)
Dutch cuisine at its best, served in a warren of small, paneled dining rooms. The building dates from the 16th century, and the rooms are authentically furnished.
✚ G5 ✉ Spoistraat 73–275 ☎ 6249998 🚊 Tram 1, 2, 5

DE KEUKEN VAN 1870 ($)
Originally a soup kitchen, this old-fashioned establishment serves huge platefuls of no-frills food at communal tables.
✚ H4 ✉ Spuistraat 4 ☎ 6248965 ◷ Mon–Fri 12:30–8; Sat, Sun 4–9 🚊 Tram 1, 2, 5, 13, 17, 20

MOLEN DE DIKKERT ($$$)
Dine in a majestic old windmill on the outskirts of Amsterdam.
✚ Off map to south ✉ Amsterdamseweg 104 ☎ 6411378 ◷ Closed Sun and lunch Sat 🚊 Bus 175

DE POORT ($$)
Since 1870, this famous restaurant has sold nearly 6 million numbered steaks. Every thousandth one comes with a free bottle of house wine.
✚ H5 ✉ Hotel Die Port van Cleve, Nieuwezijds Voorburgwal 178 ✉ 6240047 🚊 Tram 1, 2, 5, 13, 17, 20

DE ROODE LEEUW ($$)
The brasserie-style "Red Lion" serves up stews and sauerkraut dishes that are particularly good value.
✚ H5 ✉ Amsterdam Hotel, Damrak 93–94 ☎ 5550666 ◷ 10AM–midnight, last orders 8PM 🚊 Tram 4, 9, 16, 20, 24, 25

'T SWARTE SCHAEP ($$)
The "Black Sheep" is noted for its rustic atmosphere, excellent wines and varied classic and modern cuisine.
✚ G6 ✉ Korte Leidsedwarsstraat 24 ☎ 6223021 🚊 Tram 1, 2, 5, 6, 7, 10, 20

D'VIJFF VLIEGHEN ($$$)
The menu in the "Five Flies" in five 17th-century houses has an impressive collection of "New Dutch" dishes.
✚ G5 ✉ Spuistraat 294–302 ☎ 6248369 ◷ Dinner only 🚊 Tram 1, 2, 5

ELEGANT DINING

BEDDINGTON'S ($$$)

Chef Jean Beddington's imaginative French and Far Eastern cuisine in a strikingly modern setting.
🚏 G7 ✉ Roelof Hartstraat 6–8 ☎ 6765201 🕐 Closed Sun and lunch Sat and Mon 🚊 Tram 3, 5, 12, 20, 24

DE BELHAMEL ($$)

Art nouveau and classical music set the tone for polished Continental cuisine in an intimate, often crowded setting with a superb canal view.
🚏 G4 ✉ Brouwersgracht 60 ☎ 6221095 🕐 Dinner only 🚊 Bus 18, 22

BORDEWIJK ($$)

Mediterranean and Asian touches, and a spare, black-and-white interior, add zest to French dishes.
🚏 G4 ✉ Noordermarkt 7 ☎ 6243899 🕐 Dinner only. Closed Mon 🚊 Bus 18, 22

CAFÉ ROUX ($$)

Fine French cuisine in an art nouveau setting, overlooked by a Karl Appel mural.
🚏 H5 ✉ Grand Hotel, Oudezijds Voorburgwal 197 ☎ 5553560 🚇 Nieuwmarkt

CHRISTOPHE'S ($$$)

Chef Jean Christophe combines French style and US experience to great effect in his chic canalside restaurant.
🚏 G4 ✉ Leliegracht 46 ☎ 6250807 🕐 Dinner only. Closed Sun and Mon 🚊 Tram 13, 14, 17, 20

LE CIEL BLEU ($$$)

The height of stylish French cuisine on the Okura Hotel's 23rd floor.
🚏 H7 ✉ Ferdinand Bolstraat 333 ☎ 6787111 🕐 Dinner only 🚊 Tram 12, 25

DE GOUDEN REAEL ($$)

French restaurant in a 17th-century dockside building with a waterside terrace—perfect for a romantic evening.
🚏 H3 ✉ Zandhoek 14, Westerdok ☎ 6233883 🕐 Closed Sun 🚊 Bus 28, Tram 3

LA RIVE ($$$)

In Amsterdam's most expensive hotel. Robert Kranenborg is considered Holland's finest chef.
🚏 J6 ✉ Amstel Hotel, Professor Tulpplein 1 ☎ 6226060 🚇 Weesperplein

DE SILVEREN SPIEGEL ($$$)

An exquisite classic menu, complemented by one of the city's best wine lists, in a superbly restored 1614 house. Fish is a specialty.
🚏 H4 ✉ Kattengatt 4–6 ☎ 6246589 🕐 Dinner only. Closed Sun except for parties with reservations 🚊 Tram 1, 2, 5, 13, 17, 20

TOUT COURT ($$$)

This arty restaurant is a place to see and be seen.
🚏 G5 ✉ Runstraat 13 ☎ 6258637 🕐 Dinner only 🚊 Tram 1, 2, 5

HET TUYNHUIS ($$)

Sophisticated French, Portuguese, and Dutch cuisine in a converted coach house and garden.
🚏 H5 ✉ Reguliersdwarsstraat 28 ☎ 6276603 🕐 Closed Sat and Sun lunch 🚊 Tram 4, 9, 14, 16, 20, 24, 25

Opening times and prices

The restaurants listed on pages 62–68 are all open for lunch and dinner daily unless otherwise stated. They are divided into three price categories. For a main dish, expect to pay:

$$$ over f50
$$ up to f50
$ up to f25

Tipping

Most restaurant windows display menus giving the price of individual dishes including BTW (tax) and a 15 percent service charge. Nevertheless, most Amsterdammers round up a small bill to the largest whole guilder and larger ones to the nearest f5. This tip should be left as change rather than included on a credit-card payment.

INDONESIAN RESTAURANTS

A hearty meal

When the Dutch took over the Spice Islands of the East Indies in the 17th century, they got more than spices out of their new colony. They developed a taste for the exotic local cuisine that survived Indonesian independence and gives Amsterdam today an abundance of *Indonesisch* restaurants.

First-timers to an Indonesian restaurant should order a *rijsttafel*, which includes rice and a complete range of other dishes: *ayam* (chicken), *ikam* (fish), *telor* (egg), *rendang* (beef), *krupuk* (shrimp crackers), shredded coconut, and sweet-and-sour vegetables. The *rijsttafel* ("rice table") originally referred to the long list of ingredients required to prepare such a feast. It originated in early colonial days among hungry Dutch planters who, not satisfied by the basic Indonesian meal of rice and vegetables accompanied by meat or fish, continually added other dishes. Thus the rijsttafel was born—a meal that ranges from a 6- to 10-item mini-rijsttafel to a 20- to 30-dish feast.

ANEKA RASA ($$)
This airy modern restaurant offers numerous vegetarian dishes including an all-vegetarian *rijsttafel*.
🕂 H5 ✉ Warmoesstraat 25–29 ☎ 6261560 🚇 Centraal Station

INDRAPURA ($$)
A popular colonial-style restaurant. Tell the waiter how hot and spicy you want your dishes to be.
🕂 H5 ✉ Rembrandtplein 40-42 ☎ 6237329 🕐 Dinner only 🚊 Tram 4, 9, 14, 20

JAYAKARTA ($$)
In the square that is one of Amsterdam's liveliest nightlife districts; ideal for late-evening meals.
🕂 H5 ✉ Rembrandtplein 16 ☎ 6255569 🚊 Tram 4, 9, 14, 20

KANTJIL EN DE TIJGER ($$)
Modern decor and spicy, imaginative Javanese cuisine. Try the delicious *Masi Rames*, a mini-*rijsttafel* on one plate.
🕂 G5 ✉ Spuistraat 291 ☎ 6200994 🕐 Dinner only 🚊 Tram 1, 2, 5

ORIENT ($$)
This dark, opulent restaurant specializes in *rijsttafels*, with more than 20 different sorts, three of them vegetarian, and an extensive buffet on Wednesdays.
🕂 G6 ✉ Van Baerlestraat 21 ☎ 6734958 🕐 Dinner only 🚊 Tram 2, 3, 5, 12, 20

SAHID JAYA ($$)
Shady courtyard garden, especially nice in summer.
🕂 H5 ✉ Reguliersdwarsstraat 26 ☎ 6263727 🚊 Tram 16, 24, 25

SAMA SEBO ($$)
Rush mats and batik typify this Balinese setting where you can select from the menu to create your own *rijsttafel*.
🕂 G6 ✉ P C Hooftstraat 27 ☎ 6628146 🕐 Closed Sun 🚊 Tram 2, 5, 20

SARANG MAS ($$)
Modern surroundings counterpoint traditional cuisine.
🕂 H4 ✉ Damrak 44 ☎ 6222105 🕐 Daily 11.30–11PM 🚊 Tram 1, 2, 4, 5, 9, 13, 16, 17, 20, 24, 25

SPECIAAL ($$)
One of the most popular Indonesian restaurants in town, a cozy little place hidden in a back street in the Jordaan. The *rijsttafel* is a sight to behold.
🕂 G4 ✉ Nieuwe Leliestraat 140-142 ☎ 6249706 🕐 Dinner only 🚊 Tram 10, 13, 14, 17, 20

SUKASARI ($)
Colorful batik tablecloths, closely packed tables, generous portions.
🕂 H5 ✉ Damstraat 26-29 ☎ 6240092 🕐 Mon–Sat noon–9PM 🚊 Tram 4, 9, 16, 20, 24, 25

TEMPO DOELOE ($$)
One of Amsterdam's best Indonesian restaurants, notable for its western interior, exotic flowers, and some of the hottest dishes in town
🕂 H6 ✉ Utrechtsestraat 75 ☎ 6256718 🕐 Dinner only 🚊 Tram 4

FISH & VEGETARIAN RESTAURANTS

BODEGA KEYSER ($$)

An Amsterdam institution next door to the Concertgebouw, specializing in fish and traditional Dutch dishes.

G6 ⊠ Van Baerlestraat 96 ☎ 6711441 ⏱ Mon–Sat 9AM–midnight; Sun 11AM–midnight 🚃 Tram 2, 3, 5, 12, 20

DE OESTERBAR ($$)

The seasonal delights of this elegant fish restaurant include herring in May, mussels in June, and delicate Zeeland oysters throughout the summer.

G6 ⊠ Leidseplein 10 ☎ 6232988 🚃 Tram 1, 2, 5, 6, 7, 10, 20

LE PECHEUR ($$$)

A chic fish-bistro with a secluded garden. Outstanding fresh oysters, caviar, sashimi, and lobster.

H5 ⊠ Reguliersdwarsstraat 32 ☎ 6243121 ⏱ Closed Sat lunch and all day Sun 🚃 Tram 1, 2, 5

PIER 10 ($$)

Former shipping office with an innovative menu that emphasizes fish, and an unusual shipside location on Pier 10 behind Centraal Station—one of the series of jetties where ships dock on the IJ inlet.

H4 ⊠ De Ruijterkade, Pier 10 ☎ 6248276 ⏱ Dinner only 🚃 Tram 1, 2, 4, 5, 9, 13, 16, 17, 20, 24, 25 🚇 Centraal Station

VISRESTAURANT JULIA ($$)

Julia's famous fish platter, with 10 kinds of fish—baked, barbecued, and grilled—draws people from all over the region.

🚭 Off map to south ⊠ Amstelveenseweg 160 ☎ 6795394 ⏱ Dinner only 🚌 Bus 146, 147, 170, 171, 172

VEGETARIAN

BENTO ($$)

Japanese fish and organic vegetable dishes, tatami mats.

H6 ⊠ Kerkstraat 148 ☎ 4203485 ⏱ Closed Mon 🚃 Tram 16, 24, 25

BOLHOED ($)

A trendy restaurant on the edge of the Jordaan, with vegetarian pâtés, salads, and hearty dishes.

G4 ⊠ Prinsengracht 60-62 ☎ 6261803 🚃 Tram 13, 14, 17, 20

GOLDEN TEMPLE ($)

Imaginative menu of Indian, Mexican, and Middle Eastern dishes.

H6 ⊠ Utrechtsestraat 126 ☎ 6268560 ⏱ Dinner only 🚃 Tram 4

HEMELSE MODDER ($$)

Sophisticated main courses including a vegetarian selection and delicious desserts including "Heavenly Mud," the chocolate mousse from which the restaurant takes its name.

H5 ⊠ Oude Waal 211 ☎ 6243203 ⏱ Dinner only 6–10 (last admission). Closed Tue 🚇 Nieuwmarkt

OIBIBIO ($$)

New Age music sets the tone for laid-back world cuisine in chic setting.

H4 ⊠ Prins Hendrikkade 20-21 ☎ 5539328 🚇 Centraal Station

Fish and vegetables

Although the Dutch eat a lot of meat, Amsterdam with its sea-going associations has a great choice of fish restaurants. Vegetarians, too, have specialty eating places to suit all tastes and budgets, while others, most notably pizzerias and the Asian restaurants around town, offer vegetarian menu-dishes.

INTERNATIONAL RESTAURANTS

Surinamese cuisine

Explore the narrow streets of the multiracial district around Albert Cuypstraat, and you will soon realize how easy it is to eat your way around the world in Amsterdam. The many Surinamese restaurants here serve a delicious blend of African, Chinese, and Indian cuisine. Specialties include *bojo* (cassava and coconut quiche) and *pitjil* (baked vegetables with peanut sauce). Try them at Marowijne (✉ Albert Cuypstraat 68–70), or Wan Pipel (✉ Albert Cuypstraat 140).

ASIAN CARIBBEAN EXPERIENCE ($)

More than 100 dishes from all over Asia and the Caribbean.

➕ H5 ✉ Warmoesstraat 170 ☎ 6271545 🕐 Dinner only 🚊 Tram 4, 9, 16, 20, 24, 25

DE BRAKKE GROND ($-$$)

Flemish Cultural Center's darkly atmospheric restaurant, serving bountiful portions of Belgian food.

➕ H5 ✉ Nes 43 ☎ 6260044 🕐 Tue–Sat noon–11. Closed Sun–Mon 🚊 Tram 4, 9, 14, 16, 20, 24, 25

BRASSERIE RENTRÉE ($$)

An eclectic menu of French, Asian and Dutch dishes, in a romantic, candlelit setting.

➕ H4 ✉ Zeedijk 29 ☎ 6389340 🕐 Daily, dinner only 5:30–11 (last admission) 🚉 Centraal Station

CAFÉ PACIFICO ($$)

The most authentic Mexican bodega in town. Especially crowded on Tuesday, which is *margarita* night.

➕ H4 ✉ Warmoesstraat 31 ☎ 6242911 🕐 Dinner only 🚉 Centraal Station

CHEZ GEORGES ($$)

Fine Belgian cuisine in a classical, candlelit setting.

➕ G4 ✉ Herenstraat 3 ☎ 6263332 🕐 Closed Sun, Wed 🚊 Tram 1, 2, 5, 13, 17, 20

DYNASTY ($$$)

A sophisticated, sumptuously decorated garden restaurant with fine Southeast Asian cuisine.

➕ H5 ✉ Reguliersdwarsstraat 30 ☎ 6268400 🕐 Dinner only. Closed Tue 🚊 Tram 16, 24, 25

EL RANCHO ARGENTINIAN GRILL ($$)

Sizzling steaks and spare ribs in a wood-paneled, jolly-gaucho setting that brings a taste of the pampas to Amsterdam.

➕ H5 ✉ Spui 3 ☎ 6256764 🕐 11am–midnight 🚊 Tram 4, 9, 14, 16, 20, 24, 25

DE FLES BISTRO ($$)

Cozy cellar, full of large wooden tables. A real locals' hangout.

➕ H6 ✉ Vijzelstraat 137 ☎ 6249644 🕐 Dinner only 🚊 Tram 16, 24, 25

FROMAGERIE CRIGNON CULINAIR ($)

Rustic restaurant with eight different types of cheese fondue.

➕ H5 ✉ Gravenstraat 28 ☎ 6246428 🕐 6am–9.30pm. Closed Sun, Mon 🚊 Tram 4, 9, 16, 20, 24, 25

GAUGUIN ($$)

Exotic mix of Eastern and Western dishes in colorful South Seas setting.

➕ G6 ✉ Leidsekade 110 ☎ 6221526 🕐 Dinner only. Closed Mon, Tue 🚊 Tram 1, 2, 5, 6, 7, 10, 20

MEMORIES OF INDIA ($$)

Tandoori, Moghlai, and vegetarian cuisine in refined colonial setting.

➕ H5 ✉ Reguliersdwarsstraat 88 ☎ 6235710 🕐 Dinner only 🚊 Tram 4, 9, 14, 20

PAKISTAN ($$)

Holland's top Pakistani restaurant. The menu ranges from traditional, village dishes to highly spiced specialties.

✚ F5 ✉ De Clercqstraat 65 ☎ 6181120 🕐 Dinner only 🚊 Tram 3, 12, 13, 14

PASTA E BASTA ($$)

Pasta in chic surroundings, with opera classics.

✚ G6 ✉ Nieuwe Speigelstraat 8 ☎ 4222229 🚊 Tram 16, 24, 25

ROSE'S CANTINA ($$)

Excellent value Tex-Mex meals in lively, sociable surroundings. Probably Amsterdam's most crowded restaurant.

✚ H5 ✉ Reguliersdwarsstraat 38-40 ☎ 6259797 🕐 Dinner only 🚊 Tram 16, 24, 25

RUM RUNNERS ($$)

Giant palms, caged parrots, live music, spicy stews, and cocktails feel distinctly tropical.

✚ G4 ✉ Prinsengracht 277 ☎ 6274079 🕐 Mon–Fri from 4PM. Sat, Sun from 2PM 🚊 Tram 13, 14, 17, 20

SAUDADE ($$)

A Portuguese restaurant with dockside terrace, at the heart of the fashionable Entrepotdok district.

✚ L5 ✉ Entrepotdok 36 ☎ 6254845 🕐 Dinner only. Closed Tue 🚊 Bus 22

SHERPA ($)

Nepalese/Tibetan restaurant with traditional Himalayan ornaments.

✚ G6 ✉ Korte Leidsedwarsstraat 58 ☎ 6239495 🕐 Dinner only 🚊 Tram 1, 2, 5, 6, 7, 10, 20

SHIBLI ($$$)

Sit on a sofa inside a Bedouin tent, dining on an Arabian banquet.

✚ H5 ✉ Hotel Krasnapolsky, Dam 9 ☎ 4223291 🕐 Thu–Sun dinner. Closed Mon–Thu, lunch 🚊 Tram 4, 9, 14, 16, 20, 24, 25

SUKHOTHAI ($$)

Thai dishes in bamboo and palm surroundings. Try the special Nua Pad Prik Bai Kra Pauw—if you can pronounce it!

✚ H7 ✉ Ceintuurbaan 147 ☎ 6718086 🕐 Dinner only Closed Tue 🚊 Tram 3

TANGO ($$)

Small, candlelit, and on the edge of the Red Light District. Try the huge, juicy steaks.

✚ H4 ✉ Warmoesstraat 49 ☎ 6272467 🕐 Dinner only 🚊 Tram 4, 9, 16, 20, 24, 25

TEPPANYAKI NIPPON ($$)

One of Holland's most elegant and exclusive Japanese grill-restaurants.

✚ H5 ✉ Reguliersdwarsstraat 18–20 ☎ 6208787 🕐 Dinner only 🚊 Tram 16, 24, 25

TOSCANINI ($$)

The best Italian food in town. Reserve well ahead.

✚ G4 ✉ Lindengracht 75 ☎ 6232813 🕐 Dinner only 🚊 Tram 3

LE ZINC...ET LES DAMES ($$)

Home-style French cuisine in a converted canalside warehouse. The *tarte tatin* is superb.

✚ H6 ✉ Prinsengracht 999 ☎ 6229044 🕐 Dinner only. Closed Sun, Mon 🚊 Tram 4

A taste of China

Of the many superb Chinese restaurants in the city, one of the most popular is Treasure (✉ Nieuwezijds Voorburgwal 115–17), with specialties from Beijing, Shanghai, and Canton provinces. For something inexpensive but good, try Sichuan (✉ Lange Niezel 24), with its unusual Tibetan and Szechuan dishes. The Sea Palace (✉ Oosterdokskade 8), advertises itself as Europe's first floating restaurant. It is modeled on a Chinese pagoda-style palace and is the next best thing to its prototype, Hong Kong's famous *Jumbo* restaurant.

SNACKS & *EETCAFÉS*

A bite to "eet"

Try an *eetcafé* for filling homemade fare—soup, sandwiches, and omelettes. Remember that kitchens close around 9PM. Or browse market stalls for local delicacies. Most bars offer *borrelhapjes* (mouthfuls with a glass)— usually olives, chunks of cheese or *borrelnoten* (nuts with a savory coating). More substantial *borrelhapjes* are *bitterballen* (bitter balls)—fried balls of vegetable paste; and *vlamaetjes* (little flames)—spicy mini spring rolls. For a really quick snack, the many Febo company's food dispensers about town are cheap: simply put your money in and your snack comes out hot.

CAFÉ DANTZIG ($)
Giant, crusty baguettes with delicious fillings make a perfect lunch on the terrace beside the Amstel river.
✚ H5 ✉ Zwanenburgwal 15 ☎ 6209039 🕐 10AM–1AM 🚇 Waterlooplein

CAFÉ KORT ($$)
A delightfully located café-cum-restaurant on the corner of Prinsengracht and Reguliersgracht, with a charming shady terrace beside the canals.
✚ H6 ✉ Amstelveld 12 ☎ 6261199 🕐 Closed Tue 🚃 Tram 4

GARY'S MUFFINS ($)
A late-night snack store in a street of trendy bars and clubs. Also open during the day.
✚ H5 ✉ Reguliersdwarsstraat 53 ☎ 4202406 🕐 11AM–3AM (Fri, Sat 4AM) 🚃 Tram 4, 9, 14, 16, 20, 24, 25

KAAS-WIJNHUIS ($)
A charming delicatessen-cum-*eetcafé* with wines, cheeses, cold cuts, pâtés.
✚ H4 ✉ Warmoesstraat 16 ☎ 6230878 🕐 Mon–Sat 9–6; Sun noon–6 🚇 Centraal Station

LUNCHROOM DIALOGUE ($)
A warehouse cellar, away from the crowds at Anne Frankhuis next door; good for sandwiches and cakes.
✚ G4 ✉ Prinsengracht 261a ☎ 6239991 🕐 Daily 10–5 🚃 Tram 13, 14, 17

MORITA-YA ($)
Traditional Japanese snackbar with floor seating as well as tables, that's a must for sushi fans.
✚ H4 ✉ Zeedijk 18 ☎ 6380756 🕐 Dinner only. Closed Wed 🚇 Centraal Station

PANCAKE BAKERY ($)
The best pancakes in town, cooked on an old Dutch griddle.
✚ G5 ✉ Prinsengracht 191 ☎ 6251333 🚃 Tram 13, 14, 17, 20

LA PLACE ($)
A self-service "indoor market" restaurant. Choose your dish at one of the stands, watch it being cooked, then eat at one of the tables.
✚ H5 ✉ Rokin 164 ☎ 6202364 🕐 9AM–9PM except Thu 9AM–10PM, Sun noon–9PM 🚃 Tram 4, 9, 14, 16, 20, 24, 25

SMALL TALK ($$)
Near the Museumplein, this *eetcafé* is ideal for soups and snacks between gallery visits.
✚ G6 ✉ Van Baerlestraat 52 ☎ 6714864 🚃 Tram 2, 3, 5, 12, 20

TAPAS CATALÀ ($)
Enjoy a quick bite or a meal of tempting Catalan tapas dishes.
✚ G5 ✉ Spuistraat 299 ☎ 6231141 🕐 Dinner only. Closed Tue 🚃 Tram 1, 2, 5

VAN DOBBEN ($)
A renowned sandwich shop. Try the meat croquette roll that Van Dobben himself makes from a 53-year-old recipe.
✚ H5 ✉ Korte Reguliersdwarsstraat 5–9 ☎ 6244200 🕐 Mon–Thu 9:30AM–1PM; Fri–Sat 9:30AM–2PM; Sun 11:30AM–8PM 🚃 Tram 4, 9, 14

CAFÉS & TEA SHOPS

BACKSTAGE ($)
A wacky, psychedelic café run by an eccentric entertainer.
🕂 H6 ✉ Utrechtsedwarsstraat 67 ☎ 6223638 🕓 10–5:30. Closed Sun 🚊 Tram 4

CAFÉ AMÉRICAIN ($)
Artists, writers, and bohemians frequent this grand art deco café.
🕂 G6 ✉ American Hotel, Leidseplein 28 ☎ 6245322 🕓 7AM–1AM 🚊 Tram 1, 2, 5, 6, 7, 10, 20

CAFÉ ESPRIT
Designer café, all glass and aluminum, run by the clothing chain next door; popular stop for shoppers.
🕂 H5 ✉ Spui 10a ☎ 6221967 🕓 Mon–Sat 10–6 (Thu until 10PM); Sun noon–6 🚊 Tram 1, 2, 4, 5, 9, 14, 16, 20, 24, 25

CAFÉ VERTIGO ($$)
Brown café-style surroundings, where menu-dishes occasionally reflect themes at the nearby Film Museum.
🕂 G6 ✉ Vondelpark 3 ☎ 6123021 🚊 Tram 1, 3, 6, 12

GELATERIA JORDINO ($)
Bright and breezy place that does great home-made Italian ice-cream and waistline-threatening chocolate cake.
🕂 H4 ✉ Haarlemmerdijk 25 ☎ 4203225 🚌 Bus 18, 22

GREENWOOD'S ($)
Homey little English-style tearoom serving up scones with jam and cream, chocolate cake, and lemon-meringue pie.
🕂 H4 ✉ Singel 103 ☎ 6237071 🕓 Daily 9:30–7 🚊 Tram 1, 2, 5, 13, 17, 20

METZ ($)
Views from the top floor café of this department store (▶ 71) are among the city's finest.
🕂 G5 ✉ Keizersgracht 455 ☎ 5207048 🚊 Tram 1, 2, 5

NIEUWE KAFÉ ($)
The café's crowded terrace on Dam square provides a captive audience for street musicians; ideal for people-watching.
🕂 H5 ✉ Eggertstraat 8 ☎ 6272830 🕓 8:30–6 🚊 Tram 4, 9, 14, 16, 20, 24, 25

POMPADOUR ($)
The finest chocolatier in town doubles as a sumptuous tearoom.
🕂 G5 ✉ Huidenstraat 12 ☎ 6239554 🕓 Mon 1–6; Tue–Sat 9–6 🚊 Tram 1, 2, 5

LA RUCHE ($)
Treat yourself to coffee with waffles piled high with strawberries and cream in this café in De Bijenkorf department store (▶ 72), overlooking Dam square.
🕂 H5 ✉ 1 Dam ☎ 6218080 🕓 Mon–Sat 9:30–6, except Thu 9:30–9, Sun noon–6 🚊 Tram 4, 9, 14, 16, 20, 24, 25

WINKEL ($)
A popular café looking out onto the Noordermarkt (▶ 53). Great for people-watching when the markets are on.
🕂 G4 ✉ Noordermarkt 43 ☎ 6230223 🕓 Closed evenings and Sun 🚊 Tram 3, 10

Coffee shops
In Amsterdam, the expression "coffee shop" refers to the "smoking" coffee shops, where mostly young people hang out, high on hash. "Smoking" coffee shops are usually easily recognizable by their psychedelic decor, thick fog of bitter smoke, and mellow clientele. The cake on sale is sure to be drug-laced "space cake." Surprisingly, many such shops do a good cup of coffee.

SHOPPING AREAS

Shopping tips

Although Amsterdam does not compare with Paris or London for European chic, the large number of unusual specialist stores, secondhand shops, and colorful markets among its more than 10,000 shops and department stores, make shopping a real pleasure. Interesting souvenirs and gifts to take home are easy to find, whatever your budget. Most shops are open Tuesday to Saturday from 9AM or 10AM until 6PM, on Mondays from 1PM until 6PM, on Thursdays until 9PM. Many shops open noon–5PM on Sundays too. Cash is the usual method of payment, although credit cards and Eurocheques are accepted at most department stores and larger shops.

Dutch gifts

Bulbs

Made-to-measure clogs

Bottle of *jenever* (Dutch gin)

Edam or Gouda cheese

Diamonds

Leerdam crystal

Makkum pottery

An old print or map of the city

Delftware—if you want the real thing look for De Porcelyne Fles (see panel ➤ 21)

ART & ANTIQUES

Antique shops are concentrated in the *Spiegelkwartier* near the Museumplein, along and by Nieuwe Spiegelstraat, and along the Rokin. Countless galleries are scattered throughout the city, although many can be found along the main canals. The De Looier Kunst- & Antiekcentrum on Elandsgracht in the Jordaan brings together dozens of art and antiques dealers in an indoor market. Other places to buy art, though not originals, are museum shops that sell high-quality reproductions of the famous artworks on their walls, by both Dutch and international artists. Look for the best of these at the Rijksmuseum, Van Gogh Museum, Stedelijk Museum of Modern Art, and Museum het Rembrandthuis.

BOOKSTORES

Most bookshops, including the American Book Center and a branch of British chain Waterstone's in Kalverstraat, are around the university district (off the Spui) and in Leidsestraat. You will also find several specialist antique bookstores on Nieuwezijds Voorburgwal, and there is an indoor antiquarian book market at Oudemanhuispoort.

FASHION

The three main shopping thoroughfares—Kalverstraat, Nieuwendijk and Leidsestraat—are lined with international chain stores and mainstream outlets for clothing and accessories. To the south, you'll find designer stores, including Armani, Azorro and Rodier, along P C Hooftstraat, van Baerlestraat and Beethovenstraat. For more adventurous garb, head for the Jordaan.

OFFBEAT STORES

Tiny specialist stores and boutiques selling everything from psychedelic mushrooms to designer soap and kitsch toilet furniture can be found all over the city. Many are in the Jordaan and along the web of sidestreets that connect the ring canals between Leidsegracht and Brouwersgracht.

SECONDHAND

Explore the secondhand stores of the Jordaan for a bargain, or sift through local street markets, including the city's largest and wackiest flea market at Waterlooplein.

SHOPPING MALLS

There are five main shopping malls: chic Magna Plaza near Dam square; De Amsterdamse Poort, reached by metro at Amsterdam Zuidoost; Winkelcentrum Boven't IJ, reached by ferry across the IJ; Winkelcentrum Amstelveen in the southern suburbs, reached by tram 5; and Schiphol Plaza at the airport, open from 7AM until 10PM daily.

DUTCH SOUVENIRS

AMSTERDAM SMALLEST GALLERY

An original painting of the city bought here will remind you of your stay.

✚ G4 ✉ Westermarkt 60 ☎ 6223756 🚃 Tram 13, 14, 17, 20

BLUE GOLD FISH

Storehouse of fantastical gifts including jewelry, ornaments, home fixtures, and fabrics.

✚ G5 ✉ Rozengracht 17 ☎ 6233134 🚃 Tram 13, 14, 17, 20

BONEBAKKER

Holland's royal jewelers, with dazzling displays of gold and silverware. Enjoyable even if you can't afford to buy.

✚ H5 ✉ Rokin 88–90 ☎ 6232294 🚃 Tram 4, 9, 14, 16, 20, 24, 25

DAM SQUARE SOUVENIRS

Centrally-located souvenir shop with a wide choice of clogs, furnishings, pottery, and T-shirts.

✚ H5 ✉ Dam 17 ☎ 6203432 🚃 Tram 4, 9, 14, 16, 20, 24, 25

FOCKE & MELTZER

A superior gift shop, with Delft Blue porcelain from De Porcelyne Fles, as well as outstanding Tichelaars Makkumware pottery, Leerdam crystal, and locally made silver.

✚ G6 ✉ P C Hooftstraat 65–67 ☎ 6642311 🚃 Tram 2, 3, 5, 12, 20

HEINEN HANDPAINTED DELFTWARE

Tiny but delightful for its Delftware plates, tulip vases, and Christmas decorations.

✚ G4 ✉ Prinsengracht 440 ☎ 6278299 🚃 Tram 1, 2, 5, 13, 17, 20

HOLLAND GALLERY DE MUNT

Miniature ceramic canal houses, dolls in traditional costume, ornately decorated wooden boxes, and trays.

✚ H5 ✉ Muntplein 12 ☎ 6232271 🚃 Tram 4, 9, 14, 16, 24, 25

HET KANTENHUIS

Exquisite handmade Dutch lace.

✚ H5 ✉ Kalverstraat 124 ☎ 6248618 🚃 Tram 4, 9, 14, 16, 20, 24, 25

DE KLOMPENBOER

Authentic clog factory offers the city's largest selection of hand-crafted footwear.

✚ H4 ✉ Nieuwezijds Voorburgwal 20 ☎ 6230632 🚃 Tram 1, 2, 5, 13, 17, 20

METZ & CO

Expensive gifts and designer furniture. One of the city's most stylish department stores. It has a café on the top floor (▶ 69).

✚ G5 ✉ Keizersgracht 455 ☎ 6248810 🚃 Tram 1, 2, 5

DE TUIN

The Bloemenmarkt (▶ 38) is the least expensive place to buy bulbs and this stall has the widest selection.

✚ H5 ✉ Bloemenmarkt (opposite Singel 502) ☎ 6254571 🚃 Tram 4, 9, 14, 16, 20, 24, 25

Tax-free shopping

If you live outside the European Union, you may claim a tax refund of 13.5 percent on purchases of f300 or more in one shop in one day. At shops bearing the "Tax Free Shopping" logo, ask for a Global Refund Check when you pay.

You must export your purchases within 3 months of buying them. At departure to a non-European Union country, go to customs and present your purchases and receipts to have your Global Refund Check validated. You can obtain a cash refund in Schiphol's departure hall, or arrange for a charge-card credit or certified check. You should allow around an hour to do this.

If you are traveling by train or car from Holland, you need to go through this procedure at your point of exit from the European Union (if you want to take advantage of the refund scheme). You cannot validate the shopping check at Holland's borders with neighboring countries, because they are EU members.

FOOD, DRINK & DEPARTMENT STORES

Say cheese!

Think Dutch cheese and the distinctive red *Edammer* (from Edam) and *Goudse* (from Gouda) spring to mind. They can be young (*jong*) and mild, or more mature (*belegen*) and strong. Mild young cheeses such as *Leerdammer* and *Maaslander* deserve a tasting, too. Others to try are *Friese Nagelkaas*, flavored with cumin and cloves and *Gras Kaas* (grass cheese), sold in summer, which owes its especially creamy flavor to the freshness of spring's cow pastures.

DE BIERKONING
850 beers and glasses from around the world.
✚ H5 ✉ Paleisstraat 125
☎ 6252336 🚋 Tram 1, 2, 5, 13, 14, 17,20

DE BIJENKORF
Amsterdam's busy main department store, the *Bijenkorf* ("Beehive") lives up to its name.
✚ H5 ✉ Dam 1
☎ 6218080 🚋 Tram 4, 9, 14, 16, 20, 24, 25

EICHHOLTZ
Established delicatessen with Dutch, American, and English specialties.
✚ G6 ✉ Leidsestraat 48
☎ 6220305 🚋 Tram 1, 2, 5

GEELS EN CO
Holland's oldest coffee roasting and tea trading company, full of heady aromas, with a helpful staff and traditional setting.
✚ H4 ✉ Warmoesstraat 67
☎ 6240683 🚋 Tram 4, 9, 14, 16, 20, 24, 25

HENDRIKSE PATISSERIE
Queen Beatrix buys her pastries here.
✚ F6 ✉ Overtoom 472
☎ 6180472 🚋 Tram 1, 6

H P DE VRENG & ZN
Celebrated wine-and-liquor establishment, producing fine liqueurs and *jenevers* since 1852.
✚ H4 ✉ Nieuwendijk 75
☎ 6244581 🚋 Tram 1, 2, 5, 13, 17, 20

J G BEUNE
Famous for chocolate versions of *Amsterdammertjes* (the posts lining the streets to prevent cars parking on the sidewalk), and a mouth-watering array of cakes and other bonbons.
✚ G4 ✉ Haarlemmerdijk 156–8 ☎ 6248356
🚋 Tram 1, 2, 5, 13, 17, 20

MAISON DE BONNETERIE
A gracious department store, popular with wealthy ladies.
✚ H5 ✉ Rokin 140–2/Kalverstraat 183
☎ 6262162 🚋 Tram 4, 9, 14, 16, 20, 24, 25

VITALS VITAMIN-ADVICE SHOP
Vitamins, minerals, and other food supplements, plus a unique service: a computerized vitamin test that proposes vitamin supplements based on your age and lifestyle.
✚ H4 ✉ Nieuwe Nieuwstraat 47 ☎ 6257298 🚋 Tram 1, 2, 5, 13, 17, 20

VROOM & DREESMAN
Clothing, jewelry, perfumes, electronic, and household goods.
✚ H5 ✉ Kalverstraat 201-221 ☎ 6220171 🚋 Tram 4, 9, 14, 16, 20, 24, 25

DE WATERWINKEL
A hundred different mineral waters.
✚ G7 ✉ Roelof Hartstraat 10
☎ 6755932 🚋 Tram 3, 12, 20, 24

WOUT ARXHOEK
One of the best cheese shops, with over 250 different varieties.
✚ H5 ✉ Damstraat 19
☎ 6229118 🚋 Tram 4, 9, 14, 16, 20, 24, 25

ANTIQUES & BOOKS

AMERICAN BOOK CENTER
Four floors of English-language books, plus US and British magazines and newspapers, and games.
⊕ H5 ✉ Kalverstraat 185
☎ 6255537 🚊 Tram 4, 9, 14, 16, 20, 24, 25

AMSTERDAM ANTIQUES GALLERY
Six dealers under one roof, selling silver, pewter, paintings, and Dutch tiles, among other items.
⊕ G6 ✉ Nieuwe Spiegelstraat 34 ☎ 6253371 🚊 Tram 6, 7, 10

ATHENAEUM BOEKHANDEL
This bookshop, in a striking art nouveau building, stocks international newspapers and specializes in social sciences, literature, and the classics.
⊕ G5 ✉ Spui 14–16
☎ 6226248 🚊 Tram 1, 2, 5

EDUARD KRAMER
Old Dutch tiles, the earliest dating from 1580.
⊕ G6 ✉ Nieuwe Spiegelstraat 64 ☎ 6230832 🚊 Tram 6, 7, 10

EGIDIUS ANTIQUARISCHE BOEKHANDEL
A tiny shop packed with antique books on travel, photography, and the arts.
⊕ H5 ✉ Nieuwezijds Voorburgwal 334 ☎ 6243929 🚊 Tram 1, 2, 5

DE KINDER-BOEKWINKEL
Children's books, arranged according to age.
⊕ G5 ✉ Rozengracht 34

☎ 6224761 🚊 Tram 13, 14, 17, 20

LAMBIEK
The world's oldest comic shop.
⊕ G6 ✉ Kerkstraat 78
☎ 6267543 🚊 Tram 1, 2, 5

DE LOOIER KUNST- & ANTIEKCENTRUM
A covered antiques market with hundreds of stalls selling everything from quality items to junk.
⊕ G5 ✉ Elandsgracht 109
☎ 6249038 🚊 Tram 7, 10, 17, 20

PREMSELA & HAMBURGER
Fine antique jewelry and silver in a refined setting.
⊕ H5 ✉ Rokin 120
☎ 6249688 🚊 Tram 4, 9, 16, 20, 24, 25

SCHELTEMA, HOLKEMA EN VERMEULEN
The city's biggest bookstore, with a floor of computer software, and audio and video titles.
⊕ G5 ✉ Koningsplein 20
☎ 5231411 🚊 Tram 1, 2, 5

DE SLEGTE
Amsterdam's largest secondhand bookshop is good for bargains.
⊕ H5 ✉ Kalverstraat 48–52
☎ 6225933 🚊 Tram 4, 9, 14, 16, 20, 24, 25

'T CACHOT
Secondhand thrillers and crime novels in the jail of what was once Holland's smallest police station.
⊕ L9 ✉ Dorpsplein
☎ 6691795 🕐 Tue, Wed, Sat afternoons only
🚌 Bus 59, 60, 175

Going, going, gone!
Amsterdam's main auction houses are Sotheby's (✉ Rokin 102 ☎ 5502200) and Christie's (✉ Cornelis Schuytstraat 57 ☎ 5755255). Their Dutch counterpart, Veilinghuis (Auction House) de Nieuwe Zon, is at Overtoom 197 (☎ 6168586). All hold presale viewings, interesting even if you have no intention of buying.

SPECIALTY SHOPS

Magna Plaza

Amsterdam's most luxurious shopping mall, Magna Plaza, is in an imposing neo-Gothic building in Nieuwezijds Voorburgwal near Dam square. Its four floors are filled with upscale specialist shops, such as Pinokkio, for educational toys; Bjorn Borg, for sporty underwear; and Speeldozenwereld, for quaint musical boxes. There is a café on the top floor and a Virgin Megastore in the basement.

ANIMATION ART
Drawings, paintings, and figurines of famous cartoon characters from Superman to Tintin and the Smurfs.
✚ G5 ✉ Berenstraat 19
☎ 6277600 🚋 Tram 1, 2, 5

ART RAGES
The latest in contemporary pottery, jewelry and glass, by mainly European and North American craftspeople.
✚ G6 ✉ Spiegelgracht 2a
☎ 6273645 🚋 Tram 6, 7, 10

DE BEESTENWINKEL
A cuddly-toy shop for adults. Ideal for collectors and small gifts.
✚ H5 ✉ Staalstraat 11
☎ 6231805 🚋 Tram 4, 9, 14, 16, 20, 24, 25

BELLTREE
A toyshop with benign toys, many made from wood, that children should find educational and fun.
✚ G6 ✉ Spiegelgracht 10–12
☎ 6258830 🚋 Tram 6, 7, 10

CHRISTMAS WORLD
Sample the special atmosphere of Christmas in Holland all year round, amid glittering displays of candles and bells.
✚ H5 ✉ Nieuwezijds Voorburgwal 137–9
☎ 6227047 🚋 Tram 1, 2, 5, 13, 17, 20

CONCERTO
Finest all-round selection of new and used records and CDs to suit all tastes. Especially good for jazz, classical music, and hits from the '50s and '60s.
✚ H6 ✉ Utrechtsestraat 52–60 ☎ 6245467 🚋 Tram 4

CONSCIOUS DREAMS
Anything's possible in Amsterdam. This shop specializes in "magic mushrooms!"
✚ H6 ✉ Kerkstraat 117
☎ 6266907 🚋 Tram 16, 24, 25

DEN HAAN & WAGENMAKERS
A quilt-maker's paradise of traditional fabrics, tools, and gadgets.
✚ H4 ✉ Nieuwezijds Voorburgwal 97–9 ☎ 6202525
🚋 Tram 1, 2, 5, 13, 17, 20

DE FIETSENMAKER
One of the top bike shops in Amsterdam.
✚ H5 ✉ Nieuwe Hoogstraat 21–23 ☎ 6246137
Ⓜ Nieuwmarkt

FIFTIES-SIXTIES
A jumble of period pieces including toasters, records, lamps, and other mementoes of this hip era.
✚ G5 ✉ Huidenstraat 13
☎ 6232653 🚋 Tram 1, 2, 5

HAIR POLICE
Hair styles, any shape and color you like, plus far-out fashion and accessories at this trendy boutique.
✚ H6 ✉ Kerkstraat 113
☎ 4205841
🚋 Tram 16, 24, 25

HEAD SHOP
The shop for marijuana paraphernalia and memorabilia ever since it opened in the '60s.
✚ H5 ✉ Kloveniersburgwal 39 ☎ 6249061
Ⓜ Nieuwmarkt

HEMP WORKS
Designer hemp store: jeans, jackets, shirts,

shampoo and soap all made of hemp.
🔲 H4 ✉ Nieuwendijk 13 ☎ 4211762 🚃 Tram 1, 2, 5, 13, 17, 20

JACOB HOOIJ
Old-fashioned apothecary, selling herbs, spices, and homeopathic remedies since 1743.
🔲 H5 ✉ Kloveniersburgwal 12 ☎ 6243041 🚇 Nieuwmarkt

KITSCH KITCHENS
Ghanaian metal furniture, Indian bead curtains, Mexican tablecloths, Chinese pots and pans— the whole world in one colorful kitchen!
🔲 G5 ✉ 1e Bloemdwarsstraat 21 ☎ 4284969 🚃 Tram 13, 14, 17, 20

OTTEN & ZOON
Some Dutch people still clomp around in wooden *klompen* (clogs). This shop makes fine wearable ones as well as souvenirs.
🔲 H7 ✉ Eerste Van der Helstraat ☎ 6629724 🚃 Tram 16, 24, 25

OUTRAS COISAS
Ancient and modern pots and gardening tools, reflecting the Dutch passion for plants.
🔲 G4 ✉ Herenstraat 31 ☎ 6257281 🚃 Tram 1, 2, 5, 13, 14, 17, 20

PARTY HOUSE
A cornucopia of paper decorations, dressing-up clothes, masks, and practical jokes.
🔲 G5 ✉ Rozengracht 93a–b ☎ 6247851 🚃 Tram 13, 14, 17, 20

PAS-DESTOEL
Furniture and interiors designed with a touch of innocent fantasy for children.
🔲 G4 ✉ Westerstraat 260 ☎ 4207542 🚃 Tram 3, 10

P G C HAJENIUS
One of the world's finest tobacco shops, in elegant, art deco premises.
🔲 H5 ✉ Rokin 92–96 ☎ 6237494 🚃 Tram 4, 9, 14, 16, 20, 24, 25

RED EARTH
Pamper yourself with exotic body-care products made from natural ingredients and essential oils according to ancient Aboriginal recipes.
🔲 G6 ✉ Leidsestraat 64 ☎ 6221620 🚃 Tram 1, 2, 5

SCALE TRAIN HOUSE
Take home a do-it-yourself windmill or canal barge kit as a souvenir, or choose from the vast stock of model railroad components.
🔲 F5 ✉ Bilderdijkstraat 94 ☎ 6122670 🚃 Tram 3, 12, 13, 14

DE SPEELMUIS
A splendid collection of handmade wooden toys and dollhouse miniatures.
🔲 G5 ✉ Elandsgracht 58 ☎ 6385342 🚃 Tram 7, 10, 17, 20

WORLD OF WONDERS
Interior design store in the fast-gentrifying Eastern Docks area, with upscale fabrics and furnishings, and many small items to enliven your living space.
🔲 L4 ✉ KNSM-Laan 293 ☎ 4634069 🚌 Bus 32

Oibibio

This department store-cum-spiritual center (✉ Prins Hendrikkade 20–21) offers environmentally friendly clothing (in cotton, wool, and hemp), natural cosmetics and gifts, (including some made from recycled glass, paper, and leather). The store includes a bookstore, a café, and an entire floor dedicated to workshops and therapy treatments, including yoga, tai chi, and shiatsu. You can even learn to play the didgeridoo here.

FASHION

Bargains

There are often excellent bargains to be found in Amsterdam, especially during the January and July sales. Watch for signs saying *Uitverkoop* (closing-down or end-of-season sale), *Solden* (sale), and *Korting* (discounted goods).

CANDY CORSON
One of the best places in Amsterdam for quality leather accessories, especially bags and belts.
H5 ✉ St Luciensteeg 19 ☎ 6248061 🚊 Tram 13, 14, 17, 20

CORA KEMPERMAN
Elegant and imaginative, individually designed women's fashion.
G5 ✉ Leidsestraat 72 ☎ 6251284 🚊 Tram 1, 2, 5

ESPRIT
Young, trendy designs for the seriously fashionable.
H5 ✉ Spui 10a ☎ 6221967 🚊 Tram 1, 2, 5

HESTER VAN EEGHEN
Handbags, wallets, and other leather accessories in innovative shapes, styles, and colors, designed in Holland and made in Italy.
G5 ✉ Hartenstraat 1 ☎ 6269212 🚊 Tram 13, 14, 17, 20

DE KNOPEN WINKEL
With 8,000 different kinds of buttons, from around the world, the Button Shop is on hand for apparel emergencies.
G5 ✉ Wolvenstraat 14 ☎ 6240479 🚊 Tram 1, 2, 5

THE MADHATTER
Hand-made hats by Dutch designers.
H7 ✉ Van der Helstplein 4 ☎ 6647748 🚊 Tram 3, 12, 25

MEXX
Top designer boutique where you'll find many leading French and Italian labels.
G6 ✉ P C Hooftstraat 118 ☎ 6750171 🚊 Tram 2, 3, 5, 12, 20

OGER
One of the top menswear boutiques.
G6 ✉ P C Hooftstraat 81 ☎ 6768695 🚊 Tram 2, 3, 5, 12, 20

OILILY
Children love the brightly colored and patterned sporty clothes of this Dutch company.
G6 ✉ P C Hooftstraat 131–133 ☎ 6723361 🚊 Tram 2, 3, 5, 12, 20

OSCAR
All the latest footwear here, from glittery platforms to psychedelic thigh boots.
H4 ✉ Nieuwendijk 208–10 ☎ 6253143 🚊 Tram 4, 9, 14, 16, 20, 24, 25

PALETTE
The smallest shop in the Netherlands has a large selection of silk and satin shoes, in 500 colors.
H5 ✉ Nieuwezijds Voorburgwal 125 ☎ 6393207 🚊 Tram 4, 9, 14, 16, 20, 24, 25

RETRO
Way-out fashion, including a dazzling array of '60s and '70s flower-power clothing.
F6 ✉ 1e Constantijn Huygenstraat 57 ☎ 6834180 🚊 Tram 1, 3, 6, 12

SISSY-BOY
A Dutch clothing chain with stylish, affordable clothing for men and women.
G5 ✉ Leidsestraat 15 ☎ 6238949 🚊 Tram 1, 2, 5

THEATER, DANCE & MOVIES

THEATER & DANCE

FELIX MERITIS
An important avant-garde dance and drama center, and home to the Shaffy experimental theater company.

🏠 G5 ✉ Keizersgracht 324 ☎ 6262321 🚊 Tram 13, 14, 17, 20

DE KLEINE KOMEDIE
The very best cabaret and stand-up comedy, in one of the city's oldest theaters.

🏠 H5 ✉ Amstel 56 ☎ 6240534 🚊 Tram 4, 9, 14, 20

KONINKLIJK THEATER CARRÉ
The "Royal Theater" hosts long-running international musicals, revues, cabaret, folk dancing, and an annual Christmas circus.

🏠 H–J6 ✉ Amstel 115–25 ☎ 6225225 🚊 Weesperplein

MUZIEKTHEATER
An Amsterdam cultural mainstay and home to the Dutch national opera and ballet companies since it opened in 1986, Holland's largest auditorium, seating 1,689, mounts an international repertoire as well as experimental works. Guided backstage tours on Wed and Sat at 3PM (➤ 55).

🏠 H5 ✉ Waterlooplein 22 ☎ 6255455 (recorded information in Dutch; hold for operator) 🚊 Waterlooplein

STADSSCHOUWBURG
Classical and modern plays form the main repertoire of the stylish, 19th-century Municipal Theater.

🏠 G6 ✉ Leidseplein 26 ☎ 6242311 🚊 Tram 1, 2, 5, 6, 7, 10, 20

DE STALHOUDERIJ
One of the city's very few English-language theater companies, in a converted stable that seats 40.

🏠 G5 ✉ 1e Bloemdwarsstraat 4 ☎ 6262282 🚊 Tram 13, 14, 17, 20

VONDELPARK OPENLUCHTTHEATER
The open-air theater in the park offers drama, cabaret, concerts, and children's programs from June to August.

🏠 F6 ✉ Vondelpark ☎ 5237700 🚊 Tram 1, 2, 3, 5, 6, 12, 20

MOVIES

CITY 1–7
Amsterdam's largest multiscreen cinema.

🏠 G6 ✉ Kleine Gartmanplantsoen 13–25 ☎ 6234579 🚊 Tram 1, 2, 5, 6, 7, 10, 20

FILM MUSEUM CINEMATHEEK
International programs, ranging from silent movies to more recent releases.

🏠 G6 ✉ Vondelpark 3 ☎ 5891400 🚊 Tram 1, 2, 3, 5, 6, 12, 20

TUCHINSKI THEATER
Holland's most attractive and prestigious cinema, with six screens; classic art deco interior alone makes it worth visiting, no matter what's showing.

🏠 H5 ✉ Reguliersbreestraat 26–28 ☎ 6262633 🚊 Tram 4, 9, 14, 20

Tickets
For theater information and tickets, contact the Amsterdam Uit Buro's Ticketshop (✉ Leidseplein 26 ☎ 6211211 🕐 office open daily 10–6, Thu until 9; telephone answered 9–9 daily). Tickets for most performances can also be purchased from the VVV tourist offices. The daily newspapers and listings magazine *Uitkrant* have program details.

Movie guide
The city's main multiscreen cinema complexes, in the Leidseplein and Rembrandtplein areas, follow Hollywood's lead closely. The latest big US releases and British movies that become international hits are sure to show up on Amsterdam's screens after a short delay. Movies from other countries occasionally make it to the screen.

Almost all movies are shown in their original language, with Dutch subtitles.

CLASSICAL MUSIC & OPERA

Ticket time

For performances at popular venues, including the Concertgebouw and Muziektheater, you generally need to book ahead. This can be done in person or by phone to ticket reservation counters. VVV tourist offices also book tickets for a small charge, as does Amsterdam Uit Buro's Ticketshop (✉ Leidseplein 26 ☎ 6211211). Many hotels can reserve tickets for guests.

BEURS VAN BERLAGE

Home to the Netherlands Philharmonic Orchestra and Dutch Chamber Orchestra, this remarkable early modernist building that once housed the stock exchange now makes an impressive concert hall (▶ 54).
✚ H4–5 ✉ Damrak 213–279 ☎ 6270466
🚋 Tram 4, 9, 16, 20, 24, 25

CONCERTGEBOUW

One of the world's finest concert halls, the magnificent neoclassical Concertgebouw has wonderful acoustics, making it a favorite with musicians worldwide. Since the Royal Concertgebouw Orchestra made its début in 1888, it has come under the baton of Richard Strauss, Mahler, Ravel, Schönberg, and Haitink to name but a few. It continues to be one of the most respected ensembles in the world.
✚ G7 ✉ Concertgebouwplein 2–6 ☎ 6718345 🚋 Tram 3, 5, 12, 16, 20

IJSBREKER

A major international venue for contemporary classical music. There are performances of work by John Cage, Xanakis, and other modern music pioneers, and around half the concerts are devoted to modern Dutch compositions.
✚ J6 ✉ Weesperzijde 23
☎ 6939093 🚇 Weesperplein

MUZIEKTHEATER

Major operatic works and experimental opera from the Dutch National Opera and other leading international companies (▶ 55 and 77).
✚ H5 ✉ Waterlooplein 22
☎ 6255455 🚇 Waterlooplein

NIEUWE KERK

Frequent lunchtime concerts and exceptional organ recitals by visiting organists, in an atmospheric setting (▶ 37).
✚ H5 ✉ Dam ☎ 6268168
🚋 Tram 1, 2, 4, 5, 9, 13, 14, 16, 17, 20, 24, 25

OUDE KERK

Chamber music concerts and organ recitals are held in this old church, where Holland's foremost composer, Jan Pieters Sweelinck (1562–1621) was once organist. Pass by at 4PM on Saturdays, and you may hear a carillon concert (▶ 40).
✚ H5 ✉ Oudekerksplein 23
☎ 6258284 🚇 Nieuwmarkt

RAI

This convention center sometimes stages classical music and opera.
✚ G–H8 ✉ Europaplein
☎ 5491212 🚋 Tram 4

TROPENMUSEUM

Traditional music from developing countries is performed at the museum's Soeterijn Theater (▶ 48).
✚ K6 ✉ Linnaeusstraat 2
☎ 5688215 🚋 Tram 6, 9, 10, 14, 20

WESTERGASFABRIEK

A popular venue for experimental opera.
✚ F3 ✉ Haarlemmerweg 8–10 ☎ 5810425 🚌 Bus 18 Tram 10

LIVE MUSIC

AKHNATON

Funky multicultural youth center with reggae, rap, and salsa dance nights.
🔢 H4 ✉ Nieuwezijds Kolk 25 ☎ 6243396 🚋 Tram 1, 2, 5, 13, 17, 20

ALTO JAZZ CAFÉ

One of Amsterdam's best jazz clubs. Live music nightly, pricey drinks.
🔢 G6 ✉ Korte Leidsedwarsstraat 115 ☎ 6263249 🚋 Tram 1, 2, 5, 6, 7, 10, 20

BIMHUIS

The place for serious followers of avant-garde, improvisational, and experimental jazz, attracting top international players.
🔢 H5 ✉ Oudeschans 73–77 ☎ 6231361 🚇 Nieuwmarkt

BOURBON STREET

Nightly blues and jazz.
🔢 G6 ✉ Leidsekruisstraat 6–8 ☎ 6233440 🚋 Tram 6, 7, 10, 20

CANEÇAO

Brazilian bar with live salsa nightly.
🔢 G6 ✉ Lange Leidsedwarsstraat 86 ☎ 6380611 🚋 Tram 1, 2, 5, 6, 7, 10, 20

DE HEEREN VAN AEMSTEL

Prior to events such as the North Sea Jazz Festival, you can often see some of the world's great jazz performers here.
🔢 H6 ✉ Thorbeckeplein 5 ☎ 6202173 🚋 Tram 4, 9, 14, 20

HOF VAN HOLLAND

Come here for an evening of Dutch folk music and traditional songs.
🔢 H5 ✉ Rembrandtplein 5 ☎ 6234650 🚋 Tram 4, 9, 14, 20

JOSEPH LAM JAZZ CAFÉ

Traditional jazz club with live Dixieland on Saturdays.
🔢 G3 ✉ Van Diemenstraat 242 ☎ 6228086 🚌 Bus 28

MALOE MELO

This smoky yet convivial Jordaan bar, Amsterdam's "home of the blues," belts out some fine rhythms.
🔢 G4 ✉ Lijnbannsgracht 163 ☎ 4204592 🚋 Tram 3, 10

O'REILLY'S IRISH PUB

Choice whiskeys and hearty Irish fare accompanied by jolly folk music.
🔢 H5 ✉ Paleisstraat 103–105 ☎ 6249498 🚋 Tram 1, 2, 5

PARADISO

Rock, reggae, and pop concerts, in a beautiful old converted church that was once the haunt of '60s hippies. Now the discotheque offers music from the 1970s to the latest dance trends.
🔢 G6 ✉ Weteringschans 6–8 ☎ 6237348 🚋 Tram 6, 7, 10

TWEE ZWAANTJES

Traditional Dutch entertainment off the tourist track in a tiny bar full of accordion-playing, folk-singing Jordaaners.
🔢 G4 ✉ Prinsengracht 114 ☎ 6252729 🚋 Tram 13, 14, 17, 20

Melkweg

Located in a wonderful old dairy building (hence the name *Melkweg* or "Milky Way") on a canal just off Leidseplein, this off-beat arts center opened in the '60s and remains a shrine to alternative culture. Live bands play in the old warehouse most evenings, and there is also a constantly changing program of unconventional theater, dance, art, and film events.
(✉ Lijnbaansgracht 234 ☎ 6248492).

Brown Cafés & Other Bars

Ancient and modern

Brown cafés, so-called because of their chocolate-colored walls and dark wooden fittings, are reminiscent of the interiors in Dutch Old Master paintings. Here you can meet the locals in a setting that's *gezellig* (cozy). In stark contrast, there are a growing number of brasserie-like grand cafés, and chic, modern bars, with stylish, spacious interiors. Watch also for the tiny ancient *proeflokalen* tasting bars (originally distillers' private sampling rooms), with aging barrels and gleaming brass taps, serving a host of gins and liqueurs.

BROWN CAFÉS

FRASCATI
A lively, cultured crowd frequent this bar next to an experimental theater.
⊞ H5 ✉ Nes 59 ☎ 6241324
🚊 Tram 4, 9, 14, 16, 20, 24, 25

HOPPE
One of Amsterdam's most established, most popular brown cafés, with beer in one bar and gin from the barrel in another.
⊞ G5 ✉ Spui 18–20
☎ 4204420 🚊 Tram 1, 2, 5

DE KARPERSHOEK
A sawdust-strewn bar dating from 1629, and frequented by sailors.
⊞ H4 ✉ Martelaarsgracht 2
☎ 6247886 🚇 Centraal Station

HET MOLENPAD
An old-fashioned brown café. The canalside terrace catches the early evening sun.
⊞ G5 ✉ Prinsengracht 653
☎ 6259680 🚊 Tram 1, 2, 5

PAPENEILAND
Amsterdam's oldest bar resembles a scene from a Dutch Old Master painting, with its paneled walls, Makkum tiles, candles, benches, and wood-burning stove.
⊞ G4 ✉ Prinsengracht 2
☎ 6241989 🚌 Bus 18, 22

DE PRINS
Very much a locals' bar, despite its proximity to the Anne Frankhuis, with a cozy pub atmosphere and seasonal menu.
⊞ G4 ✉ Prinsengracht 124
☎ 6249382 🚊 Tram 13, 14, 17, 20

VAN PUFFELEN
An intimate sawdust-strewn brown bar with a smart restaurant in the back. You can sit on a barge moored outside, on the Prinsengracht, in summer.
⊞ G5 ✉ Prinsengracht 375–377 ☎ 6246270
🚊 Tram 13, 14, 17, 20

REIJNDERS
Brown cafés are typically on tranquil streets; Reijnders is on brash, neon-lit Leidseplein yet has retained much of its traditional style and look.
⊞ G6 ✉ Leidseplein 6
☎ 6234419 🚊 Tram 1, 2, 5, 6, 7, 10, 20

GRAND CAFÉS & STYLISH BARS

DE ENGELBEWAARDER
Jazz on Sunday from 4PM livens up a usually tranquil, arty hangout situated off the Red Light District.
⊞ H5 ✉ Kloveniersburgwal 59
☎ 6253772
🚇 Nieuwmarkt

DE JAREN
A spacious, ultramodern café, known for its trendy clientele and its sunny terraces overlooking the Amstel.
⊞ H5 ✉ Nieuwe Doelenstraat 20–22 ☎ 6255771
🚊 Tram 4, 9, 14, 16, 20, 24, 25

DE KROON
A chic, colonial-style bar, with large potted plants and wicker furniture, and an executive clientele.
⊞ H5 ✉ Rembrandtplein 17
☎ 6252011 🚊 Tram 4, 9, 14, 20

HET LAND VAN WALEM

One of Amsterdam's first modern bars.

🚩 G5 ✉ Keizersgracht 449
☎ 6253544 🚋 Tram 1, 2, 5

LUXEMBOURG

Watch the world go by over canapés or colossal club sandwiches on the terrace of this elegant, high-ceilinged bar.

🚩 G5 ✉ Spui 22–24
☎ 6206264 🚋 Tram 1, 2, 5

L'OPERA

Fashionable with the city's chic set.

🚩 H5 ✉ Rembrandtplein
27–31 ☎ 6275232
🚋 Tram 4, 9, 14, 20

SCHILLER

An evocative art deco bar enhanced with live piano music.

🚩 H5 ✉ Rembrandtplein 26
☎ 6249846 🚋 Tram 4, 9,
14, 20

PROEFLOKALEN (TASTING BARS)

CAFÉ HOOGHOUDT

Brown bar-cum-*proeflokalen* in an old warehouse lined with traditional stoneware *jenever* barrels. Tasty Dutch appetizers go with a big selection of liqueurs.

🚩 H6 ✉ Reguliersgracht 11
☎ 4204041 🕙 Noon–1AM
🚋 Tram 4, 9, 14, 16, 20, 24, 25

DE DRIE FLESCHJES

Amsterdammers have been tasting gins at "The Three Little Bottles" since 1650.

🚩 H5 ✉ Gravenstraat 18
☎ 6248443 🚋 Tram 1, 2, 4,
5, 9, 13, 14, 16, 17, 20, 24, 25

DE OOIEVAAR

A homely atmosphere pervades "The Stork," one of Holland's smallest *proeflokalen*.

🚩 H4 ✉ Sint Olofspoort 1
☎ 4208004 🚉 Centraal Station

SPECIALIST BARS

DE BEIAARD

A beer drinker's paradise—over 80 beers from around the world.

🚩 G5 ✉ Spui 30
☎ 6225110 🚋 Tram 1, 2, 5

BROUWERIJ 'T IJ

Lethally strong beer brewed on the premises of the old De Gooier windmill (► 60).

🚩 K5 ✉ Funenkade 7
☎ 6228325 🕙 Fri–Sun
3PM–8PM 🚌 Bus 22, 28

BULLDOG PALACE

Flagship of the Bulldog chain of bars and smoking coffee shops—a plush, loud bar, brashly decked out in stars and stripes. Downstairs is a "smoking coffeeshop" (► 69).

🚩 G6 ✉ Leidseplein 13–17
☎ 6271908 🚋 Tram 1, 2, 5,
6, 7, 10, 20

CYBER C@FÉ

The first of several internet cafés in Amsterdam.

🚩 H4 ✉ Nieuwendijk 19
☎ 6235146 (e-mail: visitor1@cybercafe.euronet.nl)
🚉 Centraal Station

CAFÉ APRIL

Popular, easy-going gay bar that attracts a mixed crowd of mostly male locals and tourists.

🚩 H5 ✉ Reguliersdwarsstraat
37 ☎ 6259572 🚋 Tram 1, 2, 5

Bar talk

Most of the 1,400 bars and cafés in Amsterdam are open from around 10AM until the early hours and many serve meals. *Proeflokalen* open from around 4PM until 8PM, and some serve snacks, such as nuts, cheese, meatballs, and sausage. Beer is the most popular alcoholic drink. It is always served with a head, and often with a *jenever* chaser called a *kopstoot* (a blow to the head). If you want only a small beer, ask for a *colatje* or *Kleintje pils*. Dutch for "cheers" is *Proost!*

Jenevers

Dutch gin (*jenever*), made from molasses and flavored with juniper berries, comes in a variety of ages: *jong* (young), *oud* (old), and *zeer oud* (the oldest and the mellowest), and in color ranging from clear to brownish. Other flavors may be added; try *bessenjenever* (blackcurrant), or *bitterkoekjes likeur* (macaroon). *Jenever* is drunk straight or as a beer chaser, not with a mixer.

NIGHTCLUBS

Gay Amsterdam

Clubbing is at the heart of Amsterdam's gay scene. The best-known venue is iT, a glitzy disco with throbbing techno. Gay bars and clubs abound in nearby Reguliersdwarsstraat and Halvemaansteeg. To find out exactly what's on and where it's happening, call the Gay and Lesbian Switchboard (☎ 6236565) or read the English-language *Guide for Gays* magazine.

BOSTON CLUB

Attracts a 30s–40s crowd looking for a quieter dancing experience.
✚ H4 ✉ Renaissance Hotel, Kattengat 1 ☎ 6245561 or 6275245 (hotel) 🚊 Centraal Station

DANSEN BIJ JANSEN

Student disco, playing the latest chart toppers.
✚ H5 ✉ Handboogstraat 11 ☎ 6201779 🕐 11PM–4:30AM 🚊 Tram 1, 2, 5,

ESCAPE

Amsterdam's largest disco can hold 2,000 dancers. Dazzling light show, superb sound system.
✚ H5 ✉ Rembrandtplein 11–15 ☎ 6221111 🕐 10PM–4AM (Fri, Sat until 5AM) 🚊 Tram 4, 9, 14, 20

HOLLAND CASINO

One of Europe's largest casinos.
✚ G6 ✉ Max Euweplein 62 ☎ 5211111 🚊 Tram 1, 2, 5, 6, 7, 10, 20

iT

The wildest disco in town, with outrageously dressed clientele and fierce house music. Saturday night is exclusively gay.
✚ H5 ✉ Amstelstraat 24 ☎ 6250111 🕐 11PM–4AM. Closed Sun–Wed 🚊 Tram 4, 9, 14, 20

MAZZO

A young image-conscious crowd prop up the bar of this small, trendy disco in the Jordaan, while guest DJs and live bands play the latest sounds.
✚ G5 ✉ Rozengracht 114 ☎ 6267500 🕐 11PM–4AM (Sat 5AM) 🚊 Tram 13, 14, 17, 20

MINISTRY

A café-cum-nightclub with all kinds of disco music.
✚ H5 ✉ Reguliersdwarsstraat 12 ☎ 6233981 🕐 Thu–Mon 10–5 🚊 Tram 1, 2, 5, 16, 20, 24, 25

ODEON

A converted canal house with house music on the first floor, '60s–'80s classic disco upstairs, and jazz in the basement.
✚ H5 ✉ Singel 460 ☎ 6249711 🕐 10PM–4AM (Fri, Sat until 5AM) 🚊 Tram 1, 2, 5

RICHTER

The '36 on the Richter Scale" club with "earth-quake" decor is enchanting.
✚ H5 ✉ Reguliersdwarsstraat 36 ☎ 6261573 🕐 midnight–4:30AM 🚊 Tram 1, 2, 5, 16, 20, 24, 25

RoXY

Set in an old cinema, this cool club is a favorite with Amsterdam's chic club-set.
✚ H5 ✉ Singel 465–467 ☎ 6200354 🕐 11PM–4AM (Fri, Sat until 5AM) 🚊 Tram 1, 2, 4, 5, 9, 14, 20, 24, 25

SALAD BOWL

Jazz dance, soul, disco, and hip-hop in trendy surroundings.
✚ H5 ✉ Nieuwezijds Voorburgwal 161 ☎ 4205062 🚊 Tram 1, 2, 5, 13, 17, 20

SOUL KITCHEN

Leading "non-house" club for soul and also '60s and '70s music.
✚ H5 ✉ Amstelstraat 32 ☎ 6202333 🕐 Wed–Mon 11PM–5AM 🚊 Tram 4, 9, 14, 20

SPORTS

FISHING
Obtain a permit from the Dutch Fishing Federation to fish in the Amsterdamse Bos (► 58).
✚ H6 ✉ Nicolaas Witsenstraat 10 ☎ 6264988 🚊 Tram 6, 7, 10

FITNESS
JANSEN AEROBIC FITNESSCENTRUM
Fitness center with gyms, sauna, solarium, and daily aerobics classes.
✚ H5 ✉ Rokin 109–111 ☎ 6269366 🚊 Tram 4, 9, 14, 16, 20, 24, 25

GOLF
GOLFBAAN WATERLAND
Modern 18-hole course just north of the city center.
✚ L1 ✉ Buikslotermeerdijk 141 ☎ 6361010

HORSE RIDING
HOLLANDSCHE MANEGE
Amsterdam's most central riding school dating from 1882.
✚ F6 ✉ Vondelstraat 140 ☎ 6180942 🚊 Tram 1, 6

JOGGING
There are marked trails for joggers through the Vondelpark and Amsterdamse Bos. The Amsterdam Marathon is in May, and the Grachtenloop canal race in June (► 22), when up to 5,000 run either 5, 10, or 20km along the banks of Prinsengracht and Vijzelgracht.

ICE SKATING
The canals often freeze in winter, turning the city into a big ice rink. Skates can be bought at most sports equipment stores.

JAAP EDENBAAN
A large indoor ice rink, open October to March.
✚ L7 ✉ Radioweg 64 ☎ 6949652 🚊 Tram 9

SWIMMING
The seaside is only 30 minutes away by train, with miles of clean, sandy beaches. Zandvoort is closest; Bergen and Noordwijk are also popular.

MARNIXBAD
A normal, rectangular indoor swimming pool, but with the addition of water slides and whirlpool.
✚ G4 ✉ Marnixplein 5 ☎ 6254843 🚊 Tram 3, 10

DE MIRANDABAD
Subtropical swimming pool complex, with indoor and outdoor pools, beach and wave machines.
✚ H8 ✉ De Mirandalaan 9 ☎ 6428080 🚊 Tram 25

TENNIS
AMSTELPARK TENNIS CENTER
Holland's biggest, with 42 outdoor and indoor courts, the outdoor ones floodlit, and all open to visitors.
✚ F9 ✉ Koenenkade 8, Amsterdamse Bos ☎ 6445436 🚌 Bus 125, 147, 170, 171, 172, 193

WATERSPORTS
DUIKELAAR, SLOTERPARK
A water park with sail boats, canoes, and sailboards to rent in summer.
✚ C5 ✉ Noordzijde 41 ☎ 6138855 🚊 Tram 14

Spectator sports
Soccer is Holland's number one spectator sport and the number one team is Ajax Amsterdam. Watch them play at their magnificent new stadium, the Amsterdam ArenA, ArenaBoulevard, Amsterdam Zuidoost (☎ 3111333). Other popular events include international field hockey at Wagenaar Stadium (✉ Nieuwe Kalfjeslaan ☎ 6401141) and equestrian show-jumping at RAI (✉ Europaplein ☎ 5491212) every November. Look out for a Dutch hybrid of volleyball and netball called *korfball*, and *carambole*—billiards on a table without pockets.

LUXURY HOTELS

Prices
Expect to pay over f400 a night for a double room in a luxury hotel.

Hotel tips
Two-fifths of Amsterdam's 30,000 hotel beds are in 4- and 5-star properties, making problems for people looking for mid-range and budget accommodations. At peak times, such as during the spring tulip season and summer, empty rooms in lower-cost hotels are about as rare as black tulips. Book ahead for these times. Special offers may be available at other times. Many hotels lower their rates in winter, when the city is quieter and truer to itself than in the mad whirl of summer. Watch out for hidden pitfalls, such as Golden Age canal houses with four floors, steep and narrow stairways, and no elevator; and tranquil-looking mansions with a late-night café's sidewalk terrace next door.

AMERICAN
Resplendent art-nouveau Amsterdam classic on the Leidseplein.
✠ G6 ✉ Leidsekade 97 ☎ 6245322 🚊 Tram 1, 2, 5, 6, 7, 10, 20

AMSTEL INTER-CONTINENTAL
Holland's most luxurious and expensive hotel, on the Amstel river, notable for its stately grandeur and opulent decor, is a little way from the center, but provides a motor yacht and luxury limousines to make sightseeing easier.
✠ J6 ✉ Prof Tulpplein 1 ☎ 6226060 🚊 Tram 6, 7, 10, 20

BILDERBERG GARDEN
In a pleasant leafy suburb, a short tram ride from downtown.
✠ F7 ✉ Dijsselhofplantsoen 7 ☎ 6642121 🚊 Tram 16

DE L'EUROPE
Prestigious, combining turn-of-the-century architecture with the most modern amenities, in a waterfront setting.
✠ H5 ✉ Nieuwe Doelenstraat 2–8 ☎ 5311777 🚊 Tram 4, 6, 9, 14, 16, 20, 24, 25

GOLDEN TULIP BARBIZON PALACE
Modern luxury deftly concealed within a row of 17th-century mansions. Many split-level suites with ancient oak beams.
✠ H4 ✉ Prins Hendrikkade 59–72 ☎ 5564564 🚇 Centraal Station

GRAND HOTEL KRASNAPOLSKY
Built in the 1880s, the "Kras" has belle-époque grace in its public spaces and modern facilities in its rooms.
✠ H5 ✉ Dam 9 ☎ 5549111 🚊 Tram 1, 2, 4, 5, 9, 13, 14, 16, 17, 20, 24, 25

GRAND WESTIN DEMEURE
Once a 16th-century royal inn, then the City Hall, now a luxury hotel.
✠ H5 ✉ Oudezijds Voorburgwal 197 ☎ 5553111 🚇 Nieuwmarkt

HILTON
Modern efficiency, on a leafy boulevard in the south of the city. The honeymoon suite was the scene of John Lennon and Yoko Ono's weeklong 1969 love-in for world peace.
✠ F7 ✉ Apollolaan 138–140 ☎ 6780780 🚊 Tram 16

MARRIOTT
An easy walk to the main museums, shops, and nightlife centers.
✠ G6 ✉ Stadhouderskade 19–21 ☎ 6075555 🚊 Tram 1, 2, 5, 6, 20

PULITZER
Twenty-four 17th-century houses, once the homes of wealthy merchants, have been converted into this luxurious canalside hotel.
✠ G5 ✉ Prinsengracht 315–331 ☎ 5235235 🚊 Tram 13, 14, 17, 20

RENAISSANCE
Modern, with extensive business facilities and own disco, near Dam square and Centraal Station.
✠ H4 ✉ Kattengat 1 ☎ 6212223 🚊 Tram 1, 2, 5, 17, 20

MID-RANGE HOTELS

AMBASSADE

Amsterdam's smartest
B&B, in a series of gabled
canal houses.
✚ G5 ✉ Herengracht
335–353 ☎ 6262333
🚊 Tram 1, 2, 5

AMSTERDAM

Fully modernized behind
its 18th-century facade, on
one of the city's busiest
tourist streets.
✚ H5 ✉ Damrak 93–94
☎ 5550666 🚊 Tram 4, 9, 14,
16, 20, 24, 25

AMSTERDAM HOUSE

Quietly situated small
hotel beside the Amstel.
Most rooms have a view of
the river.
✚ H5 ✉ 's-Gravelandseveer
3–4 ☎ 6246607 🚊 Tram 4,
9, 14, 16, 20, 24, 25

CANAL HOUSE

Antique furnishings and a
pretty garden make this
small, family-run hotel on
the Keizersgracht a gem.
✚ G4 ✉ Keizersgracht 148
☎ 6225182 🚊 Tram 13, 14,
17, 20

LA CASALO

A converted houseboat
with just four rooms.
✚ J7 ✉ Amsteldijk 862
☎ 6423680 🚊 Tram 4

DOELEN HOTEL

Amsterdam's oldest hotel,
the place where
Rembrandt painted the
"*Night Watch*," with small
rooms, but well-equipped.
✚ H5 ✉ Nieuwe Doelenstraat
24 ☎ 5540600 🚊 Tram 4, 9,
14, 16, 20, 24, 25

ESTHERÉA

A well-considered blend
of wood-paneled canalside
character with efficient
service and modern
facilities.
✚ G5 ✉ Singel 303–309
☎ 6245146 🚊 Tram 1, 2, 5

JAN LUYKEN

A well-run, elegant
town-house hotel in a
quiet back street near
Vondelpark and the
Museumplein.
✚ G6 ✉ Jan Luijkenstraat
54–58 ☎ 5730730
🚊 Tram 2, 3, 5, 12

MAAS

A charming, family-run,
waterfront hotel round the
corner from Leidseplein,
near museums, stores, and
nightlife. Some rooms
have waterbeds.
✚ G6 ✉ Leidsekade 91
☎ 6233868 🚊 Tram 1, 2, 5,
6, 7, 10, 20

REMBRANDT RESIDENCE

On Amsterdam's most
celebrated canal.
✚ G5 ✉ Herengracht 255
☎ 6236638 🚊 Tram 13, 14,
17, 20

SEVEN BRIDGES

Small and exquisite, with
a view of seven bridges,
lots of antiques, and
owners who treat their
guests as though they
were family friends.
✚ H6 ✉ Reguliersgracht 31
☎ 6231329 🚊 Tram 16,
24, 25

TULIP INN

Strikingly modern
Amsterdam School-style
architecture. Good
facilities for visitors with
disabilities.
✚ G5 ✉ Spuistraat 288–292
☎ 4204545 🚊 Tram 1, 2, 5

Prices

Expect to pay from f200 to f400
a night for a double room in a
mid-range hotel.

Bed and breakfast, apartments, and boats

If you want to rent an apartment
in Amsterdam, contact Amsterdam
House (✉ Amstel 176a
☎ 6262577); you can take your
pick of luxury apartments in
converted canal houses, or even a
houseboat. Bed and Breakfast
Holland (✉ Theophile de
Bockstraat 3, ☎ 6157527) will
set you up in a private house.

85

BUDGET ACCOMMODATIONS

Prices

Expect to pay up to f200 a night for a double room in a budget hotel. Hostels and campsites are considerably cheaper.

Camping

There are several campsites in and around Amsterdam. The best-equipped one is a long way out, in the Amsterdamse Bos (✉ Kleine Noorddijk 1, ☎ 6416868). Vliegenbos is just a ten-minute bus ride from the station, close to the River IJ (✉ Meeuwenlaan 138, ☎ 6368855). Contact the VVV for full details.

ACACIA
An inexpensive, cheerful, family-run hotel in the Jordaan, with studio rentals and a houseboat that sleeps four.
➕ G4 ✉ Lindengracht 251
☎ 6221460 🚋 Tram 3

AGORA
A small, comfortable, 18th-century canal house furnished with antiques and filled with flowers from the nearby Bloemenmarkt.
➕ H5 ✉ Singel 462
☎ 6272200 🚋 Tram 4, 9, 14, 16, 20, 24, 25

AMSTEL BOTEL
One of Amsterdam's few floating hotels, with magnificent views over the old docks.
➕ J4 ✉ Oosterdokskade 2–4
☎ 6264247 🚋 Centraal Station

ARENA
A large hostel and information center for youthful travelers. It has a café and restaurant (with garden terrace), and puts on dance nights, concerts, exhibitions, and other events.
➕ J6 ✉ 's-Gravensandestraat 51 ☎ 6947444 🚋 Tram 3, 6, 10

DE FILOSOOF
Each room in this unique hotel is named after the great philosophers and decorated accordingly.
➕ F6 ✉ Anna van den Vondelstraat 6 ☎ 6833013
🚋 Tram 1, 6

HOKSBERGEN
A basic hotel in an old canal house, an easy walk from the main city sights.
➕ G5 ✉ Singel 301
☎ 6266043 🚋 Tram 1, 2, 5

NJHC CITY HOSTEL VONDELPARK
A wide range of modern options, from dormitories to family rooms.
➕ G6 ✉ Zandpad 5, Vondelpark ☎ 5898999
🚋 Tram 1, 2, 5, 6, 20

NOVA
A clean, simple, central hotel, with a friendly young staff.
➕ H5 ✉ Nieuwezijds Voorburgwal 272–276
☎ 6230066 🚋 Tram 1, 2, 5

OWL
Family-owned hotel with bright, comfortable rooms and a garden, in a quiet street near Vondelpark.
➕ G6 ✉ Roemer Visscherstraat 1 ☎ 6189484
🚋 Tram 2, 3, 5, 12, 20

PRINSENHOF
Quaint, comfortable, and clean. One of the city's best budget options.
➕ H6 ✉ Prinsengracht 810
☎ 6231772 🚋 Tram 4

SINT-NICOLAAS
Rambling former factory and comfortable, if spare, facilities.
➕ H4 ✉ Spuistraat 1a
☎ 6261384 🚋 Tram 1, 2 ,5, 13, 17, 20

VAN OSTADE BICYCLE HOTEL
Small hotel that rents bikes and gives advice on how to discover hidden Amsterdam by bicycle.
➕ H7 ✉ Van Ostadestraat 123 ☎ 6793452 🚋 Tram 3, 12, 20, 24, 25

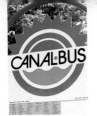

AMSTERDAM
travel facts

ARRIVING & DEPARTING

Before you go

- EU nationals and citizens of the USA, Canada, Australia, and New Zealand need a valid passport or national identity card to stay for up to three months. Nationals of many other countries require a visa.
- There are no vaccination requirements.

When to go

- Most tourists visit between April and September.
- From late March until late May is the time to see Holland's tulips in bloom.
- June, July, and August are the sunniest months, but you can never be sure of good weather. Many people come in June for the Holland Festival.
- In winter, temperatures can drop so low that the canals freeze over.
- Christmas is always a busy tourist season.

Arriving by air

- Amsterdam has one international airport (Schiphol), 11 miles from the center. Many international airlines operate scheduled and charter flights here, including Delta, Northwest (in alliance with Dutch national carrier KLM), and United Airlines from the US, British Airways, KLM uk, British Midlands, Aer Lingus, and KLM.
- Airport information ☎ 0900/0141.
- Trains leave the airport for Amsterdam Centraal Station every 15 minutes from 6AM until midnight, then hourly through the night. The ride takes 20 minutes and the one-way fare costs f6.25.
- A taxi from Schiphol Airport to the center of Amsterdam costs around f70.

Arriving by sea and rail

- The major ferry ports, IJmuiden, Rotterdam, and Hook of Holland, have good rail connections with Amsterdam. Regular sailings from the UK are offered by Stena Line, Scandinavian Seaways, and P&O North Sea Ferries.
- There are good rail connections with most European cities.
- Train information ☎ 0900/9292.

Arriving by car

- Amsterdam is well served by highways. From the A10 ring road, S-routes (indicated by blue signs) go into the city center.
- In the center, many streets are one-way, particularly in the canal area.
- Watch out for bicycles and trams.
- Street parking is very difficult in the center. It is metered Monday to Saturday from 9AM to 11PM, Sunday noon to 11PM, and expensive (f2.75–4.75 per hour). Use parking lots instead.
- Always lock your car securely, and never leave valuables in it.

Customs regulations

- EU nationals are not required to declare items intended for personal use.
- For Americans and other non-EU nationals the limits are:
  200 cigarettes or 50 cigars or 250g of tobacco
  1 liter liquor or 2 liters fortified wine or 2 liters non-sparkling wine
  50ml perfume, 500g coffee, and 100g tea plus other goods to the value of f200.

Departing by air

- Airport tax is included in the price of your ticket.
- There are numerous duty-free shops at Schiphol Airport.

ESSENTIAL FACTS

Electricity
- 220 volts; round two-pin sockets.

Etiquette
- Shake hands on introduction. Once you know people better, you might exchange three pecks on alternate cheeks instead.
- Remember to say *hallo* and *dag* (goodbye) when shopping.
- Dress is generally informal, even for the opera, ballet, and theaters.
- Although service charges are included in bills, tipping is customary. Round-off bills to the nearest guilder, or five guilders for larger bills.

Insurance
- Take out a comprehensive policy before you leave home.

Women travelers
- There are no particular risks for women traveling alone. For information and advice contact the Vrouwenhuis (Women's House) ✉ Nieuwe Herengracht 95 ☎ 6252066

Money matters
- The guilder (formerly called the florin) is abbreviated in numerous ways: f, fl, Hfl, Dfl, NLG. 1 guilder=100 cents.
- On January 1, 1999, the euro became the official currency of The Netherlands, and the Dutch guilder became a denomination of the euro. Dutch guilder notes and coins continue to be legal tender during a transitional period. Euro bank notes and coins are likely to start to be introduced by January 1, 2002.
- Banks may offer a better exchange rate than hotels or independent bureaux de change. GWK offer 24-hour money-changing services at Schiphol Airport and Centraal Station.

National holidays
- January 1; Good Friday, Easter Sunday and Monday; April 30; Ascension Day; Pentecost and Pentecost Monday; December 25 and 26.
- May 4 and 5—Remembrance Day (*Herdenkingsdag*) and Liberation Day (*Bevrijdingsdag*)—are World War II Commemoration Days but not public holidays.

Opening hours
- Banks: Mon–Fri 9 until 4 or 5. Some stay open Thu until 7.
- Shops: Tue–Sat 9 or 10 until 6, Mon 1 to 6. Some open Thu until 9 and Sun noon until 5. Some close early Sat, at 4 or 5.
- State-run museums and galleries: most open Tue–Sat 10 to 5, Sun and national holidays 1 to 5. Many close on Mon.

Places of worship
- Roman Catholic: Parish of the Blessed Trinity, Heilige Familie-kerk (✚ L8 ✉ Zouiersweg 180 ☎ 4652711)
- English Reformed Church: (✚ H5 ✉ Begijnhof 48 ☎ 6249665)
- Jewish: Jewish and Liberal Community Amsterdam: (✚ H9 ✉ Jacob Soetendorpstraat 8 ☎ 6423562)
- Muslim: THAIBA Islamic Cultural Center: (✚ Off map ✉ Kraaiennest 125 ☎ 6982526)

Student travelers
- For discounts at some museums, galleries, theaters, restaurants, and hotels, students under 26 can obtain an International Young Person's Passport (CJP—Cultureel Jongeren Passpoort), cost f20, from: AUB ✉ Leidseplein 26 ☎ 6211211; and NBBS ✉ Rokin 66 ☎ 6240989.

Time differences

- Amsterdam observes Central European Time, 6 hours ahead of New York and 9 hours ahead of Los Angeles.

Toilets

- There are few public restrooms. Use the facilities in hotels, museums, and cafés. There is often a small charge.

Tourist offices (VVV)

- The five main Vereniging Voor Vreemdelingenverkeer (VVV) offices all have multilingual staff, city maps and brochures. They will also make hotel, excursion, theater, and concert reservations for a small fee. They are:
  Centraal Station VVV
  (✚ H4 ✉ Centraal Station, Platform 1)
  Stationsplein VVV
  (✚ H4 ✉ Stationsplein 10)
  Leidseplein VVV
  (✚ G6 ✉ Leidseplein 1)
  Stadionplein VVV
  (✚ E8 ✉ Van Tuyll Van Serooskerkenweg 125)
  and Holland Tourism International at Schiphol Airport (✚ Y12).
- For inquiries ☎ 0900/4004040.

Visitors with disabilities

- Facilities, especially in the hotels and museums along the canals, are not very good. Check in advance for facilities at tourist attractions, theaters, and restaurants.
- VVV brochures include details of hotels and tourist attractions with access and facilities for people with disabilities.
- SGOA (Stichting Gehandicapten Overleg Amsterdam) provides information on suitable accommodations (✚ G6 ✉ Quellijnstraat 84, 1072 ZA Amsterdam ☎ 020/5777955 ☎ 020/5777950 ☎ 020/5777960 ✉ sgoa@xs4all.nl)
- There is a special taxi service for wheelchair users ☎ 6134134.

PUBLIC TRANSPORTATION

How to use the buses and trams

- The majority of buses and trams start from Centraal Station.
- Seventeen different tram lines run frequently from 6AM on weekdays (slightly later at weekends) until midnight when night buses take over, running hourly until 4AM. Day tickets are valid during the night following the day on which they are issued.
- If you need a ticket, board at the front and pay the driver.
- Take care when getting off. Many stops are in the middle of the road.

The Metro/light rail

- There are only three lines, all terminating at Centraal Station. They are used mainly by commuters from the suburbs. The most useful city-center station is Nieuwmarkt.

Buying and using tickets

- The GVB (Transportation Authority) network is divided into zones.
- The same ticket system is valid for tram, bus, and Metro.
- If you intend to use public transportation frequently, buy a ticket of 15 or 45 strips (*strippenkaart*), available at GVB and Dutch Railways ticket counters and the VVV. For each ride, a strip must be stamped for each zone you want to pass through, plus one for the ride: for example, from Centraal Station to Leidseplein is two zones, so you need to stamp two strips of your *strippenkaart*, plus one more. Zones are shown on maps at tram, bus, and Metro stops.
- On buses: tell the driver the number of zones you want and your ticket will be stamped.

- On the Metro or light railway: before boarding, fold back the appropriate number of strips and punch your ticket in the yellow ticket machines on the station.
- On trams: either ask the driver to stamp your ticket or do it yourself in a yellow punch-machine. Some trams have a conductor at the back who sells and stamps tickets.
- For a single trip, purchase a "one-hour" ticket, from the driver of the bus or tram, or from a machine at the Metro entrance. Buy day and other tickets, 2-, 3-, 8-, 15-, and 45-strip cards from Metro and train station ticket counters, VVV offices, newsagents, and bus/tram drivers.
- All tickets are valid for one hour after the time stamped on them, and include transfers.
- Don't travel without a valid ticket: you could be fined f60 plus the ticket price.
- For further information and maps, contact GVB (➕ H4 ✉ Stationsplein ☎ 0900/9292)

Getting around by bicycle

- The best way to see Amsterdam is by bicycle. To hire one costs from f12.50 a day, f60 a week.
  Damstraat Rent-a-Bike (➕ H5 Pieter Jacobszoondwarsstraat 11 ☎ 6255029 ⏰ Daily 9–6)
  Bikes-a-Gogo (➕ G5 ✉ Elandsstraat 111 ☎ 6277726 ⏰ Mon–Sat 9–6)

Taxis

- It is difficult to hail a taxi in the street. Go to a taxi stand outside major hotels, tourist attractions, and Centraal Station. Fares are high, so add only a small tip.
- Taxicentrale (☎ 6777777) runs a reliable 24-hour service.
- Water taxis can be hailed, or ordered from Water Taxi Centrale (➕ H4 ✉ Stationsplein 8 ☎ 6222181)

MEDIA & COMMUNICATIONS

Mail

- Postage to US and European destinations costs f1.60 for letters up to 20g, and f1 for postcards. Other destinations may be more.
- Purchase stamps (*postzegels*) at post offices, tobacco stores, and souvenir shops.
- Post boxes are bright red and clearly marked "ptt post."

Post offices

- Most post offices open weekdays 8.30 or 9 until 5.
- Main Post Office: ➕ G5 ✉ Hoofdpostkantoor PTT, Singel 250–256 ☎ 5563311 ⏰ Mon–Fri 9–6, Sat 9–1
- Postal Information: ☎ 0900/0417

Telephones

- Most public telephones take phonecards, costing f10, f25, or f50, available from telephone centers, post offices and railway stations.
- Phone calls from the Netherlands to the US cost about f0.58 ($0.28) per minute.
- Information: ☎ 0900/8008
- International information: ☎ 0900/0418
- Numbers starting 0900 are premium rate calls.
- Local and international operator: ☎ 0800/0410
- To phone abroad, dial 00 then the country code (USA and Canada 1, UK 44, Australia 61, New Zealand 64), then the number.
- Low rates: USA and Canada 7PM–10AM and weekends; UK and Ireland 8AM–8PM and weekends; Australia and New Zealand midnight–7AM, 3–8PM and weekends.
- Most hotels have International Direct Dialing, but it is expensive.
- At the Telecenter (➕ G5 ✉ Raadhuisstraat 48), you can make

calls and pay afterwards with cash, credit card, traveler's check, or Eurocheque.

Newspapers and magazines

- The main Dutch newspapers are *De Telegraaf* (right wing), *De Volkskrant* (left wing), and *NRC Handelsblad*.
- The main Amsterdam newspapers (sold nationwide) are *Het Parool* and *Nieuws van de Dag*.
- *Vrij Nederland* is a (very popular, left-wing) weekly news magazine.
- Listings magazines: *What's on in Amsterdam*, *Agenda* and *Uitkrant*.
- The *Wall Street Journal*, *USA Today*, and *International Herald Tribune* are widely available.

Radio and television

- News is broadcast on Dutch Radio 1 (747kHz), classical music on Radio 4 (98.9mhz), and pop on Radio 3 (96.8mhz). BBC Radio 4 (long wave) is on 198kHzAM and the World Service (medium wave) is on 648kHzAM.
- There are five main Dutch TV channels and numerous cable and satellite stations, including NBC, Sky, CNN, and MTV.

EMERGENCIES

Emergency phone numbers

- Police: ☎ 112
- Ambulance: ☎ 112
- Fire Service: ☎ 112
- Tourist Medical Service: ☎ 6245793 (day), 5923355 (24hr)
- Automobile Emergency (ANWB): ☎ 0800/000888
- Lost credit cards: American Express ☎ 5048666, Diners Club ☎ 5573557, Master/Eurocard ☎ 030/2835555, Visa ☎ 6600611
- Sexual Abuse (◉ 24 hours): ☎ 6116022
- Crisis Helpline (◉ Mon–Thu 9AM–3AM, Fri–Sun 24 hours) ☎ 6757575

Embassies and consulates

- American Consulate: ⊞ G6 ✉ Museumplein 19 ☎ 6645661
- British Consulate: ⊞ F7 ✉ Koningslaan 44 ☎ 6764343
- Canadian Embassy: ✉ Sophianlaan 7, The Hague ☎ 070/3111600
- Australian Embassy: ✉ Carnegielaan 4a, The Hague ☎ 070/3108200
- New Zealand Embassy: ✉ Carnegielaan 10, The Hague ☎ 070/3469324
- Irish Embassy: ✉ Dr. Kayperstraat 9, The Hague ☎ 070/3630993
- South African Embassy: ✉ Wassenaarseweg 40, The Hague ☎ 070/3924501

Lost Property

- For insurance purposes, report lost or stolen property to the police as soon as possible.
- Main lost property offices: Centraal Station (⊞ H4 ✉ Stationsplein 15 ☎ 5578544 ◉ 7AM–11PM daily); Police Lost Property (⊞ K7 ✉ Steffersonstraat ☎ 5593005 ◉ Mon–Fri noon–3.30)
- For property lost on public transport, GVB (⊞ H4 ✉ Prins Hendrikkade 108–14 ☎ 5578544 ◉ Mon–Fri 9–4)

Medicines

- For non-prescription drugs, bandages and so on, go to a *drogist*.
- For prescription medicines, go to an *apotheek*, open Mon–Fri 8:30–5:30.
- Details of pharmacies open outside normal hours are in the daily newspaper *Het Parool* and all pharmacy windows.
- The Central Medical Service (☎ 020/5923434) can refer you to a duty GP or dentist.
- Hospital outpatient clinics are open 24 hours a day. The most central is Onze Lieve Vrouwe Gasthuis (⊞ J6 ✉ 1e Oosterparkstraat 279 ☎ 5999111 ▣ Trams 3, 6, 10)

Precautions

- Pickpockets are common in busy shopping streets and markets, and in the Red Light District. Take sensible precautions and remain on your guard at all times.
- At night, avoid poorly lit areas and keep to busy streets. Amsterdam is not dangerous, but muggings do occur.

LANGUAGE

Basics

yes	ja
no	nee
please	alstublieft
thank you	dank u
hello	hallo
good morning	goedemorgen
good afternoon	goedemiddag
good evening	goedenavond
good night	welterusten
goodbye	dag
breakfast	het ontbijt

Useful words

good/bad	goed/slecht
big/small	groot/klein
hot/cold	warm/koud
new/old	nieuw/oud
open/closed	open/gesloten
push/pull	duwen/trekken
entrance/exit	ingang/uitgang
men's/women's bathroom	heren/damen wc
free/occupied	vrij/bezet
far/near	ver/dichtbij
left/right	links/rechts
straight ahead	rechtdoor

Restaurant

breakfast	het ontbijt
lunch	de lunch
dinner	het diner
menu	de kaart
winelist	de wijnkaart
main course	het hoofdgerecht
dessert	het nagerecht
the check, please	mag ik afrekenen

Numbers

1	een	15	vijftien
2	twee	16	zestien
3	drie	17	zeventien
4	vier	18	achtien
5	vijf	19	negentien
6	zes	20	twintig
7	zeven	21	eenentwintig
8	acht	22	tweeëntwintig
9	negen	30	dertig
10	tien	40	veertig
11	elf	50	vijftig
12	twaalf	100	honderd
13	dertien	1,000	duizend
14	veertien		

Days and times

Sunday	Zondag
Monday	Maandag
Tuesday	Dinsdag
Wednesday	Woensdag
Thursday	Donderdag
Friday	Vrijdag
Saturday	Zaterdag
today	vandaag
yesterday	gisteren
tomorrow	morgen

Useful phrases

Do you speak English? Spreekt u engels?

Do you have a vacant room? Zijn er nog kamers vrij?

with bath/shower met bad/douche

I don't understand Ik versta u niet

I'm sorry Sorry

Where is/are …? Waar is/zijn …?

How far is it to …? Hoe ver is het naar …?

How much does this cost? Hoeveel kost dit? …

Do you take (credit cards/traveler's checks)? Accepteert u (credit cards/reischeques)?

What time do you open? Hoe laat gaat u open?

What time do you close? How laat gaat u dicht?

Can you help me? Kunt u mij helpen?

INDEX

Citypack
Amsterdam

Important note

Time inevitably brings changes, so always confirm prices, travel facts, and other perishable information when it matters. Although Fodor's cannot accept responsibility for errors, you can use this guide in the confidence that we have taken every care to ensure its accuracy.

Copyright   © 1997, 1999 The Automobile Association
Maps copyright   © 1997, 1999 The Automobile Association
Fold-out map   © Falk-Verlag AG
                         © Kartographie GeoData

Published in the United States by Fodor's Travel Publications, Inc.
Published in the United Kingdom by AA Publishing

Fodor's is a registered trademark of Random House, Inc.

ISBN 0–679–00443–2
Second Edition 1999

FODOR'S CITYPACK AMSTERDAM

AUTHOR *Teresa Fisher*
REVISER *George McDonald*
CARTOGRAPHY *The Automobile Association*
Falk-Verlag AG
COVER DESIGN *Fabrizio La Rocca, Allison Saltzman*

Acknowledgments

Teresa Fisher wishes to thank the Netherlands Board of Tourism, the VVV, British Midland, KLM UK, Hotel Maas, Hotel Nova, Damstraat Rent-a-Bike and Bikes-a-Gogo for their assistance in preparing this book.
The Automobile Association wishes to thank the following photographers, libraries, and museums for their assistance in the preparation of this book: Anne Frankhuis 31a; Mary Evans Picture Library 38b; Museum het Rembrandthuis 44a, 44b; Museum Willet-Holthuysen 42; Eddy Posthuma de Boer 31b, 39, 46; Rex Features Ltd 12; Rijksmuseum Foundation 28a, 28b; Spectrum Colour Library 13a, 19, 20, 45; Van Gogh Museum 26a, 26b; Wyn Voysey 1, 61b; Zefa Pictures 6, 8, 50, 51. The remaining photographs were taken by Ken Patterson and are in the Automobile Association's own Picture Library.

Special sales

Color separation by Daylight Colour Art Pte Ltd, Singapore
Manufactured by Dai Nippon Printing Co. (Hong Kong) Ltd.
10 9 8 7 6 5 4 3 2 1

Titles in the Citypack series

- Amsterdam ● Atlanta ● Beijing ● Berlin ● Boston ● Chicago ● Dublin ●
- Florence ● Hong Kong ● London ● Los Angeles ● Miami ● Montreal ●
- New York ● Paris ● Prague ● Rome ● San Francisco ● Seattle ● Shanghai ●
- Sydney ● Tokyo ● Toronto ● Venice ● Washington, D.C. ●

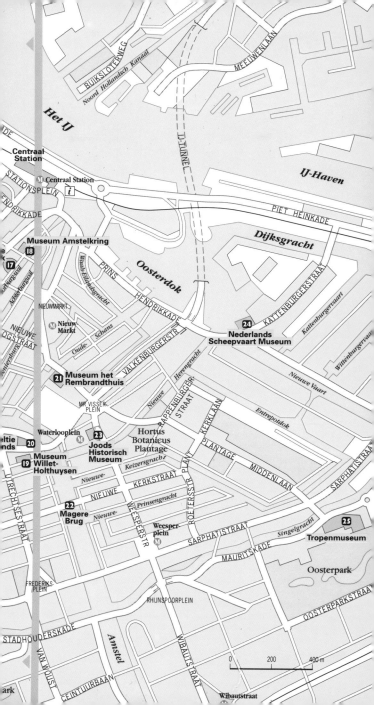

Het IJ

BUIKSLOTERWEG

Noord Hollandsch Kanaal

MEEUWENLAAN

IJ-TUNNEL

Centraal
Station

IJ-Haven

M Centraal Station

STATIONSPLEIN

i

PIET HEINKADE

ENDRIKKADE

Museum Amstelkring

Dijksgracht

18

PRINS

Oosterdok

KATTENBURGERSTRAAT

17

Achtergracht

NIEUWMARKT

Nieuw-
Markt

Oude Schans

HENDRIKKADE

Waals-Eilandsgracht

24

Nederlands
Scheepvaart Museum

Kattenburgervaart

NIEUWE
OGSTRAAT

VALKENBURGERSTR

Nieuwe Vaart

Wittenburgervaart

Museum het
Rembrandthuis

21

Herengracht

Nieuwe

RAPPENBURGER
STRAAT

KERKLAAN

Entrepotdok

MR VISSER
PLEIN

Waterlooplein

 Itie
nds

20

M

Joods
Historisch
Museum

23

Hortus
Botanicus
Plantage

PLANT

PLANTAGE MIDDENLAAN

SARPHATISTRAAT

Museum
Willet-
Holthuysen

19

Keizersgracht

Nieuwe-

NIEUWE KERKSTRAAT

ROETERSSTR

Magere
Brug

22

UTRECHTSESTRAAT

NIEUWE

Prinsengracht

WEESPERSTR

Nieuwe-

25

Tropenmuseum

Weesper-
plein

M

SARPHATISTRAAT

Singelgracht

MAURITSKADE

Oosterpark

FREDERIKS
PLEIN

Oosterpark

RHIJNSPOORPLEIN

OOSTERPARKSTRAA

STADHOUDERSKADE

Amstel

0   200   400 m

VAN WOUST

WIBAUTSTRAAT

ark

CEINTUURBAAN

Wibautstraat

Amsterdam

AMSTERDAM

The Citypack map covers the city in detail, while the Citypack guide gives you just the information you need to experience the best of Amsterdam:

- Top attractions and their must-see sights

- Where to find windmills and canals

- Itineraries for walks and excursions

- The best museums and monuments, parks and green spaces, markets, children's activities, and freebies

- Restaurants, hotels, shopping, nightlife— an unabashedly opinionated selection, with pithy descriptions of each recommendation

- Offbeat sights even locals don't know

- Tips on getting the most from your visit

The author: Teresa Fisher is a freelance journalist and frequent visitor to Holland. She writes regularly for a variety of newspapers and magazines.

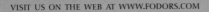